D1346135

Thirty Four

William Hastings Burke

Wolfgeist PUBLISHING

First published in 2009
by Wolfgeist Limited
Suite 116, 30 Red Lion Street
Richmond upon Thames, Surrey, TW9 1RB
United Kingdom
www.wolfgeistpublishing.com

Typeset by Wolfgeist Limited
Printed and bound in Latvia by SIA Jelgavas Tipogrāfija, Jelgava

British Library Cataloguing in Publication Data. A catalogue
record for this book is available from the British Library.

ISBN 978-0-9563712-0-1

For Da

CONTENTS

Acknowledgements vi

The List of Thirty Four viii

One: The Compass 1

Two: Neverland 6

Three: Blue Eyes, Brown Eyes 13

Four: Birth 32

Five: A Boy and a Study of Books 59

Six: Émigré 82

Seven: The King of Sweden 107

Eight: Baron von Mosch 128

Nine: Bredow Straße 154

Ten: 'Reason for Arrest: Subject is brother of

    Reichsfeldmarschal Goering' 171

Eleven: Schwarz, Rot und Gelb 195

Twelve: The Contented Pariah 205

Thirteen: From One to Another 215

Notes 220

ACKNOWLEDGEMENTS

First and foremost, I am eternally indebted to all the people who so graciously invited me into their homes and shared their family narratives. For they are the true authors of this history. I would like to especially thank Elizabeth Goering for so generously sharing her family's memories and photographs of her father.

I am grateful to all the archivists and historians who helped me to scale the mountain of data that stood before me. They include Adam LeBor for his guidance in the initial stages of my research, Lawrence H. McDonald and Jon Taylor of the US National Archives, Dr Vladislav Krátký of the Škoda Museum, Sabine Stein of the Stiftung Gedenkstätten Buchenwald und Mittelbau-Dora-Archiv, Dr Margot Fuchs of the Historisches Archiv der Technische Universität München, Per Svensson and the good people at the National Archives of the UK and the Czech State Archives.

Many thanks go to Nick Mooney and Byron Matthews for their South American 'reconnaissance missions', and Lalo Walsh and Beth Porter for their encouraging comments during the editing process. I cannot thank Dustin Gould enough for his linguistic skills, expert photography, constant support and the *Gaudi* he produced along the autobahn.

I would like to extend my sincere thanks to the army of translators who so willingly helped me to decipher the stacks of documents and letters I accumulated along the way. The Kolars, Ladislav Douda and Andrey Lipattsev helped me with translations in Czech, as did Clare Allgeier in French and Marta Castorino in Italian. Susanne Seeburger, Kathrin Borgerding, Klaus Keller and my flatmates ensured that my cases and syntax in German were always in order.

Cheers, thanks a bunch, *Vielen Dank* and *tusen takk* to all my friends around the world who so kindly put up with my sleeping on their couches and raiding their fridges. My heartfelt thanks go to Sarah Lambe and the 'Teds' at O'Kellys for accepting me into their surrogate — albeit dysfunctional — family.

I cannot express enough gratitude to my (biological) family for the understanding and belief that they showed me in my seemingly bizarre and endless endeavour. I am especially grateful to my mother for instilling in me a thirst for history and to my father for his inspiring, 'can-do' attitude. I would also like to thank my brother-in-law for allowing me to comfortably finish off the last chapters of the book.

Most of all, I am indebted to my eldest sister, editor, mentor, friend and confidant, who, ever since birth, has kept me under her wing and helped me to realise my goals. The fact that I have even got to this point, writing these acknowledgements, I owe to her.

To Albert for reinforcing my faith in humankind.

THE LIST OF THIRTY-FOUR

1. Ehepaar Dr Alsegg
2. Alfred Barbasch
3. Ehepaar Benaroya
4. Ehepaar Benbassat
5. Prof. Dr med. Bauer
6. Prof. Dr med. Charvat
7. Prof. Dr med. Diviš
8. Prokurist Gratien
9. Dr ing. W. Grüss
10. Michael Hohensinn
11. Ing. Vilem Hromadko
12. Erzherzog Joseph Ferdinand
13. Ing. Georg Kantor
14. Dr med. L. Kovacs
15. Frau Franz Lehár
16. Fräulein M. Likar
17. Frau Direktor V. Maschek

The List of Thirty-Four

18. Dr med. Medvey
19. Frau de Montmollin
20. Dir. Jan Moravek
21. Frau Hans Moser
22. Familie Serge Otzop
23. Inspektor Pernkopf
24. Familien Pilzer
25. Familie Pollak
26. Mann von Henny Porten
27. Dr Kurt v. Schuschnigg
28. Gen. Dir. Bruno Seletzky
29. Major Frank Short
30. Franz Šimonek
31. Hans Stahl
32. Gen. Dir. Karel Staller
33. Dr Vilem Szekely
34. Dir. Franz Zrno

ONE

THE COMPASS

I t's his name. That's why he is condemned to this blackest of holes. It is May 1945 — he doesn't even know the exact date — and he is a ward of the US Army at the 7th Army Interrogation Center in Augsburg, Bavaria. The complex is a converted apartment block in the suburb of Bärenkeller. It is now populated by the Allies' first haul of the Nazi elite, preparing to answer for their crimes in Nuremberg. Ten will hang in a little over a year's time.

In his makeshift cell he prepares to draft his own defence. As he rises from his bed to a writing desk set by a barred window, a crippling pain courses down his back; he suffers from a deteriorating kidney condition that goes unnoticed by his warders. His wife and baby daughter anxiously await word of him back in Salzburg, clueless as to his whereabouts or welfare.

He stands accused of complicity in the Nazi regime, an accusation of macabre irony. For this is the same regime he denounced with his whole being and one that only five months before had accused him of subversive behaviour. He was labelled by the Gestapo a 'public enemy', a perennial thorn in their side. Jew or gentile, political or apolitical, Aryan or Slav, rich or poor, he protected them in the streets, freed them from concentration camps and ran them across borders. But his warders are blind to all of this; they only see his name.

You see, he is the younger brother of a fellow inmate in cell number five, the prize catch of them all, the former Reichsmarschall and Commander of the Luftwaffe, Hermann Göring. Albert Göring — this is the condemned man's name — reported at the end of the war to the American Counter Intelligence Corps (CIC) in Salzburg and was subsequently bundled off to this prison. Here he begins to tell his interrogators his story: a story filled with the kind of heroism, espionage and head-spinning audacity that could only be the fanciful notions of a madman. He tells them how he eschewed all the splendours of Nazi royalty – a league his name gave him instant entrée into. He alleges that he manipulated this status to attack the regime from within. He regales them with tales of near escapes from the Gestapo, of saving old Jewish ladies in the street, of money smuggling syndicates and aiding Jewish refugees ... only to be rebuffed by his interrogators. One interrogator, Major Paul Kubala, concludes: 'The results of the interrogation of Albert GOERING, brother of the REICHSMARSCHALL Herman [sic], constitutes as clever a piece of rationalization and 'white wash' as SAIC [Seventh Army Interrogation Center] has ever seen. Albert GOERING's lack of subtlety is matched only by the bulk of his obese brother.'[1]

And so he sits in his cell with five sheets of paper and thirty-four names to convince his accusers of the unfathomable. He starts with the title *Menschen, denen ich bei eigener Gefahr (dreimal Gestapo-Haftbefehle!) Leben oder Existenz rettete* — People whose lives or existence I saved at my own peril (three Gestapo arrest warrants). He then proceeds to write, in alphabetical order, a list of thirty-four names of just a collection of the people who he rescued from Nazi persecution. He includes their titles, professions, previous addresses, citizenships, places of last contact, current addresses, assistance provided and race. Lastly, he signs his name and hands the list to his warders; his fate now resting in their hands.

It is sixty years later and I am sitting in the US National Archives in Washington DC. In my hands is the very list Albert crafted all those years ago. These five unassuming, coffee-stained pages are my first real brush with Albert Göring.

But I'm getting ahead of myself. Rewind and I'm back in my home town, Sydney, Australia, before the grand Main Quad within the University of Sydney, at my graduation ceremony. My parents are there, trying their best to operate the camera. My thesis supervisor shakes my hand, and strangers wish me luck. Where to now? they all ask. Doctor of Philosophy or finance? No, I will neither be continuing on to a PhD nor tackling the Windsor knot. Instead, I bring to light an idea that I've been toying with for some time. I tell them about a story that has plagued me ever since I chanced upon a documentary* alleging that Hermann Göring — Nazism personified — had an anti-Nazi brother.

The idea that the monster we learn about in history class could

---

The Real Albert Goering, 3BMTV, 1998.

have had a brother with an Oskar Schindler-type story was close to unbelievable. A quick poke around my local library, a more thorough search in the university library and the all-knowing Google, and very little came up to substantiate or repudiate the claim. There had to be more to this. Or could the heroism of one man be completely obliterated because of his brother? The name Göring started to take on so many layers that history itself seemed flawed.

A month after graduation, I booked an around-the-world ticket and left Sydney with a clear destination in mind but no certain way of reaching it. On the face of it, it looked like the proverbial back-packers' adventure or even a boy avoiding impending adulthood. But for me, it was the beginning of a mission; a fact-finding mission to cut through the rumour and conjecture that has shrouded the truth of Albert's story.

And the mission begins here, at the US National Archives, with these five dog-eared pages resting in my hands. Sitting in this sterile reading room of tweed coats and moustaches, I try to imagine myself there with Albert, in that cell so many years ago. I want to know why he chose to document these particular names and not the hundreds of others he rescued. The Habsburg Archduke Joseph Ferdinand (number twelve) is noted, as is the ill-fated Austrian Chancellor Dr Kurt von Schuschnigg (number twenty-seven). All prominent individuals and hence people who could easily be tracked down, even today.

The list begins to read like a map, as though Albert had unwittingly condensed and plotted the entire narrative of his war years into these thirty-four names; each name a coordinate on the blueprint of his story. My boy's own adventure then crystallises into something far more serious. The paper trail and crumbling files are just that: a preserved relic. *The List of Thirty-Four* is far more than paper. It is the flesh and blood of those who stand as testament and guardian to the story of Albert Göring. It's then I realise their voices will be the compass of my journey.

TWO

NEVERLAND

From my window I can see a cloak of fog roll over the Schwarzwald, blanketing the ancient, black forest with a mythical aura found only in fairytales. It's easy to imagine a small girl in a red riding cape being led astray or a princess with a complexion as white as snow hiding out with seven of her short-statured friends. This is the realm of the Brothers Grimm and my new home in Germany. It's from here that I intend to trace the story of the brothers Göring.

I live in a share house in the picture book suburb of Wiehre, in the folkloric city of Freiburg, cradled between the borders of Switzerland and France. I can have breakfast in Germany, lunch in Switzerland and dinner in France. It is a sort of Neverland for hippies, greens, punks, kaffiyeh-clad students high on idealism or just those trying to escape the harsh realities of the outside world. Inside this womb they meander through life blissfully oblivious to all the evils and obligations of the 'adult' world.

When I first moved to this centuries-old university town, I imagined being immersed in a scholarly milieu, one that might issue forth future Friederich Nietzches, Günter Grasses and Karl Marxes. But swap languages and throw in a few frat parties, and Freiburg, as I quickly realised, has the same 'one big (beer-fuelled) family' feeling of the last university town I lived in: 'Happy Valley', USA, the home of Pennsylvania State University where I spent an exchange year. And though that European sophistication I thought I was upgrading to is yet to evidence, Freiburg has a lot to recommend it: starting with Jägermeister shots for less than a euro.

To keep me afloat and fund my research, I have taken a job at the local Irish pub. It's a dream job except for one snag: my boss keeps scheduling me on for only a handful of shifts a week. As a result, I have been forced to submit to involuntary vegetarianism. Carbohydrates dominate the menu; real and sachet mash potato, pasta and more pasta. Forget the Atkins Diet, so far I have lost ten kilos in six months.

But where my job lacks in financial remuneration, it compensates with a healthy dose of banter and shenanigans, *craic*. The staff and regulars at the pub are an eclectic bunch of expats. Irishmen, Kiwis, Scots, Russians, Canadians, Englishmen, Spaniards, Welshmen, South Africans, Americans and Aussies, all carrying some kind of émigré story; a past life, a spouse, an over-bearing parent or even an arrest warrant they are escaping. And this pub, set in this Neverland city, is their unofficial embassy: a home and surrogate family where they take refuge in the warmth of their mutual transience, language, alcoholism and, above all, sense of humour. This, in a seemingly humourless, Germanic world, provides them with a type of sanity — but then again, when they are well lubricated with German beer, they all tend to go insane.

That's at least what the horrified faces of the German customers suggest. On Saturday nights, the regulars, ten pints full, dance and sing on the bar, whilst on the floor the Germans quietly sit, staring at these crazed Ausländer (foreigners) in shock as they sip on their hot chocolates, *Kiba*s (cherry and banana juice) or one and only *Banana-weizen* (wheat beer shandy with banana juice). After six months here, I still struggle to come to grips with the groups of twentysomething males opting for hot chocolates — with whipped cream, of course — at midnight on a Saturday … in an Irish pub!

AROUND THE CORNER FROM my apartment is Goethestraße, and in the tradition of its namesake, it is the bricks and mortar of German Romanticism. Stroll down Goethestraße and you will be greeted by lavish town houses reminiscent of New York Brownstones, except much smaller and quainter. Spires and gables branch off flat rooftops, and grand balconies extend from pastel façades bordered by earth brown, quoined brick work. All that is missing from this scene are gilded horse-carriages alighted by well-to-do residents with powdered wigs. But do not be fooled by the façade and architecture, these are not old edifices.

Indeed, except for the Münster (cathedral), almost every building in the *Stadtmitte* of Freiburg is a post World War II construction. For Freiburg bore the brunt of two major indiscretions during World War II — one dealt out by their trigger-happy brothers and the other by their estranged cousins. The 10th of May 1940: a thick grey blanket consumed the Schwarzwald, schoolchildren were playing in school yards, local farmers were offering their produce on the Münster-platz, the bells of Herz-Jesu-Kirche had just given a performance in Stühlinger, when a hail of Krupp steel rained down on the surrounding area of the *Hauptbahnhof* (central train station). Strangely, there were no air-raid sirens. No warnings from the authorities. No ominous signs of an attack. Why should there be any reason to worry when from overhead came the soothing rumble of Heinkel He 111s, and the mighty black-and-white Balkenkreuz pierced through the clouds. Yet Balkenkreuz or no Balkenkreuz, on this dreary spring day fifty-seven Freiburgers ceased to be Freiburgers — twenty-two of whom were children. Why? Some say because of poor visibility and nascent navigation technology. Some say because of overzealous Luftwaffe crewmen who, raring to impress their Führer in striking that first blow, mistook German Freiburg for French Dijon. Or some even had the audacity to blame those 'bloody Tommys' from across the Channel — Propaganda Minister Goebbels comes to mind.

Around four years later, the second indiscretion could officially be accredited to those 'bloody Tommys'. Misinformed that a large mass of German troops were ready to be deployed from Freiburg, four hundred and forty-one Royal Air Force (RAF) bombers dumped one thousand nine hundred tons of British steel on what was supposed to be Freiburg's railway infrastructure on the 27th and 28th of November 1944. The RAF's definition of railway infrastructure apparently included apartment buildings, churches, book shops, restaurants, bakeries, cafés, parks, university buildings and schools ... the whole city centre. That is, except for the tallest structure of Freiburg, the mighty Münster, that still dominates the city's skyline. In the wake of the raid and amid the rubble, this cathedral of God stood alone, defiantly, as though giving Churchill the big finger.

[9]

Unlike the previous air raid, the citizens of Freiburg had, this time, some sort of warning. It was neither the air-raid sirens nor the radio reports that first caused most of its citizens to head into their bunkers. It was but a single drake, a mere bird, albeit a bird of apparently great foresight, authority and persuasion. Before the first RAF plane could be seen or heard — at least for the human eye and ear — this bird flapped its wings, squawked to the heavens and made such a great commotion that its onlookers took notice and scuffled underground. For this reason many Freiburgers survived the onslaught, although the remains of that one brave, feathered Freiburger were found tangled among a heap of debris.

Just outside the Altstadt, across the Leopoldring, over the footbridge into Stadtgarten, past the gondola that winds up to Schlossberg and the triangular roofed amphitheatre, in a pond inhabited by toadstool fountains, is a black marble statue of that famous drake at its finest moment, arched up, bill pointing to the sky, crying out its message of premonition. "The Creature of God Laments, Charges and Scolds," is inscribed at the base of the statue.

This very line could also be aptly engraved onto a statue for Albert Göring — if there ever was one. Like the Drake of Freiburg, Albert had an animal instinct for looming danger and was compelled to protect those in peril. He lived in Munich, the birth city of the Nazi movement. He shared the same university lecture halls as Himmler and heard the earliest rumblings of a burgeoning student nationalist movement. He watched his brother fall deeper in with Hitler's clique and witnessed his speech darken with hate. In short, he was afforded intimate knowledge of what these future leaders of Germany intended for the nation. So he gave alarm, voiced his distress and admonished his countrymen to take heed. But unlike that prophetic drake, he found himself utterly ignored.

THERE IS A COMMOTION rumbling outside my door. My flatmates must be preparing to launch their *Putzoffensive*, cleaning offensive, as they call it. I share an attic with four German students: a punk-rocker-cum-primary school teacher, a linguist, a future opera director and a classical violinist. They are a quirky set who have become my self-appointed guides in Freiburg, always eager to lend me a hand with my German or to assist me with my many struggles with the officious *Stadtamt* (municipal offices). On the surface they are like a group of twentysomething men anywhere in the western world: they like a drink and are always up for a good time. But when it comes to cleanliness and orderliness a certain Germanic streak dominates. Typical of most German student WGs (share houses), they have constructed a colour-coded, rotating *Putzplan* (cleaning roster) in the shape of a wheel. And once that wheel clicks over to Sunday, all men report to duty in the kitchen and wage war on grime and mess. Today, though, I have been granted leave on account of my solo mission on the bathroom yesterday.

Over the drone of the vacuum cleaner comes a knock on my door and then "Vill". What now? Did I not slay enough scum? No, the linguist flatmate just wants to give me a letter uncovered in the cleanup. It's from Eckhardt Pfeiffer, an editor of a regional newspaper in Franconia, Northern Bavaria (the region where Albert and Hermann Göring grew up), a local historian and supposedly a pundit on the Göring family. I had sent him a letter more than five months ago, hoping that he could offer me some leads.

The letter is typically written in formal German, albeit with a friendly and sympathetic tone. Its content, however, is sparse in substance. All he can offer me is that Albert attended a high school in Hersbruck. It is almost a carbon copy of the many replies I have received since I began this whole project. They normally begin with 'May I congratulate you on your endeavours to tell the story of Albert Göring' but end with either 'I regret to inform you that we only have very limited information regarding Albert' or 'We are unfortunately unable to supply you with any information as our [enter family member] passed away [enter date] and has taken all his/her information with him/her to the grave.' I am beginning to believe I am twenty years too late.

But then I resolve to be proactive: if the information won't come to me, I will just have to go to the information. And with that I call my boss and tell her that I will be going away for a couple of weeks to Franconia. "When?" she asks in her usual no-nonsense, Irish fashion. "As soon as you start to give me more shifts and I can raise the money." She hangs up.

THREE

BLUE EYES, BROWN EYES

Early morning, bitterly cold, I wait for Dustin, an American friend who, as a stranger in his own country, has been enjoying voluntary exile in Europe for the past ten years. He commands a better knowledge of German than me and has agreed to join me as my research assistant/interpreter. Dustin finally appears, luggage is checked, maps deployed, wheels turn and the bonnet points to the autobahn.

We leave behind the clear blue sky of Baden Württemberg for a thick Bavarian mist. The autobahn disappears as do the rolling valleys, church steeples, neatly packed villages, suspension bridges poised over waterless obstacles and ploughed fields with hardened, frozen soil. We drive in a throng of BMWs and Mercedes-Benzes threatening to lift off. The Fränkischer Autobahn climbs through

Swiss-like mountain ranges and coniferous forests, earning it the name of the Fränkische Schweiz (Franconian Switzerland). Past it we reach Veldenstein Forest, host to Burg Veldenstein (Veldenstein Castle), the first stop on our expedition back into Albert and Hermann's childhood.

The road to Burg Veldenstein is a quaint country road, not unlike those found in the English countryside. Sections of light green pastures, with handfuls of dairy cows penned in by knee-high, mossy stone walls, are broken up by clumps of dense woodland and green-bearded rock faces. It is easy to picture a fox hunt streaking by, with a young Hermann Göring in the lead. He would be on horseback, decked out in full hunting regalia complete with Tyrolean hat, chasing the bark of bloodhounds, the fear of the fox spurring on both hound and boy-hunter. We leave this gentleman's playground for a series of one-road villages inhabited by a collection of houses, the village church and roadside shrines to Jesus. This is Pope Benedict XVI, or rather, Joseph Alois Ratzinger's home base, the heart of German Catholicism.

We wind along a cliff-side road with the river Pegnitz meandering below and a mass of rock threatening from above. Around one more sharp bend and the commanding image of Burg Veldenstein appears. The castle sits high atop an imposing cliff. Man-made and natural defences are in perfect harmony: stone parapets nestle into the jagged and steep escarpment, circular bastions protrude from each crook of the mountain — an attack from the low ground would be suicide. At the centre of the compound is the castle's high-reaching central tower, its gaze bearing down onto the village Neuhaus an der Pegnitz below. It is omnipresent, ever-watchful, securing submission from its subjects. Burrowed into its base is a rabbit warren of wooden doors, which appear to lead right into the depths of the mountain and in turn the confines of the castle. Are these secret medieval passageways once used to smuggle in mistresses or, perhaps later, Hermann Göring's art loot?

We take a right around the front face of the castle and motor up the mountain until we come to a stop in a field where two young boys are playing football. The older boy, standing at the penalty spot, slams balls pass the younger boy in goal. He is forced each time to chase after the ball as it runs down the hill. I wonder whether Hermann and Albert once battled against one another in this very park. The athletic and older Hermann of course taking the spotlight at the eleven-meter mark, whilst the more delicate Albert being on the receiving end, feeding his brother's ego with each scurry down the hill. With the early evening air brisk and scented with wood fires, we walk back down to the gates of Burg Veldenstein and peer into Albert and Hermann's childhood.

WITH ARYANISM THE CURRENCY of the day, the German historian Barron Otto von Dungern released, in 1938, an article on the family tree — or more appropriately, the Aryan credentials — of Hermann Göring. It was part of a series chronicling the family trees of other famous Germans, such as Arthur Schopenhauer and Rudolf Heß. For many Germans, proof of sixteen Aryan ancestors was considered, at the time, an acceptable number to buffer them against the hysteria of the Nuremberg laws.[1]

Dungern turned out to be a creative genealogist. He took out his secateurs and hacked through unions and births as far back as the 12th century. He started at the bottom of the family tree, pulling out weeds and meaningless roots, until he came upon the prize root of the Hohenzollern and Wittelsbach royal houses. He clipped on, looking for a robust, commanding branch, a branch representing conquest and high achievement. Sure enough, he revealed an offshoot to the 'Iron Chancellor', modern Germany's founding father, Otto von Bismarck. Halfway through, his cutting technique took on a more artistic flair, and its fruit was an abstract piece of art, to say the least: a sinuous vine leading to Herr German Literature himself, Johann Wolfgang von Goethe. He pruned further along the extremities of the tree, right to the point where its leaves began to brush against a neighbouring tree, and there he managed to uncover a regal branchlet to Kaiser Wilhelm II, the grandson of Queen Victoria.[2] At the end, with a pile of dead, useless roots and weeds surrounding him, a glistening Aryan knight stood before him.

Discarding this Nazi propaganda and rummaging through all these forgotten, genealogical off-cuts, you would find a more fitting representative of the Görings' ancestry to be a high-ranking, Prussian bureaucrat with an affinity to the land, who occasionally flirted with royalty.

A more appropriate juncture to begin an exploration into the Görings' lineage is, perhaps, the birth of Michael Geringk of Schlawe in 1694. Michael Geringk, one of the ancestors that the Görings were particularly proud of, once served the King of Prussia, Frederick the Great. From the post of regimental quartermaster he rose through the ranks to become the *Commissarius Loci* (economic controller) of the Ruhr. In between raising funds for the Prussian war effort and languishing in French custody as a political hostage during the Seven Years' War, Michael Geringk managed to father a son named Christian Heinrich Göring — the first to adopt the modern spelling of the Göring family name. Christian Heinrich led a humble but reputable life in the Rhineland where he raised Albert and Hermann's grandfather, Wilhelm Göring. Wilhelm brought great prestige to the Göring family, not through conquests on the battlefield or by climbing the rungs of public office but through his courting exploits in the ballrooms of high society. For he managed to secure the hand of Caroline de Nerée, a member of a noble Dutch family with French Huguenot blood.[3]

On the 31st of October 1838 in Emmerich, a stone's throw from the Netherlands, the Göring Family tree grew a new branch. On this branch the name of Heinrich Ernst Göring, Albert and Hermann's father-to-be, was penned in. With his father being a highly respected judge, Heinrich was destined for a career in law; a presumption he would initially shun. Despite graduating from the prestigious Heidelberg and Bonn universities in law, the twenty-seven-year-old Heinrich donned the Prussian Army uniform in the Austro-Prussian War of 1866. It took only seven weeks for the cartographer to brandish his worn quill and draft a new map of Europe, a map now favouring the victorious and ever-expanding Prussian Empire over the dwindling Austrian Empire. The Prussians again kept the cartographer busy in 1871 with their victory in the Franco-Prussian war, and again Heinrich was there, helping to push the boundaries of the Prussian Empire and in turn conceive modern Germany. As a reward for his participation on the battlefield, Heinrich was awarded the position of district judge and then later circuit judge in the newly founded German Empire.[4]

But then discontentment and melancholy descended upon him. His initial disenchantment of the legal system resurfaced. Even worse, he had just lost his wife Ida of ten years and mother of his first five children, one of whom had died as an infant. He succumbed to depression. He became jittery; an honorary circuit judge was not enough. He wanted a new assignment. He wanted a fast ticket to the top of German society, and one such ticket was the new Consular

Service of the Foreign Office in Berlin. He knew that the German Empire was growing, and he was well aware of Kaiser Wilhelm I's desperation to share drinks with his British and French counterparts at the 'Colonial Club'. Chancellor Bismarck, a friend of Heinrich's, encouraged him to travel to London and learn from the best, that is, to learn all the ins and outs of the very successful British model of colonial administration.[5]

Yet before he could leave, he needed to find a wife, a companion with whom to share his new endeavour and, not to mention, the rearing of his children. This void was filled by a pair of arresting blue eyes. This nineteen-year-old buxom blonde with a peasant but nevertheless attractive face was Franziska Tiefenbrunn, the daughter of Peter Paul Tiefenbrunn, a well-respected yeoman in the Tyrolean town of Reutte. An engagement, born not necessarily out of love but convenience, was thus brokered between the Prussian judge and the humble Tyrolean Fräulein. Already pregnant with her first child (Karl Ernst), Franziska joined Heinrich on his journey across the Channel. At St James Church in London on the 28th of May 1885 Franziska Teifenbrunn — over twenty years Heinrich's junior — became Fanny Göring.[6] Now well-versed in colonial governance and ready for an assignment, Heinrich won the respect of Bismarck and was duly appointed that same year as '*Reichskommissar von Deutsch-Südwestafrika*' (Reich Commissioner of current day Namibia).

DUSTIN AND I ENTER through the outer gates of the castle as the bells of the nearby church begin to toll. At the entrance is a shuttered up ticket booth and kiosk with pictures of frosted ice creams. The castle grounds are winter-still. Only the squawk of ravens that have taken nest upon the castle's central tower hint at life. We push on along a cobbled road until we come to the main gate proudly displaying the castle's address marker, a stone engraving of a medieval crest.*

At yet another gate, a bitumen driveway, flanked on each side by two flagpoles, runs to the site of what must have been the Görings' living quarters but now is home to Hotel Veldenstein: a triple-storey, architectural hodgepodge with an algae-green façade, arched white windowpanes, terracotta tiles and a bright red front door that looks to be borrowed from Willy Wonka's factory. Unsure of what to expect behind this porthole, I turn the door knob.

An Alsatian greets us with exposed fangs and a growl that erupts into a deafening bark. Then from down the hall comes the equally stinging bark of Frankish dialect. The voice announces the hulking figure of a man not at all pleased to see us. His face contorts into an ingratiating 'school photo smile', a lame attempt to mask severe discomfort. We ask whether they are opened for dinner, and after a moment of hesitation, he responds in a deep voice, "*Natürlich* — of course. Come this way."

He leads us into a riotous celebration of taxidermy: a dining room brimming with mounted stag antlers, chamois heads and stuffed pheasants, and accented by a tropical parrot, a vulture and an owl enshrined in glass. Featured alongside are some of the weapons responsible for these stiff, permanent poses. Crossbows, pikes, swords, shields and even a full suit of armour. Apart from King Ludwig II and Jesus, we sit alone. The crackle and pop from a fire at the far end of the room intermittently pierces the crypt-like silence. Afraid to offend this quiescence, our conversation is reduced

---

*I later found out that it is Prince Bishop Henneberg's coat of arms, which also documents the reconstruction of the castle in 1486.

to whispers. We mainly discuss how bizarre the setting is and how we might pry information from our Northern Bavarian host. The bizarre becomes surreal when speakers resting on the heads of monk figurines suddenly blare out oom-pah music with a medieval twist, followed by the *Braveheart* soundtrack.

Our host pops in and out of the room, and each time he enters we try to engage in general conversation about the weather or the town, but he just shrugs us off with one-sentence answers and busies himself. The door opens once again, but this time a young waitress walks in with a bun of blonde hair and a warm smile. A transformation takes place. The mounted fauna no longer fix us with ghostly gazes. The warped oom-pah/Celtic music dulls. The room grows warmer. We feel welcomed. After exchanging a few pleasantries with the waitress, we learn that our surly host is Herr Betzeld, the very man who I must — but by no means want to — ask about the previous famous occupants of this castle.

Herr Betzeld proves to be as reticent on the subject of Albert Göring as he is on everything else we enquire about. He even goes as far as to warn us that no one in the town, or the world, for that matter, knows anything about Albert. On that note, we thank him and leave for the town centre to look for a bed for the night and test his theory.

IN MODERN-DAY NAMIBIA, downtown in the nation's capital of Windhoek, a street sign with the lettering of 'Göring Street' marked for more than a century one of the city's major thoroughfares. This sign was one of the few legacies of the five years that the territory between the Orange and Cunene River in South-West Africa was governed by Reichskommissar Heinrich Göring. Accompanied by a chancellor (Herr Nels) and a police chief (Herr Goldamer) but no Frau Consul — Fanny Göring was in Germany giving birth to her first child Karl Ernst — Heinrich Göring landed in September 1885 at Walvisbay.[7] He was there on a sales trip: he was given the arduous task of selling protection treaties to the local inhabitants, namely the Herero and Nama tribes. These were to enable private German trading companies to exploit the area's plentiful resources and Lutheran missionaries to instil the word of god without the threat of a spear in the back. The only problem was that the product that Heinrich had to sell was not all that appealing to the local consumers. In fact, they were so dissatisfied with the concept that they regularly attacked German trade outposts, including the Göring homestead.

Along with the intolerable heat and the scarcity of water, this took a toll on Fanny who, with her new born baby Karl Ernst, had now reunited with her husband in Africa. Her health was further compromised after the birth of her second child, Olga, proved near fatal for her. Yet the care of a young Austrian doctor with the aristocratic title of 'von' ensured that she would live to bear two more influential Görings. Dr Hermann von Epenstein stayed by her bedside day and night, occasionally getting a glimpse of those mesmerising blue eyes. He was besotted. And upon her awakening in the company of her saviour, a mutual infatuation ensued.[8]

Faced with a quick end to his young career as a statesman, Heinrich decided to temporarily abandon his initial soft approach and engage in some aggressive marketing by employing the muscle of Imperial Troops, which were bolstered by his own police force of sympathetic natives. But as soon as order was restored, Heinrich resumed a gentler approach to native management. He did not share the conventional opinion towards 'savages' espoused by civilised Germany. Rather, he saw the indigenous population as human beings who should be treated accordingly, a doctrine he would impose on his subordinates.*[9] Carrot imports thus began to outweigh stick imports. The Imperial ear became unclogged. Coercion was replaced by diplomacy. Treaties were signed with Xs. Relationships between the colonisers and the colonised began to consolidate almost to a point of friendly cooperation. After Heinrich's five years as Reichskomissar to South-West Africa, German sovereign territory had spread five hundred miles inland.[10]

In the end, though, the protection treaties' defects began to resurface again. Imperial Germany could no longer honour its side of the bargain, namely providing protection. The chieftain of the Nama tribe, Hendrik Witbooi, did not respect the royal seal of a far distant king and launched attack after attack on rival Herero cattle posts. The local tribes, most notably the Herero, lost faith in their white-skinned protectors and subsequently opted for a renegotiation of terms. This ultimately meant that Heinrich and his contingent had to temporarily abandon the young colony.[11]

Heinrich returned in 1890 to a very different Germany: a Bismarck-free Germany, a Germany in the hands of the young and brash Kaiser Wilhelm II, a Germany rife with conservatism. Such notions of equal rights to man — black or white, savage or civilised — as those held by Heinrich were not well received. Heinrich's protestations or attempts to defend his native friends were met by accusations of his being a socialist, which, at the time, was the equivalent of being charged as a communist in McCarthyist USA.[12]

Heinrich chose to flee his beloved fatherland, even if that meant

*In contrast, less than twenty years later, Heinrich's sucessors − namely, Lieutenant General Lothar von Trotha − oversaw a policy of genocide against the Herero and Nama tribes. Between 1904 and 1907, tens of thousands of men, women and children were murdered either through forced starvation or poisoning.

dragging his wife and three children — the second daughter Paula had just been born — through another testing colonial life. Heinrich took the post of German Consul General to Haiti and Minister Resident at Port-au-Prince in 1891. In this Caribbean setting, with civil unrest brewing all around, Heinrich's warrior spirit and Fanny's blue-eyed mystique fused together to conceive their fourth child. Nine months later, the 12th of January 1893, at Marienbad Sanatorium in Rosenheim, Bavaria — not too far from Hitler's birth town of Braunau am Inn on the Austrian/German border — a boy was born, Hermann Wilhelm Göring. His first name was borrowed from Fanny's guardian and increasing focus of admiration, the young Austrian doctor from their days in Africa, Dr Hermann von Epenstein. Epenstein was there by Fanny's side to witness Hermann's birth. Hermann's middle name was either a tribute to the late Kaiser Wilhelm I or to the pride of the Göring family, Grandfather Wilhelm Göring.

Baby Hermann only had six weeks to get acquainted with his mother as Fanny's presence was immediately requested at Heinrich's side in Haiti. Frau Graff, a close family friend living at the town of Fürth near Nuremberg, acted as Hermann's surrogate mother until the Görings returned some three years later. This separation between mother and babe would seemingly have a great effect on both juvenile and adult Hermann.

According to Hermann's eldest sister Olga Rigele, the reunion between Hermann and his estranged parents was by no means a happy occasion. On the train platform, when the Graffs were greeting the Görings with open arms, three-year-old Hermann just turned his back on the whole affair. When Fanny Göring tried to lift him in her arms, he squirmed, flailed his arms around, burst into tears and beat his arms on his biological mother's chest. And as for the old stranger standing aside from the commotion, his own father, he did not as much as bat an eyelid his way.[13]

Tired and aged after his Haiti posting, Heinrich worked for a few more months in the Foreign Office, before retiring to the Berlin suburb of Friedenau. At first Heinrich, now surrounded by his 'people', Prussian civil servants and army officers, relished retired life. On Sundays he would take the children to Potsdam to be awed by the pomp and might of the parading Prussian Army — a spectacle igniting Hermann's life-long obsession with the military and warfare.[14] But for a man hung up on progress and achievement, he did not take well to the static of retirement. Whilst as a dissatisfied law graduate, Heinrich had turned to the Army; as a disenchanted consul to South-West Africa, he had turned to the Caribbean; and as a restless retiree, he now turned to the bottle. To further complicate things his alcoholism was accompanied by bouts of bronchitis and pneumonia. And whilst Heinrich was withering away, his wife and old friend from Africa, Epenstein, spent an increasing amount of time together.[15]

Amidst this tangle of family controversy, a brown-eyed boy by the name of Albert Günther Göring was born in Friedenau on the 9th of March 1895. From birth Albert carried the mantle of 'black sheep' in the Göring family. Yet this label would come to define his life. His eternal resistance to the status quo, that is, to all that he abhorred, would see him renounce his Fatherland upon the advent of Nazism in 1933. It would lead to his declaring war on the Nazi regime. It would push him on to the road as a political exile and a fugitive of the Gestapo. And, most importantly, it would mean life for hundreds of would-be victims of Nazism.

Almost immediately after Albert's birth and citing 'Heinrich's ailing health', Epenstein suggested the Göring family take up residence at his newly purchased castle, Burg Veldenstein. This Franconian castle, once home to prince-bishops and conquering Swedish and Bavarian knights, was acquired in 1897 by this modern Austrian knight, Ritter* von Epenstein, for twenty thousand marks. By 1914 Epenstein had spent a further million marks on its reconstruction. Though retired as a doctor, this sum was very much affordable for the wealthy Epenstein, who inherited the bulk of his estate from his father. Senior Dr Epenstein, a physician at the court of King Frederick Wilhelm IV of Prussia and a real estate speculator, was well placed in Prussian society, despite being Jewish. This minor 'mark' on his social standing was diminished when he converted to marry the daughter of a wealthy, catholic merchant. Junior Dr Epenstein was thus born a catholic, raised as a catholic and lived his life along strict catholic lines.

Quite small in stature and prone to chubbiness, Epenstein was not a particularly handsome man, but his elegant clothes, speech and manner and his intriguing anecdotes of travel in far-off exotic lands rendered him a more than worthy beau.[16] He also boasted an impressive real estate fortune, which included properties around Berlin, Burg Veldenstein and another medieval castle in the Austrian Hohe Tauern Mountains, Burg Mauterndorf.

He frequently threw dinner parties at both castles. Not just any old black-tie affair, these parties had all the trimmings of a medieval feast. He had staff dressed in old court uniforms, meals announced by the blow of a hunting horn, copious amounts of food and wine served, whilst the melody of an army of minstrels added

---

*The title of Ritter, or Knight, was given to him by Emperor Franz Josef of the Habsburg Empire.

to the merriment. Whilst the alcoholic and virtually senile Heinrich received no invitation to such shindigs, Fanny Göring often played hostess, sometimes right up until breakfast the next morning. When Epenstein came to visit the Görings at Veldenstein, he would request the choicest of the castle's twenty-four rooms, which also happened to be a short late-night scamper away from Fanny's room.[17] This increasingly suspicious behaviour began to give rise to rumours among the local townsfolk and family friends that Epenstein and Fanny were having an affair.

"We never had any doubt about it," comments Professor Hans Thirring, a godson of Epenstein who also enjoyed his summers at Burg Mauterndorf with the Görings. "Everyone who stayed at Mauterndorf accepted the situation, and it did not seem to trouble Hermann or the other Göring children at all. Like all the rest of us, they went in fear and trembling of Pate [godfather] Epenstein."[18] There is also an argument that this liaison led to Albert's conception. It has been speculated that the affair properly began around one year before Albert's birth. Furthermore, Epenstein conveniently elected to become the godfather of all the Göring children upon the birth.[19] As Albert's older sister Olga Rigele recollects: "Pate had made Hermann his favourite godchild then, but after Albert's birth he was always fussing over him."[20] The rumours only intensified as Albert grew up and people began to notice a certain physical likeness between the godson and godfather. "The result of this relationship people say was a son: Albert. And the rumour went around that this boy looked exactly like Epenstein," says Mia Haunhorst, an ex-neighbour in Neuhaus an der Pegnitz.[21] Those same dark, brown eyes and hair, that same central-European physiognomy, were coincidences people could not overlook. If there is any truth to these rumours, Albert was a quarter Jewish, which, according to the Nazi Aryan purity laws, would have required his transportation to a concentration camp.

In later years, however, it became obvious that Hermann was Epenstein's favourite. Albert was said to be 'a sad boy, apt to whine and cry before even being hurt'.[22] A cautious child, he preferred a book and the security of the indoors. No military haircut for Albert; he sported a shoulder-length, pageboy haircut. Hardly the model son of a swashbuckling, globe-trotting Austrian knight.

On the other hand, Hermann was a confident — perhaps, even over-confident — young boy. If he was not leading the Boer contingent of the local village boys in a mock Boer War battle or on a great hunt, he was taming a mountain. By the age of ten he had scaled the cliffs of Burg Veldenstein, and by thirteen he had reached the peak of Austria's highest mountain, the 3798m Groß Glockener. He was also not afraid to defend his hero, Epenstein. On one occasion, a boy on holidays in Mauterndorf questioned Epenstein's aristocratic title by taunting Hermann that Epenstein had only "won his title from the Kaiser with money, rather than with brave deeds". Hermann quickly responded to this insolence by giving the boy a bloody nose. Somehow, Epenstein had heard about this incident, and the next day "the boy and his parents disappeared from Mauterndorf." As a reward, "Hermann was given the special treat of spending the day alone with his hero, hunting chamois in the mountains."[23]

NOW IN THE TOWN centre, Dustin and I are in search of accommodation. We try the first building with the sign *Gasthof* (guest house) we see. We enter through the *Gaststube* (salon) doorway, ducking under a low beam and come to a room which, despite being abuzz with conversation and activity only moments ago, is now as cold and hostile as the winter night outside. Tables of middle-aged men stop their games of skat and place their beers down; all eyes are on us. We are the same old faces asking the same old questions that chafe them in the warmer months. Except now it's the middle of winter. We are encroaching on their holidays. A little unnerved, we continue to the bar presided over by a portrait of the crazy-eyed King Ludwig II and a stern-faced barman. In the most polite and formal German we ask if they have a spare room, but the barman fixes us with the same 'what are you doing here' look as his patrons and mutters: "We don't do rooms."

We decide to try another *Gasthof* across the street called the Hexenhäusle — the Witches' House. Déjà vu! We pass under the same old low doorway, get the same old stares from middle-aged skat players, walk to the same old bar with the same old portrait of King Ludwig II and hear the same old answer of 'We don't do rooms'. But this time the barman gives us an amicable look and helpful directions to a *Gasthof* that does 'do rooms'. Each bar scene reminds me of a country pub back home in Australia. You could be welcomed with smiles and some chit chat or scorned as though you were trespassing on sacred ground.

The Hexenhäusle is the former. As we walk through an isle of booths, one punter, who seems to have stolen comrade Lenin's goatee and bald pate, invites us for a drink. After telling him that we have to first find accommodation, he jests with the deviant smile of a dirty old man whether we wanted a "*Zimmer ohne oder mit Frauen?*" "Tonight, without ladies," we reply. "What about one quick drink?" he pushes. "Ok, maybe one small one," we oblige. Besides, there is something about this guy's worn and tired eyes that hint at having seen a few things in their day.

He steps behind the bar and pours in porcelain steins two unfiltered beers from the local brewery, Kaiserbräu — so it turns out our punter is no common punter but rather a very privileged one: the punter who owns the bar. He hurries us to a table with two pensioner-aged men having an argument. Our Bavarian friend introduces them to us as being from Süddänemark (South Denmark), meaning that they really come from Northern Germany — the subtle cultural and dialectical idiosyncrasies between different regions of Germany is always a favourite source of humour among Germans. Their accents were indeed a testament to their origin as we could understand their *Hochdeutsch* (textbook German more commonly associated with Northern Germany) perfectly well, whilst the local dialect of our host took a bit of getting used to.

Since I have moved to Germany, I have been struggling with not only the dialectical nuances of the German language but also its logic. With each new word I learn, I am amazed at how literal, blunt, sterile and, dare I say, unimaginative the German language can be. How instead of developing a whole new noun in its entirety two already existing words are simply combined to make another. Hence: *Stinktier* (smelly animal: skunk), *Tintenfisch* (ink fish: squid), *Leichenwagen* (dead body wagon: hearse), *Süßstoff* (sweet stuff: sweetener), *Handschuhe* (Hand shoes: gloves), *Hungersnot* (Hunger emergency: famine), *Selbstmord* (Self murder: suicide) and so on. The same logic can also be applied to verbs. At times it seems that every sentence can be completed by applying the verb *machen* (to make). *Saubermachen* (make clean: to clean), *freimachen* (make free: to clear), *kurz machen* (make short: to shorten), *Party machen* (make party: to party) ... WHEN IN DOUBT JUST ADD *MACHEN*!

With banter flying between us, the Northern Germans and the Bavarians, we truly '*Party machen*'. Our table is never scarce of laughter nor is my stein ever empty of beer; each member of the group keeps insisting on buying me another stein. At a break in the laughter, they ask us what we are doing here. "Göring," we reply. Our jovial host's eyes light up. A cigarette in his mouth and with a voice hoarse with decades of smoke, our host reveals himself to be a font of information on the Görings. Living here for all of his seventy-one years, he tells us that as a child he remembers how Hermann used to visit this very *Gasthof*, even though his father, the owner at the time, was not a Nazi party member. And this fact, he tells us, nearly brought him into strife with the Nazi government. On one occasion, the local party leader came to the *Gasthof* to collect his father for interrogation. "But he was out hunting!" our host concludes with a cough and a chuckle.

As our host reels off his wartime memories, one in particular plays out in technicolour, even though more than sixty years have passed. He tells us how Hermann used to arrive in his *Bundeszug* (government train) filled with art treasures and spoils 'procured' from various museums and private galleries around Europe. Pointing with his stubbed index finger — which he flaunts rather than conceals — to where the castle stands, our host jokes that such was the mass of booty that, once hauled up and installed, the castle seemed transformed on each visit. On one visit it would resemble a Silesian or Bohemian castle; on another the Louvre.

He breaks into a croaky laugh which devolves into an all-out coughing fit. He self-medicates with a cough-lozenge and another cigarette. Resuming, he clarifies that, despite this blemish to his character, Hermann was well-liked by the townspeople. He tells us that Hermann used to fund the communion and confirmation ceremonies of the town's children, providing them with all the expensive garb and paraphernalia.

Trying to steer him back on track, I remind him that I am mainly interested in Hermann's younger brother Albert. The one who saved Jews and political dissidents? Whether a little crazier than we first thought or simply hard of hearing, he maintains his narrative on Hermann and tells us in a tone missing his usual cheer: "Hermann's best friend at school was a Jew, but no one knows why his stance changed." But what about Albert? "Oh, Albert!" he responds back with a blank face. "No one knows much about Albert." Herr Betzeld was right. It seems that, just as in the history books, as far as the people of Neuhaus an der Pegnitz are concerned Albert Göring never existed.

As we leave, I look up again at Albert's childhood home, Burg Veldenstein, and imagine young Albert sitting by one of the many archer's slits, keeping to himself, peering out the window down at the lives as disparate from his as the town is distant from its towering castle.

FOUR

BIRTH

The next bend is always out of sight, each corner a mix of thrill and white-knuckle terror. The light fades as we ascend higher and higher into the Hohe Tauern Mountains. Time is escaping us. Scattered patches of snow become whole ski fields. Skiers careen down shadowy slopes; others dangle on chairlifts suspended over the road. Gradually, the mountain jaws open to a verdant alpine valley dotted by huts snuggled into the mountainside.

It is day three of our journey into the landscape of the Göring brothers' childhood, and Dustin and I are driving on route 99, in the Lungau region of Austria, two hours' drive south from Salzburg. It is the very road that Hermann used to tear down in his bulging 38' 540K Mercedes-Benz and centuries earlier, Roman traders were forced to travel upon. Intercepting these traders is the ancient toll station of Burg Mauterndorf, Dr Hermann von Epenstein's second residence and Albert and Hermann's summer fairytale castle.

The castle is the first visible edifice as you approach the town of Mauterndorf. It sits on a modest rise above the town, reaching nowhere near the heights of Burg Veldenstein. There is also a notice-able absence of the watch towers, secondary walls, archer slits and other defensive measures that punctuated Burg Veldenstein. In its place is an attractive façade of mellow cream stone walls contrasted by mustard quoined brickwork and dark brown, shingled spires; and now, with a dressing of spotlights, it is all the more radiant. Rather than a fort designed to repel treasure-hungry raiders it is more a welcoming manor masking a tax office, as though to lure in unsuspecting traders and then sting them with a toll.

We cross a small wooden bridge built over a relatively shallow moat, empty of water but full of thick grass. An information board tells some of the castle's history. It was originally built as a Roman toll gate before the Salzburger Domkapitel (Chapter) took owner-ship in the 13th century, later reinforcing it in the 15th century to provide protection for the market town of Mauterndorf. It remained in the hands of the Domkapitel until 1806 when the government assumed ownership. Neglected by the authorities, the structure fell into gradual decay. In this state, eager to offload the non-revenue-contributing artefact, the state of Salzburg sold the castle in 1894 to Epenstein for a modest sum.

The castle is supposed to be haunted. On stormy nights, when the wind whistles through the corridors, the long-dead inmates, who perished in the bowels of the castle, are said to scream and seek revenge for all those cold, damp, hungry nights that they were once consigned to. Well, so goes the myth. But right now, with a witches' full moon looming, the myth seems more than plausible. Prepared to take our chances with the ghosts, we continue up the path and come to the rear entrance. We peer through a cast-iron gate with spear-like tips into the castle's courtyard, but this is as far as we can delve; the castle is shut due to winter closing hours.

Slightly dejected, we decide to head into town and find something to eat. The main road through town has nothing main about it. The half-bitumen and half-cobbled stone road is so narrow that two ordinary cars cannot pass each other. We rattle down this channel of terraced houses and quaint boutiques, until we park by the town's church — the same church that Epenstein and his entourage, including Albert and Hermann, would have over-run every Sunday. It being a Sunday evening and a tiny village, little is open. We approach one of the few inhabitants out and about, an elderly lady wearing the traditional hair style of long grey plaits along with a full length fur coat. She tells us that a *Gasthof* down the road might be open.

"*Grüß Got!*" the innkeeper greets us with the same phrase that Albert liked to use, whether addressing a dear friend or a less-than-impressed, Nazi official. "*Wir wollten nur fragen, ob Sie die Küche auf haben?*" we enquire whether they are serving food yet. Much to the displeasure of our growling stomachs, she tells us that dinner will not be served for another hour. Believing all is lost, we make plans for our journey home.

HERMANN, ILL AT EASE in the confines of the classroom, did not take well to school, let alone to pedagogic authority. After all, how could he respect such an authority when at the time he only recognised three masters: his beloved godfather, Mother Nature and, above all, himself. In later years, Hermann would extract great amusement to think that he, the all-powerful Reichsmarschall, could have ever felt the sting of the school teacher's cane.[1]

Initiating what would become an endless escapade of entering and exiting various schools, Hermann began his education in a local kindergarten in Fürth. His tenure at this school only lasted a few temper tantrums, forcing his parents to employ the help of a private tutor for the next four years. Still showing signs of rebellion, it was decided that the stern stick of the German boarding school system was the only resort for such a wayward child. So eleven-year-old Hermann was shipped off to one such school in Ansbach.

Hermann immediately disliked his new environment. The slop dealt out at the school dining room did not agree with Hermann's already refined pallet — no doubt adopted from his godfather. It was in fact so abhorrent that he mobilised his fellow students in a revolt against the school's cuisine, which ended in miserable failure. Humiliated by his first attempt at politics, he took flight. He reportedly sent his bedding ahead to Burg Veldenstein, sold his violin for ten marks for his train fare and suddenly appeared back home.[2] He was hastily sent back and forced to endure further culinary abuse, despite his protestations.

The only respite that Hermann received during these boarding school years came on summer holidays when he could visit his summer home of Burg Mauterndorf. For Hermann the forests and mountains surrounding Mauterndorf were his true classroom, one dictated by the lessons of nature and man's will against it. As the days grew shorter and the air became crisper, he was dragged back every year to what he considered hell. He particularly detested his music classes where he was forced to play the violin, not the piano which his parents had originally enrolled him to play. Hermann's hatred for not only string instruments but also the entire institution festered for sometime until finally the opportunity arose to vent it.

One day in class the students were asked to write an essay about their heroes. Whilst most children wrote about the Kaiser or Bismarck, Hermann chose to write about one of the only men he admired: his godfather, Hermann von Epenstein. The next day he was asked to the principal's office, and there he was reprimanded for writing a piece championing a Jew. The Epenstein name was listed in the semi-Gotha of the time, a publication of all noble families in Europe with Jewish ancestry. And it was apparently a document that the principal had readily at hand. Hermann was forced to write a hundred lines of: 'I shall not write essays in praise of Jews.'[3]

That was nothing compared to the punishment that came at the hands of his fellow peers. Hermann was bullied and forced to walk around the schoolyard in shame with a sign attached to his neck stating: '*Mein Pate ist Jude*.' 'My godfather is a Jew' was a statement that Hermann had never heard before nor would ever accept. The following morning Hermann once again fled Ansbach, though not before avenging his hero's reputation by cutting the strings of every string instrument in the school band.[4]

Somehow this lesson in anti-Semitism failed to create a building block in Hermann's moral foundations. Many years later, as the second most powerful man in the Third Reich, Hermann condoned and assisted in anti-Semitic acts of persecution committed by his own regime. His brother Albert, who seems to have been spared such a brutal childhood lesson, would many years later in Anschluss Vienna rip off a similar sign hung around an elderly Jewish lady's neck that had been strapped on by Hermann's own brown-shirts.[*]

Hermann's final boarding school coup compelled his parents and

---

*See chapter five.

godfather to call on the Army. It was clear that no ordinary civilian teacher could curtail Hermann's wild spirit. A man in a Prussian military uniform, a conqueror of both the might of the Austro-Hungarian and French forces, was seen to be the only force equal to the rebellion of Hermann Göring. So Epenstein called in favours, provided the funds and managed to get Hermann enrolled in a military academy in Karlsruhe.

Being packed off to military school was a dream come true for Hermann, who even from a very young age showed an affinity for all things martial. Hermann, in his Boer uniform consisting of khaki shorts and a wide-brimmed hat, spent hours in his room re-enacting battles from the Boer Wars. Many years later, as a real-life military commander, Hermann told King Boris of Bulgaria that during such battles in his room he would employ the use of a mirror to double his forces.[5] This begs the question whether Hermann, the Lufftwaffe commander, facing a dwindling supply in his inventory, salvaged his old mirror from his childhood when reporting the state of Luftwaffe affairs to Hitler in the closing years of the war.

Hermann flourished in his new environment, attaining in March 1911 a 'quite good' in Latin, English and French, a 'good' in cartography and comprehension, a 'very good' in history, maths and physics and an 'excellent' in geography.[6] His report card read: 'Goering has been an exemplary pupil and he has developed a quality that should take him far: he is not afraid to take a risk.'[7] With such a report card, Hermann was offered a place at the renowned cadet college in Lichterfelde, near Berlin. This was the breeding ground for Germany's future officers.

In December 1913 Hermann not only attained the title of officer with relative ease but was also awarded *magna cum laude* in each subject. A month later, the now ensign Göring was assigned a commission in the Prinz Wilhelm Regiment No. 112 in Mülhausen (now Mulhouse), located then in the south-west of Germany, on the French/German border.[8]

Languishing in his Nuremberg gaol cell, Hermann shared with the American psychiatrist Leon Goldensohn his thoughts on the dispositional differences between Albert and himself: "He was always the antithesis of myself. He was not politically or militarily interested; I was. He was quiet, reclusive; I like crowds and company. He was melancholic and pessimistic, and I am an optimist. But he's not a bad fellow, Albert."[9] In many respects this was a relatively accurate appraisal of, at least, Albert the schoolboy.

Albert quietly satisfied the demands of his teachers but rarely exceeded them. He was considered studious, competent in certain subjects and, unlike his brother, well behaved. He preferred to sit in the back of the class daydreaming, perhaps about the operas and theatre performances he was occasionally taken to by his godfather. Through these outings he developed a love for music and the arts. In particular, he had a gift for music, playing the piano and other instruments at quite a proficient level.

This whimsical, artistic and inconspicuous student drifted through his early school years, not in the halls of the finest boarding and military schools like his brother but amongst the common folk at the local *Volksschule* (elementary school) in Velden and then at a *Progymnasium* (junior high school) in Hersbruck. At the age of eleven he was presented with the same dilemma that German children today have to contend with: join the ranks of the normal Gymnasium system and receive a classical education or enter the *Realgymnasium* and focus on more vocational subjects. Albert chose the latter and found himself in 1906 at a *Realgymnasium* in Munich, immersed in the world of physics and mechanics. Months before the outbreak of World War I, he completed his *Abitur* (secondary school leaving exams), paving the way to university.

In 1913, when Albert was coming into his final *Abitur* year and Hermann was about to sit for his officer exams in Lichterfelde, the sixty-two-year-old Hermann von Epenstein visited the Görings at Burg Veldenstein. There he told both Heinrich and Fanny Göring that he had fallen in love with a young Fräulein — forty years younger than him — and they were soon to wed. Well aware of Epenstein's ways, his soon-to-be bride, Lilli, demanded that he renounce his bachelor lifestyle, which meant formally ending his long-time affair with Fanny. When Epenstein delivered this news to Fanny in Burg Veldenstein, Heinrich emerged from his den and confronted them about all those years they had betrayed and neglected him. His tirade ended with a declaration that he could no longer live under a roof provided by an adulterer and Judas.

The Görings, splitting at the seams, left Burg Veldenstein in the spring of 1913 for a modest existence in Munich.[10] Suffering not only from diabetes and a range of other illnesses but also of a broken heart, the old Reichskommisar shortly thereafter departed his Fatherland and family on the 7th of December for his final posting. It was only after Heinrich's death, when they got a chance to look through his personal documents, that the brothers got to know their true father. Far from the senile drunk they had known as children, they saw a man who had achieved much glory on the battlefield and along the colonial road for the Fatherland. And so both brothers stood beside their father's grave in the family's plot in the Waldfriedhof in Munich, overcome by unfathomable guilt and regret. The guilt was said to be so great for Hermann that his strict Prussian military composure slipped away and a tear ran down his face.[11]

Then the war broke out ...

OUR STOMACHS YEARN FOR a schnitzel. Our heads ache for a bed. We decide to cut our losses and head back to the car. Along the way we spot a café open. Café Claudio is only a small café filled with families and couples. All dressed in their Sunday best, they have just come from mass at the church across the street. We are met by a greeting in unison which I am not familiar with, though it must be the local equivalent of *Gutend abend*! We sink into a leather booth at the far corner of the café.

Gazing around the room I come across a group of well-dressed elderly townsfolk sitting at an adjacent booth. The women wear fine jewellery and matching emerald-green shawls. A man with thin, grey hair looks to be kitted out in the traditional, local Lungau garb: a light grey, collarless, woollen cardigan and a green string bowtie. Not engaging in conversation, he appears content to let the women do the talking whilst he devotes his attention to the glass of red wine and cheese platter in front of him.

There is something about this man that triggers a flash of recognition in me. It is his pair of large 1970s steel-framed glasses. I have seen those glasses somewhere before. I search my mental hard drive until a folder opens and I can attribute those glasses to the man I saw on the British documentary on Albert. It is Herr Hohensinn, a local resident who had shared his memories of the Görings in Mauterndorf. How our fortunes have changed. One minute we were contemplating an early escape, tails between our legs; the next minute we are staring at potentially the next piece to the puzzle, sipping red wine only a couple of meters away.

"*Hallo, Guten Abend! Es tut mir leid zu stören,*" I apologise for

interrupting their conversation after approaching their table. I introduce myself and politely enquire whether he was in fact the same
man that I had seen on the documentary. Yes, I have the right man.
He then begins to tell me a few things about the Görings and
Epenstein, all in clear Hoch-Deutsch, although at times he slips back
into his local dialect. Of course, like everyone else, he tells me right
from the start that no one really knows too much about Albert. He
does say enough for me to ask if I could interview him properly with
a recording device. He shows some hesitancy until his wife interjects:
"Sure, we live just across the street. Come over in an hour or so."

AFTER A MAN WEARING a funny feathery hat and his wife
were struck down by the Black Hand during a leisurely drive
through Sarajevo, a few ultimatums crossed back and forth, treaties
and alliances were assured, and a blank cheque signed by Kaiser
Wilhelm II was delivered to Kaiser Franz Joseph, Hermann's
childhood military board game came to life on the 1st of August
1914. Stationed in Mülhausen on the heavily fortified German/
French border in Alsace-Lorraine, the twenty-one-year-old officer
saw action within hours of Germany declaring war on France.
Unfortunately for Hermann he was on the wrong end of the action.
Part of a decoy incorporated in the Schlieffen Plan, Hermann's Prinz
Wilhelm Regiment No, 112 was ordered to retreat back to the other
side of the Rhine in the traditional German zone, whilst the bulk
of the German forces were in forward motion, steamrolling through
Belgium en route to Paris.

Once the signal for attack was finally granted to Hermann's regiment, he at last had the chance to engage the enemy. But a few skir-
mishes later he was dealt a cruel blow: he was incapacitated by an

acute case of rheumatoid arthritis. These aches and pains in his joints would serve Hermann well, however disheartening it may have been for him at the time. It was this condition that forced him to rest in Freiburg, and it was here that he met Bruno Lörzer, a young *Luft-streitkräfte* (air force) aspirant. Lörzer invited him on board his Albatros B990 as observer, and during one reconnaissance flight over Verdun he took vivid and invaluable pictures of the French battery at Côte de Talon. It was these photos that won him the Iron Cross First Class on the 25th of March 1915 and the chance to train as a pilot.[12] And it was this course that propelled him into the celebrity of a World War I fighter ace, an achievement which would foment his rise to power on the political front in years to come.

In 1916 Hermann's plane was shot down, consigning him to a year of idleness, an anxious wait until he was fit enough for active duty. In February 1917 he was able to join the Jagdstaffel (fighter squadron) 26. Dressed in full metal armour, he had finally become the Teutonic knight of his childhood dreams. Hermann proved to be just as lethal in the air as he was hunting in the woods and mountains around Mauterndorf or Veldenstein. By June 1918 he had notched up twenty-one hits. For this he was awarded an accolade that would ensure him free beer in any German beer hall and true love in any young Fräulein's heart: the Pour le Mérite.

Hermann all of a sudden burst into the realm of German celebrity. His face was all over front pages of newspapers and on magazine covers. His portrait was passed between the sticky fingers of children trading World War I fighter ace cards. He was a hero. He was a rare glimmer of hope for the German people. His rise to fame was beginning to mirror that of the most feared and respected pilot in the world, Manfred Albrecht Freiherr von Richthofen, the Red Baron.

On the 21st of April 1918, the hitherto untouchable Red Baron was shot down by anti-aircraft fire.*[13] Richthofen was succeeded by Wilhelm Reinhard, but he would not hold the reins for long. They slipped out of his hands whilst flight-testing a new Albatross plane, the very plane that Hermann had tested only minutes before. And so another twist of fate saw the appointment of 'No. 178.654, 8. 7. 18 Oberlt. Hermann Göring' as the commander of the Red Baron squadron on the 8th of July 1918.[14]

On the 14th of April 1945, the RAF paid Berlin's little brother city of Potsdam one of their famous visits. Left in their wake was a deep imprint, not only on the landscape of Potsdam but also German military history. For amid the concrete rubble laid Germany's Heeresarchiv (Military Archive), including centuries of military records and, most importantly for my purposes, the slender personnel file of Albert Göring. What still stand today as evidence of Albert's involvement during the war are his military-medical records at the Landesamt für Gesundheit und Soziales (National Office of Health and Social Affairs) archive in Berlin, documenting the exact dates of his enlistment, discharge and war wounds as well as his middle name of Günther, which had hitherto escaped documentation.

Albert's military record begins on the 2nd of August 1914 in a Bavarian enlistment hall where he gave himself up to the Kaiser and Fatherland; a declaration that was by heredity in his blood but not, perhaps, in his heart. He was assigned a position in the Bavarian 6th Reserve-Division as a communication engineer or, as they were

---

*Whilst the Red Baron's hit was once accredited to a Canadian pilot Roy Brown, it is now widely considered that the fatal blow came from anti-aircraft fire – his bullet wound suggests that it came from a 303 round shot in an upward direction. Miller (1998) purports that it was actually an Australian Sergeant Cedric Popkin of the Australian 24th Machine Gun Company who shot the Red Baron down with his Vickers gun.

referred to back then, 'Pionier'.

It was by no means a glorious role like his brother's, but nevertheless an essential one, especially in relation to the blitzing Schlieffen Plan. For every meter of territory gained a meter of communication cable had to be laid, and a break in this progress meant a break in direction and momentum. Without quick and accurate information on the status of the line ahead, the Schlieffen Plan could have easily derailed. Even when the Schlieffen Plan did finally come to a muddy halt, the role of the signalman did not lose its significance. The reliable dissemination of information between the frontline and the generals in their distant châteaux could either foil an enemy attack or mean the difference between a successful and failed offensive.

Accordingly, communication infrastructure was a prime target for enemy assaults. It was Albert's job to implement preventive measures, such as planting cable two meters into the ground, to counter these attacks, and to then repair any disruptions he could not safeguard against. The latter job meant that Albert had to scurry about in the midst of artillery bombardment, find broken connections and quickly repair them whilst dodging enemy sniper fire. Such were the perils of the job that Albert spent most of the war in and out of military hospitals.

Pionier Albert Göring sustained his first war wound during the First Battle of Ypres and was sent off the line on the 14th of November 1914 to a military hospital in Dortmund. Just over two weeks later he was then sent home — and quite literally home as he was housed at the recently converted Burg Veldenstein military hospital. After recovering in the regal splendour of his childhood castle, he was sent back to the Western Front, most likely to the Flanders region along the Hindenburg Line. Albert remained there in the squalid trenches amongst the lice-infested rats and the resultant trench fever, through the frostbite of winter and mud of spring, and under the never-abating cloud of looming death, until he very nearly succumbed to it. Taking part in Ludendorff's last-ditch, spring offensive in 1918, he was struck down by a bullet to the stomach.

The now 1st Lieutenant and Communications Unit Leader of the 103rd Bavarian Division was consigned once again to the bedlam of the World War I military hospital. On the 27th of July he was temporarily interned at a hospital at Montigny en Ostrevent in the French region of Nord-Pas de Calais, before being shifted to another hospital at the town of Péruwelz in the Belgian province of Hainault. With the war all but over and a bullet wound to nurse, Albert hobbled back to Munich on the 15th of August 1918 with his discharge papers in hand.[15]

Today, the whole mess of World War I seems so distant and inconceivably brutal that it is hard to fathom the pain and tragedy that Albert or any other soldier had to endure. In my house the closest we came to understanding it was through the stories passed down by our great-grandfathers and granduncles who shed blood for country and empire on the beaches of Gallipoli and in the quagmire of France. In particular, it was the story of Great-granduncle Les and his portrait that brought this far-away war home. To this day his portrait sits in my family's living room. It is of a fresh-faced man of the age of twenty, proudly adorned in his new khaki, eagerly awaiting his imminent departure for his 'adventure' at the Somme. The portrait stood in my family's home for the duration of the war. It stood there whilst he waited along the line for that fateful whistle; whilst he was bombarded in no man's land and felled by shrapnel; whilst he was bundled off onto a ship bound for England and left to die from his stomach wound, only to miraculously survive. His portrait stayed hanging until he could stand the memory no more and took it down at the age of eighty. The night he took it down he passed away peacefully in his sleep.

The bullet wound inflicted on Albert did not seem to win him the same status in the Göring family folklore as Hermann's exploits, though it was felt by millions of men from both sides who endured this common hell. They could all understand what it meant for Albert to have survived this murderous war that took twenty million lives. Like Great-granduncle Les, the pain of the war and his wound would haunt Albert until his death.

The war took an immense physical toll on all involved, soldier or civilian, but it also weighed heavily on their hearts and minds, especially on those of the vanquished. When that infamous piece of paper was signed on that infamous day on the 28th of June 1919, Hermann, the true soldier, monarchist and patriot of the brothers, plummeted to the ground, as though the Treaty of Versailles was one final Allied artillery round. His heart and pride had been ripped out. He was on foreign ground: he was part of the losing team. His beloved Kaiser was replaced by squabbling liberals and industrialists. He was no longer the war hero but a nonentity without a home. He felt betrayed. This state of mind would dictate the rest of his life and push him towards the man who he would come to think had all the answers: Adolf Hitler.

By contrast, Albert, the professional civilian, would have been happy that the madness was over and life could resume. To facilitate this transition he enrolled in university in the summer of 1919, at what is now named the Technische Unversität München. As his brother rumbled with Bolsheviks and planned a coup with the Freikorps, Albert immersed himself in mechanical engineering studies for the next eight semesters.

[46]

But even Albert, ever disinterested in politics, could not have escaped the political turmoil of the day. Albert's university was just as rife with anti-Weimar Republic, anti-Treaty of Versailles, National Socialist rhetoric as the streets of Berlin and beer halls of Munich. Heinrich Himmler, Albert's future arch-nemesis, attended the same university at the exact time period as Albert. Himmler, an agronomic student, was an active participant in the fraternity scene, the playground of a budding student nationalist movement. Albert surely had an inkling as to the direction his countrymen, with his brother at the helm, were moving.

But these concerns were not the main focus of his time and energy. For the time being, he occupied himself elsewhere: captivating the hearts of women. Like his mentor Epenstein, Albert found himself initially attracted to regal blood and showed a penchant for women bearing the aristocratic title of 'von'. On the 16th of March 1921 he married the twenty-one-year-old Maria von Ummon.

"*ER KOMMT GLEICH*," BLARES Frau Hohensinn's voice through the intercom at the front door. Herr Hohensinn and his memorable steel frame spectacles welcome us in. We follow him through a hallway cluttered with sleds, Christmas decorations and a large, disquieting wooden crucifix of Christ, before winding up a spiral staircase to a kitchen filled with the aroma of freshly baked *Lebkuchen* (gingerbread) — the smell of Christmas in Austria and Germany. Hohensinn moves away an industrial-sized sewing machine from the kitchen table and gestures for us to take a seat opposite him.

After having a good laugh about our little chance meeting and chatting about our previous failed visit to the castle, he begins to tell us a little about Epenstein. Apparently the reconstruction of

Burg Mauterndorf did not take all that long at all. "Why?" we ask. "Because he had so much money," Hohensinn cuts straight to the point. He said that Epenstein was not well-known in Mauterndorf as he spent most of his time in Berlin. Yet they certainly knew his money very well, which, like Hermann in years to come, ensured that he would always be revered by the townsfolk. He was known, for example, to have funded the construction of a local kindergarten. I enquire about the rumour of Epenstein being Albert's real father, and he replies: "All rumours! Some people say that Albert was a son of Epenstein. They are rumours that no one can verify. I would say that it is just gossip." He breaks into full-body laughter as he mentions how such gossip can be perpetuated by the usual culprits: old ladies mingling in supermarkets and church.

The topic of Hermann comes up, and he describes town parades filled with all the hoopla and spectacle only a character like Hermann Göring could inspire. Every time Mauterndorf's favourite son came to visit, his motorcade would be warmly greeted by crowds of townsfolk and children throwing bouquets of flowers into his convertible Mercedes-Benz. On one such visit, Hohensinn tells us, Hermann received more than just flowers.

As was the case in England, the Nazi government had established a children evacuation program, Kinderlandverschickung (KLV), whereby city families vulnerable to air raids could send their children to stay with families in the countryside. The Hohensinns participated in such a program and housed a young girl from the bomb-ravaged Rhineland. This girl was, to say the least, free-spirited. Pointing to a balcony outside the window, Hohensinn describes how this girl and his older sister had a favourite game of throwing water — or anything at hand, for that matter — on unsuspecting passersby below. On one such occasion Hermann Göring happened to be passing by with his entourage in tow. The girls launched a water attack on Hermann's open-air Mercedes. As Hohensinn relates the story his eyes and mouth grow round with disbelief as if he is re-witnessing the whole event.

Officers quickly swarmed the house only to discover that the perpetrators were just a couple of little girls. Once it was known that it was just children at play from an honourable household that hosted a child of the Reich, Hermann laughed it off as kids being kids. He may have sympathised with them as he himself had been known to engage in such mischievous and cheeky pranks as a child. Hohensinn's shocked demeanour slowly makes way for laughter until he abruptly stops, slides his hands down the table as if gesturing to us to come closer to him, lowers his voice and says that the local Nazis failed to see the humour in the event and never forgave his family for the incident. He then makes the point that these were the same Nazis that never opened their doors to the fleeing children of the Reich.

Hohensinn is a natural storyteller, bubbling with excitement as he theatrically unfurls anecdotes and memories. He effectively employs his hands, flailing them above his head to emphasise the enormity and significance of an event or placing them on the table in front of him when he wants to say something in earnest. He knows exactly when to pause or slow his speech to stress a point. In only a matter of sentences his mood and appearance jumps from jubilation and cele-bration to sadness and despair. This has become a common thread in my interviews with survivors of war. Having lived through such emotionally testing times, they oscillate easily between highs and lows, and I am transported on every up and down of this emotional roller-coaster.

Again Hohensinn slides his hands down the table, and the

interview takes a more serious turn, one I did not expect. "And when my father was taken to the concentration camp because he refused to join the party; that was at the time a reason. It was an offence to the Führer. My father was an opponent of the Nazis, and maybe he wasn't so clever. He didn't have any idea how brutal the regime was. It wasn't so well known," Hohensinn explains before saying, "and the Gestapo always came in the night. ... You have probably heard before. They throw a stone on the window, then you have to go see what is happening, and that is how my father was taken!"

His father was sent to Dachau concentration camp where he shared a bunk with a Dr Gorbach who would later become the chancellor of Austria and a regular visitor of the Hohensinns. Whilst his father endured hard labour in Dachau, his family, under immense stress, had no knowledge as to his whereabouts. The Hohensinns were good family friends with the local family Rigele, and the head of this household was a Frau Olga Rigele, née Göring, the older sister of Hermann and Albert. Frau Hohensinn rushed to the Rigeles to seek help, and in a few months father Hohensinn was miraculously released. Once reunited with his family he would not utter a word of his experiences. His silence was born out of trauma as well as fear, for at the gates of Dachau his captors left him with a chilling warning: "If you say one word what happened here, we will be seeing you again!" It was only long after the war that his father would talk about his experiences there.

"And with Albert, this Albert," Hohensinn gasps with disbelief and excitement, "I only found out later from this interview that my father is on this list from Albert!" This list was none other than *The List of Thirty-Four*, and the interview was with the makers of the British documentary I had recognised him from. This is as big a surprise for me as it was for Hohensinn. The documentary did not mention Hohensinn as a member of the list nor did it point to Albert ever intervening on his behalf.

"It can only be that Frau Rigele had called Albert, and through Hermann he had intervened," Hohensinn clarifies. "And this family were no Nazis. ... Hermann always had an ear for his family," he further adds. According to Hohensinn's story then, Frau Hohensinn had brought her husband's arrest to the attention of Frau Olga Rigele, who then contacted Albert in Bucharest where he was working for Škoda. Albert then, either personally or with Hermann's help, secured father Hohensinn's release from Dachau.

He also speculates that Albert knew whilst writing up the list that his father would help Albert should he be ever called to testify in Albert's defence. His father could sympathise with Albert as they shared a common cause and experience: both were terrorised by the Gestapo. Like Albert, Hohensinn's father was arrested by the Gestapo on multiple occasions. The local Gestapo could not accept that he be allowed to resume as an influential businessman and Nazi opponent after his release from Dachau.

After Hohensinn's father was released from a Gestapo prison in Salzburg, Hermann Göring came to visit. During this visit Hermann, the all-powerful Reichsmarschall, asked him what it was like in Dachau, and trusting Hermann, he explained everything that he witnessed there. "Göring was actually shocked!" Hohensinn reveals with a curious tone. "It was not his concern. One must consider that these people, like Göring, were primarily busy with the war. They had to worry about a lot of other things: the Front. And then there were the criminals, who were responsible for these matters: Himmler and so. The camp commandants were the biggest criminals!"

Back in the car on the way to Freiburg, I can't get Hohensinn's last comments out of mind. Hermann Göring, the man who brought the whole concept of the concentration camp to Germany, shocked at what was occurring at Dachau concentration camp?

In 1933, as the then Commander-in-Chief of the Prussian Police and Gestapo, Hermann established the first concentration camps in Germany. They were conceived in response to the Reichstag Fire (27th of February 1933) and the need to accommodate the sudden influx of thousands of new political prisoners. The blame for the fire was conveniently placed on the Communists, the Nazis' political rivals. The camps would continue in this vein as a vital and brutal tool in eliminating political dissidents — or anyone opposing the regime's doctrine, for that matter — and consolidating power. Hermann, well-versed in the history of the Boer Wars, borrowed the concept from a British model instituted by Lord Kitchener during the Second Boer War.

I try to consider Hohensinn's perspective, however contentious as it may be. It is true that Hermann's portfolio was stacked high: he was the Reichsmarschall, President of the Reichstag, Commander of the Luftwaffe, Plenipotentiary of the Four Year Plan, Chief Executive Officer of his industrial empire, Reichswerke Hermann Göring AG, and, for good measure, the Reich Minister for Forestry and Hunting. It is true that Hermann handed over the Gestapo to Himmler in 1934, along with the control of the concentration camps.

It is also true that he was a member of a regime strictly demarcated, steeped in inter-party conflict and secrecy, and populated by paranoid leaders vehemently protecting their portfolios from any outside interference. At constant loggerheads, Himmler and Hermann were engaged in a cut-throat power struggle. Only superficial pleasantries were exchanged between the two; anything more could be used as ammunition against each other. To this end, Himmler would not dare share any information surrounding the affairs of the SS with Hermann, just as Hermann would never divulge to Himmler details of the state of the Luftwaffe or war economy.

Yet it is hard to fathom how Hermann, as powerful and politically shrewd as he was, would not have learnt through other sources what was truly taking place in the camps. With access to his own telephone-tapping unit, the Forschungsamt, he could not have been ignorant of Himmler's work. His own brother Albert had many a time shared his concerns with him. But then again, Albert didn't need documents or telephone taps to tell him he had to act.

1923, A TELLING YEAR for the Göring family. It was a year of two marriages, a graduation, a funeral, a divorce, a failed coup d'état and an exile. The first marriage occurred on the 3rd of February in Stockholm between Hermann and his Swedish sweetheart Carin von Kantzow, who, as her name suggests, came from aristocratic stock.

After the war, there came a period of political and social unrest. The streets were flooded with disenfranchised ex-war heroes like Hermann. And amid this cataclysm, Hermann, the man who once held nothing but disdain for politics and politicians, became political. He joined the ranks of the Freikorps (paramilitary units formed in the wake of World War I) in Berlin and let his voice be heard. Though his speeches were well received, Hermann's political career, at this stage, was not meant to be. His political aspirations fizzled out along with the Freikorps' disorganised and failed 1920 Kapp Putsch.

With no cause defining his existence, no Kaiser or Kaiser's army,

Hermann was rendered inert. But a hand of fate broke through all the anarchy, pulled Hermann to his feet and guided him back to familiar territory: the cockpit of an aeroplane. This helping hand belonged to the Dutch aeronautical genius, Anthony Fokker. Fokker was at the time desperate for pilots of Hermann's calibre, who could extract the best out of his planes and impress prospective Scandinavian clients — a growing market at the time. In the summer of 1920, Hermann left his consultant position at Fokker and indulged his wild spirit. He enlisted the help of four of his old fighter-pilot comrades and treated Scandinavia to some of the death-defying aerobatic displays they were once so famous for. They were revered again, their faces all over magazine covers.[16] Hermann had salvaged his pride.

The Scandinavian winter was looming, and so Hermann sought a job providing steady income. He found work at the Swedish airline Svenska Lufttrafik in Stockholm, chauffeuring the rich and famous. On one unforgiving winter's night, Hermann was forced to stay overnight at the castle of his wealthy passenger, Count Eric von Rosen. It was here in Count von Rosen's medieval castle in Rock-elstad, Northern Sweden, a setting evoking childhood memories of Burgs Mauterndorf and Veldenstein, that Hermann, the Teutonic knight, found his Nordic princess, Carin von Kantzow.[17] Though already spoken for and the mother of an eight-year-old boy, both princess and knight were instantly besotted. Love struck, Carin divorced her officer husband Nils von Kantzow in December 1922 and shortly thereafter travelled south to be reunited with her new beau in Munich.

Next came the graduation. After spending his last three semesters assisting Professor Krell in a study into crane and elevator design, Albert graduated in 1923 with a degree in mechanical engineering and a grade of 'Very Good'.[18] He was now free to leave Munich, the hotbed of National Socialism, for a graduate position at the I.G. Farben factory in Wolfen, Eastern Germany.[19] This was the same company which would leave a large stain on world history, being the company that supplied Zyklon B gas to the Nazi extermination camps. At the time of Albert's employment, however, the company with Farben in its name could only be guilty of colouring the world with their paint and dye products.

Jubilation gave way to tribulation when pneumonia ended the life of sixty-four-year-old Fanny Göring on the 15th of July 1923. Now older, married and hardened by war, the brothers found themselves again standing side by side at the family plot. Except this time, they did not embrace. They were beginning to separate politically and ideologically. Albert was well aware of his brother's political leanings, his early affiliations with the Austrian with that toothbrush moustache and his membership to the National Socialist Party. Years later in Austria, Albert would tell his friend Albert Benbassat: "Oh, I have a brother in Germany who is getting involved with that bastard Hitler, and he is going to come to a bad end if he continues that way."[20] This conflict of interests would lead to twelve years of silence between the two brothers. As Hermann later explained: "We never spoke to each other because of Albert's attitude toward the party. Neither of us was angry at the other. It was a separation due to the situation."[21]

The premature end of Albert's two-year marriage to Maria von Ummon followed shortly. Behind this divorce was another lady with a 'von' title, but unlike Albert's younger first wife, she was a dame of the age of thirty-seven, nine years his senior. Immediately after his divorce, Albert married Erna von Miltner on the 10th of September 1923. Given the proximity of Albert's second marriage to his divorce, a strong argument could be made that his relationship with Erna had begun long before Maria had taken Albert's ring off. This was only the beginning of Albert's capricious and at times scandalous liaisons with women.

Around the same time Albert was at the altar declaring his love for Erna, Hermann was in a Munich beer hall declaring his love for Hitler and National Socialism. Now living in Munich with his new bride, Hermann fell back into the political scene. Both Carin and Hermann became curious about a short-statured man causing shockwaves in Munich's political circles. As Hermann later described his first encounters with Hitler to the American psychiatrist Leon Goldensohn in Nuremberg:

> I was against the Versailles Treaty and I was against the democratic state, which failed to solve the problem of unemployment and which instead of making Germany a powerful nation was turning it into a small, minor state. I am a German nationalist and have high ideals for Germany. ... I met Hitler in 1922 at a meeting and was not too impressed with him at first. Like myself, he said very little at this first meeting. A few days afterward I heard Hitler give an address in a Munich beer hall where he spoke about a greater Germany, the abolition of the Versailles Treaty, arms for Germany, and a future glory of the German people. So I joined forces with him and became a member of the National Socialist Party.[22]

At this stage Hitler and the National Socialists only had a small following and were not taken seriously by the bigwigs of German society: the military, the industrialists and the established order. Hitler needed to recruit a big name; a respectable name familiar to every German household; a name that the elite would respect; and a name he could use to hitch a ride all the way to the Reichstag. The name of Hermann Göring fitted the bill. And Hermann, in return, was presented with a man full of enthusiasm and hope; a man who shared his opinions and was not afraid to speak up; and a man he saw capable of bringing much needed change. In Adolf Hitler, Hermann found a leader.

And so an infamous love affair blossomed in the year of 1922, and as with all classic love stories, a test of devotion was required. This test came on a Friday afternoon, the 9th of November 1923, in Munich, at the Odeonplatz in the front of the Feldherrenhalle. Two bullet wounds to the groin and hip proved Hermann true. These bullets came from the guns of Bavarian state police officers called to quash the coup labelled the Beer Hall Putsch — Hitler's first attempt at prying power away from the Weimar government. This day marked the beginning of four very long, dark years for Hermann. Having escaped the scene of the crime and with a warrant out for his arrest, Hermann was an injured fugitive, country-hopping from Germany to Austria to Italy to Sweden. He was in exile from his Fatherland and reality. In constant physical and emotional pain, he was reduced to a morphine addict, his mental state swinging between comatose and lunatic rage. This earned him multiple stays in various Swedish mental institutions. His only saviour was his loyal wife Carin.

Meanwhile, things were looking bright for Albert. He had just moved north with his new bride to Dessau, where he began a new job, in 1925, at Professor Junkers Kaloriferwerk. Although famous for his exploits in the aviation field, the manufacturing of boilers and heating elements was Professor Junkers' bread and butter. This was the division Albert found himself in. In 1928 Albert's role at Junkers was expanded when he was promoted to the position of representative to Austria, Hungary and southern Czechoslovakia.[23] This meant a move to Vienna but, more importantly, a move away from his brother's *Sturmabteilung* (SA: Nazi paramilitary organisation) thugs and their hate-imbued rhetoric.

Prague one day, Budapest the next, Albert was in his element, wooing clients in the finest restaurants and cafés that each city had to offer. "He always said that he felt most comfortable in the triangle between Vienna, Prague and Budapest — at that time the very hub of Europe," recounts Edda Göring, Hermann's only daughter and Albert's niece. "That was where he was working. That was where he had most of his friends. It was his world. He fitted in very well there; he was elegant, charming, bright and amusing."[24]

Amid the heady delights of the cabaret scene and the Bohemian grandeur of Eastern Europe's cafés and clubs, Albert shrugged off his old skin and brother's shadow at the same time. He emerged a complex man: part phantom hero, part unapologetic hedonist, part ruthless cad. It is here I feel I can stretch my arm out and shake hands with more than an antique sketch of a man or his collection of notes. In the shadow of 1930s Europe, the true and realised Albert Göring introduces himself.

FIVE

A BOY AND A STUDY OF BOOKS

Viennese *Volksmusik* and laughter reverberates across an otherwise lifeless Bucharest street. An aroma of freshly made coffee and tobacco floats out into the thick summer air, taunting envious neighbours stricken by rations. World War II is playing out across the continent, yet an atmosphere of hilarity and conviviality pervades the Benbassat household this evening. This is always the case when their most cherished friend pays them a visit. Sharing jokes and anecdotes of his encounters with the SS, belting out one classic Viennese folk song after another, or just giving that cheeky but reassuring smile, Albert Göring could always turn the sombre into the samba.

From across the street comes the sound of two male voices in song. A glass of wine in one hand and a cigarette in the other, one of Europe's most notorious bon vivants swaggers onto the balcony to investigate the intrusion. The source: two somewhat intoxicated Wehrmacht (German Army) officers trying to give their own drunken rendition of the Wienerlied (Viennese folksong).

"Grüß Gott," they greet each other. "Who are you, what's your name?" one officer enquires. "Albert Göring," he answers. Recognising the famous last name, the two officers both half-jokingly ask: "Are you related?" "Yeah, he's my brother," he calmly responds. Immediately their slouched postures stiffen, their faces tighten, their jovial mood sobers as their regimented Wehrmacht selves engage and roar in unison, "Heil Hitler!" They are, after all, in the presence of the brother of the Reichsmarschall. Yet, being a man who loathes the Hitler-centric rituals of Nazism, Albert Göring simply raises his middle finger and casually says in Viennese dialect: "*Leck mich im Arsch!*" — kiss my arse![1]

I WANDER DOWN A wide street lined with pickup trucks and town cars, all left at neat, forty-five-degree angles. A stranger walking by tips his hat and says: "How you doin'?" The low thud of hip-hop music causes heads to turn as a late-seventies Caddy crawls past. It is a sticky, summer afternoon in Greenville, South Carolina.

Not one to turn down a chance to take in a bit of local history, especially one filled with such drama and senseless tragedy, I follow signs to the local confederate museum. Some people seem to never let things go. The middle-aged curator with his Stonewall Jackson beard, beer belly and Vietnam veteran apparel is a classic candidate. "Not a lot of people know that there was a large contingent of coloured soldiers in the Confederate Army. They say the war was over slavery, but we had free slaves fighting for the confederacy," he confides with the tone of a sore loser. Crazy eyed, edging closer as though he can sense a Yankee spy in our midst, he whispers: "Did you know that the North only abolished slavery in 1865? Lincoln's proclamation only applied to the rebel states." I am deep in Dixieland, a world away from Anschluss Austria, Antonescu Romania and Albert Göring. Yet here in this Southern American setting lives the next piece to Albert Göring's story: Jacques Benbassat. An old family friend and number four on *The List of Thirty-Four*, he is one of the few people left who knew Albert Göring as friend and mentor.

"Hellooo," a woman calls out in a nasally, New York accent as she opens the security door. This must be Doris, Jacques Benbassat's wife of over forty years. She is slight, her bobbed hair frosted with grey, her youthful, dark eyes straining through the lenses of her glasses, as though sizing up her visitor.

"Hi, is Jacques home?" I ask, standing at the foot of the stairs.

"No, Jacques is not here. He is at the doctor's. Who are you anyway? What do you want with Jacques?"

"I had arranged with Jacques yesterday to interview him at 11am; I think I may have spoken with you yesterday when I called."

"No, he told me nothing about this."

"Okay, do you know when he will be back?"

"I don't know," she answers. An awkward silence ensues until I manage to induce an invitation inside by asking if she could call him on his 'cell-phone'.

I follow her through a dimly lit hallway to the kitchen, nearly tripping over a stairlift pitched at a puzzling-low angle. The smell of grandma's house welcomes. The kitchen is a sea of white walls, populated by a school of tropical fish playing follow the leader. The fish halt at a classic World War II US propaganda poster of a lady dressed in overalls and flexing a disproportionately large bicep muscle, and below which bold type proclaims: WE CAN DO IT. Next to an antique fridge Doris picks up an equally vintage phone and asks me what number I would like to call. "Jacques' cell phone," I answer, not sure that she heard me at the front door. Looking at me with a very peculiar look, she chuckles: "Jacques doesn't have a cell phone, silly!" Doris glances at me again, and I recognise the look of incomprehension. It is more than old age, it must be Alzheimer's.

Jacques finally hobbles in with the aid of a walking stick, though there is not much of him to be propped up. Scarce of muscle or fat, his wrinkly skin droops off his bones like a worn shirt draped over a chair. All that covers his face and head are a few long white hairs, clinging on for dear life. Etched across his face are lines that herald a man forced to flee two countries, endure a world war and evade two brutal regimes baying for his blood. Survival meant living long enough to piece together the inconceivable horrors visited upon him, his family and his people. He has persevered through all that man has thrown at him, but now nature conspires to take up where man left off. She has struck him down with lung cancer. He was never a heavy smoker nor did he work in any carcinogenic environments; his plight is another underserved trial that life has pitched at him.

With painstaking care he takes a chair opposite me and places over his protruding ears a set of bubble-lens spectacles. After apologising to me as though he is to be personally blamed for his illness, I break the ice by commenting on how green the area is, an observation most Australians tend to note in foreign countries where rainfall is not a celebrated event. He jokingly replies: "Well, that's why it's called Greenville." Apart from feeling quite stupid, I am pleasantly surprised; despite his struggle with a life-threatening disease, he can still crack a joke.

As he relays various mischievous stories from Albert Göring's life and his own, I can't help seeing a parallel between the two characters. They both seem to be lovable scallywags at heart. Perhaps it stems from Albert's prominent presence in Jacques' formative years. Albert often visited the Benbassat family home where he played the role of 'uncle' to Jacques, the adoring boy. He was also present on skiing holidays in the Austrian Alps with the Benbassats, imparting dark humour and lascivious tales to Jacques, the then young US Army recruit stationed in postwar Germany. "One day we were sitting around, shooting the breeze, you know, and he was sort of down a little bit because he couldn't find a job," Jacques says, recalling a conversation that he had with Albert after the war in Badgastein, Austria. "So he [Albert] says, 'You know, I've been thinking that all my friends who I have done favours for, don't you think they would bring me expensive wreaths if I died?' I said: 'Probably.' He said: 'Wouldn't it be a nice idea if they sent me the money NOW?'"

IT WAS A CRANE that first drew the two Alberts together. Albert Benbassat — Jacques' future stepfather, the aspiring local Viennese businessmen — required the services of Albert Göring — the young Junkers engineer/sales representative by day and bon vivant by night — to supervise the operation of his crane. Whilst a crane would bring them together, a mutual love of fine wine, coffee and curvaceous beauties fostered a relationship that would endure the reign of two fascist regimes and a major world war, and last right up until Albert Göring's death. They both mixed with Bohemian high society in Vienna, Prague and Budapest, which, along with Paris and Berlin, were the cultural and entertainment hubs of Europe. "Lots of charm!

And his thing is that he was happy with a cup of coffee and a glass of wine," says Jacques. "He did alright with the ladies. ... He loved anything that is a little bit exotic. But, he didn't like thin girls. ... He used to look at the girls and say, 'much too thin, I like them fat!'"

Jacques' voice is an almost inaudible croak. Due to his treatment he has temporarily lost his voice, and he breaks, at times, into a fit of hiccups, as though he is having trouble simply processing the air that he breathes. But when he starts to talk about an event that excites him, his symptoms fade, his voice regains authority, and his face is animated. It is as if revisiting his past is therapeutic for him.

Right up until the Anschluss, Albert was a common fixture at the Benbassat household where he always stole the limelight by serenading them with a musical performance or sharing a tale. "I do remember him coming over to the house often. My father always received him well. ... He was into happiness really. Into music. He played the guitar, he played the piano, everything sort of improvised, but he managed," remembers Jacques.

Although Jacques was still too young to know at the time, it was around this stage in his life that Albert Göring first interceded to help those persecuted by the Nazi regime. "I think the first favour was when Hermann Göring asked Albert Göring to fix a job for a friend of his wife in Austria," Jacques says. Instead of Hermann doing a favour for Albert, which would become the norm in the years to come, it was Albert who first did a favour for Hermann.

As the Junkers representative to Austria, Hungary and southern Czechoslovakia, Albert dealt regularly with the Austrian film conglomerate Tobis-Sascha Filmindustrie AG, supplying them with the chemicals needed to preserve their film. Conversation on his visits was not restricted to chemicals, though. On one occasion in 1934 they talked about Albert joining the studio in the role of a technical director. Albert eagerly accepted the position, though not before securing the blessing of his old firm.

At the time Albert was in self-imposed exile in Austria and had become a newly naturalised Austrian citizen. He took this bold action as a direct protest to the 1933 Nazi takeover of the country of his birth. Though offered all the spoils of the Nazi elite, Albert shunned everything the party stood for. His opposition was more than rhetoric; being one of the first people to see the Nazi party for what it truly was and the threat it posed to Germany, he put his ideals into action. This was not the norm. Seduced by the promise of full employment, economic prosperity and the resurrection of national pride, many stayed, conveniently ignoring the brutal Nazification of German society and early signs of the evils to come. Indeed, many Jewish Germans chose to stay. Whilst an initial spike in the year of the Nazi takeover (1933) is evident, Jewish German emigration estimates show a general downward trend henceforth: from thirty-seven thousand in 1933 to twenty-three thousand in 1934 and twenty thousand in 1938.[2]

The man who worked to woo Albert to Tobis-Sascha was company president Oskar Pilzer. Along with his three brothers, Kurt, Severin and Viktor, Oskar had merged Sascha Filmindustrie AG and Tobis-Tonbild-Syndikat AG, having bought the former in 1932 and the latter a year later. After this merger, Tobis-Sascha took the mantle of the largest film concern in Austria. Though, size engendered envy, and envy inspired plans, plans namely in Goebbels' Propaganda Ministry to snatch a piece of this pie. The Jewish Pilzer brothers were by no means ignorant of this threat, not to mention the possibility that their religious heritage might one day be used against them by Austria's anti-Semitic neighbour. This awareness no doubt played heavily on their decision to employ Albert Göring, the staunch Nazi opponent and younger brother of the Reichsmarschall.

Indeed, within just a year of the company's conception, a takeover attempt was made by Goebbels' Propaganda Ministry, only to be warded off by the Pilzer brothers. Vexed but not deterred over this failed bid, Goebbels suffocated his opponent through a ban on all film imports from non-Aryan firms to Germany. With the company now in a groggy spin, Goebbels unleashed a knockout blow. He instigated a freeze on one of Tobis-Sascha's German bank accounts, containing more than one million Reichsmarks, held at a Nazi puppet firm, the bank Creditanstalt (CA). The Pilzer brothers were forced on the 27th of January 1937 to surrender their company to the very firm that had put them in that position in the first place: CA. Although valued at more than thirty-three million schillings at the time, the brothers were bullied into accepting an offer of a mere one thousand schillings. To add insult to injury, they never saw a schilling of this token amount.[3]

Albert was not the only one with a show-business connection. After losing his adoring wife and confidante Carin in 1931 to tuberculosis,* Hermann found love again four years later in Emmy Sonnemann, a theatre actress who had starred in numerous plays at the prestigious Berlin State Theatre. With the Jewish community heavily represented in the German arts, Emmy had many Jewish friends and colleagues who, in the years after the Nuremberg laws of 1935, came to rely on the grace of their politically influential friend. One such colleague was one of Germany's first film stars, Henny Porten. Whilst Henny herself was not Jewish, her husband Dr William von Kaufman was. According to Nazi racial laws, this

---

*Such was his devotion to his first love that Hermann began in 1933 the construction of Carinhall, a hunting estate complete with a mausoleum.

would consign her to the same 'Untermensch' (sub-human) status as her husband. Henny, once the sweetheart of German cinema, found herself in completely foreign territory: she could not find work anywhere.

That was until a chance meeting with Emmy Göring in a Hamburg hotel changed her fortunes. Upon hearing Henny and her husband's plight, Emmy was appalled, and it was not long before she made her first protestations to Hermann. Hermann agreed to help by calling his sympathetic, younger brother in Vienna. "Albert, do you have a say in the film business? Can you do anything for Porten? ... Emmy believes that someone has to help her!" Hermann found himself in a strange position, requesting the help of little brother Albert.[4] Albert gladly obliged and arranged Henny a contract at his production studio. This may not have given her the opportunity to participate in a production there, but it did provide her and her husband financial security.[5] The Porten name is scribbled in at number twenty-six on *The List of Thirty-Four*.

Later in January 1945 and after being ousted from their living quarters in Neuruppin (north-west of Berlin), Henny and her husband were once again helped by Emmy and Hermann when they arranged an apartment for them in the peaceful and relatively SS-free town of Joachimsthal — situated in the state of Brandenburg, on the lake Werbellinsee.[6]

According to Emmy, in her memoirs titled *My Life with Göring*, that was not the only time that the Reichsmarschall had intervened on behalf of one of her acquaintances. She writes: 'I had occupied myself with the case of a Jewish woman doctor from Vienna .... We had succeeded in keeping her out of trouble but suddenly it seemed she was on the verge of being taken to a camp. Something had to be done quickly. I called Hermann .... He advised me to apply to

Baldur von Schirach in Vienna and ask him, at the formal request of the Reichsmarshal, to prevent this internment.' Emmy duly called Schirach and delivered Hermann's request. She also asked whether the doctor would be allowed to 'dispense with wearing the yellow star', but no sooner had she finished the sentence than an 'S.S. man listening on the line broke in' and said: 'The Reichsmarshal did not say anything about the yellow star.'[7]

Göring family folklore works hard to distance Hermann from the anti-Semitic policies of Nazism. Their protestations hinge on the fact that many of Albert's interventions on behalf of Jew and gentile depended on Hermann's direct help. Hermann's daughter, Edda Göring, comments: "It was like this: he [Albert] could certainly help people in need himself financially and with his personal influence, but, as soon as it was necessary to involve higher authority or officials, then he had to have the support of my father, which he did get."[8] Without the protection and, at times, outright support of his brother Hermann, Albert could not have evaded the Gestapo nor rescued as many people as he did, especially the more prominent ones. Albert's very life and actions throughout the war stands as a testament to this Göring family stance.

Yet Hermann's willingness to help and protect his family, occasionally assisting them in their whims, does not mean that Hermann sincerely cared for the plight of the Jews. It was more a case of family above party as well as a means to stroke his ego by demonstrating his power. Whilst he sporadically alleviated the plight of the persecuted to better his family's perception of him, he consistently enabled the persecution to improve his standing within the party. If propagating anti-Semitism on the public stage meant political advancement, he would gladly do so. As Jacques sums it up: "He [Hermann] was no more anti-Semite than anybody else; he just used it where it was convenient."

THE GERMAN WORD 'ANSCHLUSS' roughly translates to mean a political union. It is the word commonly used to describe the period in Austrian history — from 1938 to 1945 — when Austria was a member state of the Third Reich. Yet in actuality there was no political union between Germany and Austria in the sense that each country had equal control of the governing of the Germanic empire. Nor was the union's formation absent of any duress. Rather, the events of the 12th of March 1938 in Austria could be more appropriately labelled as a military annexation, just like all the other military annexations made by the Nazi war machine throughout Europe.

Pressured to secede power by Hitler's ultimatums, Austrian Chancellor Dr Kurt von Schuschnigg made one last attempt to assert Austrian independence. On the 9th of March he called a referendum, which was to be held on the 13th. He hoped to put Austria's fate into the hands of the Austrian people and asked them to vote for or against the proposed Anschluss. Hitler immediately sought to hijack the event, denouncing its authority and even claiming that it would be riddled with fraud. And then on the morning of the 11th of March he issued a final ultimatum, demanding that Schuschnigg hand over power to the Austrian National Socialist Party. This was a smoke-screen. Hitler had already given the order for German troops to march over the Austrian border one hour before the deadline. Then, with the support of German troops, the Austrian National Socialists launched an armed coup, deposing Schuschnigg and his government. In an attempt to legitimise their assumption of power and the Anschluss, Arthur Seyss-Inquart, the new nonelected Chancellor of Austria, reintroduced Schuschnigg's referendum, although it would prove to be anything but an example of democracy.

On the day of the referendum, Albert tried to counter this

attempt to derail the democratic process. "They had SS and SA officials standing at the voting locations," Jacques relates. "There was a booth in which you could vote secretly, but the first people in line were usually Nazis. They came up. They proudly said: 'I don't need the booth.' Voted yes. And then the people behind them didn't dare, in front of all these Nazi officials, to go and use the booth. When [Albert] Göring came and identified himself as everybody had to, they said: 'You certainly won't need the booth.' He said 'On the contrary, I need the booth' [and] went into the booth and voted no. And thereby [he] enabled the people behind him to use the booth without fear and vote with their conscience."[9] Albert's efforts were, however, made in vain. The referendum ended with an emphatic 'yes' to the Anschluss, as evidenced by the 99.73% of votes cast in approval of the 'union'.

Once Seyss-Inquart had both hands on the reins and a swarm of brown and black shirts had populated the streets, Nazi sympathisers sprung out of the woodwork. With ethnic tension already levelled at the minorities of the old Habsburg Empire — the Poles, Czechs, Hungarians, Ukrainians and, of course, Jews — Nazi fervour ignited. The self-proclaimed 'true' Austrians took it upon themselves to violently assert their Aryan dominance.

As a schoolboy in the third grade, Jacques found himself in the middle of this storm. "Every morning we had to recite the Lord's Prayer, and this was always followed by [a] reading from *Mein Kampf*," Jacques recalls. "And shocking stories, you know. How the Jews always played a terrible role. And there was one other kid in my class who was not Jewish, but he was baptised [as a Jew]. And unfortunately for him he was the class nerd. He was the only kid that wore long stockings, and he had glasses, but they were too big."

Just as Jacques is about to get to the crux of the story, Doris wanders into the room. She has a charm about her that reminds me of George Costanza's mother in *Seinfeld*. The Alzheimer's gives her feisty manner a sort of black humour.

"Why are you whispering? You don't want me to hear?" Doris mimics Jacques' whispering as though she has stumbled across a conversation of extreme confidentiality.

"Because I can't speak!" he responds abruptly.

"What did they say about your voice in the hospital?"

"They said it was beautiful."

"When are you going to get it back?"

"A couple of days."

"A couple of weeks?"

"A couple of days!" he strains his voice to correct her.

"Oh, days. I don't like to read lips."

"What don't you like?"

"I like to hear."

"Sorry I can't help you."

After the little quarrel, Jacques' voice is even hoarser as he returns to his story: "And we had this teacher who as soon as the Anschluss happened had the swastika on. And he caught them [the class bullies] going after the nerd, and he laid into them. He laid down the law for them. He said: 'This is not what National Socialism is all about. This is not about persecuting people.'" How wrong and naïve this teacher proved to be. "I guess there were a lot of them [who] didn't know what was going to happen," adds Jacques. "They didn't know how bad it was going to be."

SOME INDICATION OF NAZI persecution was, however, already evident on the streets of Vienna, where it was not uncommon to see

[71]

the SA or even Viennese civilians publicly humiliating members of the local Jewish community. Apart from cutting off the *payot* (sidelocks) of the orthodox Jews, one particularly sadistic ritual involved forcing old Jewish ladies to scrub the cobbled streets of Vienna on their bare knees.

"Albert Göring happened upon such a scene," Jacques recalls a story that his stepfather Albert Benbassat had told him, "With some Austrian SA standing around and Viennese mob lashing and mocking a few old women who were scrubbing the street. So Göring simply arrived, he just took off his jacket, he grabbed the brush from one of the women, knelt down and started to scrub. And when the SS grabbed him and asked him for his papers, and when he showed him the papers, that was the end of that scene."[10]

This for any other person would have been suicide. The fear of receiving a beating, sharing the same fate as the persecuted, or, even worse, being alienated and labelled one of 'them', would normally prevent any other mortal from voicing their concerns. But Albert was no mere mortal. He was Nazi royalty, but at the same time, he was not afraid to sully his royal status by undertaking such actions. In saying that, his bravery in such circumstances should not be overlooked. Göring or no Göring, any individual publicly defying the authority of the common SA thug was liable, in the heat of the moment, to a beating or arrest, no matter the consequences. Any Jewish survivor of those days would tell you that this kind of defiance would have been no easy task, even for Albert Göring.

Albert was in fact arrested by the Gestapo the next time he intervened on behalf of the persecuted in the streets of Vienna. Albert came to the aid of a "seventy-five-year-old grandmother" of a Jewish owner of the then besieged "paint shop S. Raber in the Wehringerstraße". Jeered on by a crowd, a group of SA thugs was ridiculing her, having placed around her neck a sign proclaiming 'I am a Jewish sow.' Albert came upon the commotion and broke into a fit of rage and disbelief. His innate sense of righting wrong kicked in. And so he "fought his way through the crowd" to the centre of the scene.[11] "I went in at once and liberated her, and while I did so, got into trouble with two SA men; and I hit them, and was arrested immediately," Albert explained to Lieutenant William (Bill) Jackson during his interrogation at Nuremberg.[12]

Albert, unlike most unfortunates subjected to SS hospitality, did not spend too long in custody. He was promptly released on account of his name and the influence of powerful friends living in Vienna. Yet before his release, he was warned that "such a thing must never happen again".[13] He must not have found this admonishment particularly threatening as this two-step of issuing and quashing arrest warrants would repeat itself a total of four times throughout the duration of the war.

The doorbell rings, and Jacques gets up to let in a pair of air-conditioner repair men. "Heeellooo, I'm coming innn," the taller of the air-conditioner men announces in a slow southern drawl.

"What is he going to do? Speak, what is he going to do?" Doris asks with a touch of angst and urgency in her voice, wearily looking around for what she thinks to be an intruder prowling about the house.

"He is going to fix the air-conditioning. Have you noticed that it is warm. It's not working," Jacques says in a weary, humouring tone.

"I am going to go upstairs. What is he doing up there?" asks Doris, who at this stage is in a fit of paranoia after seeing the air-conditioner men walk upstairs to assess the problem.

"He's fixing the air-conditioning," he repeats.

"Oh, we better go up and see."

"Yes, yes, yes!!"

"What did you tell him to fix?" she turns around to ask again at the foot of the stairs.

"The air-conditioning!!!!!" he yells.

Yes, there is a macabre horror to Alzheimer's, but Jacques and Doris seem to have settled into a comfortable sort of sitcom comedy. He humours her as long as it is humanly possible, and she keeps delivering her knockout lines with her blunt, Jewish matriarch's force. Lung cancer, Alzheimer's, Holocaust survivors … somehow Jacques and Doris make it all seem a long way from tragedy.

THE PRESSURE BEGAN TO mount on the Benbassat household in Vienna, with each day of the Anschluss presenting a new threat. Owning five apartment buildings, Albert Benbassat had managed to build a small real estate empire before the Anschluss. Yet the Anschluss entailed not only a political annexation but also an economic one. Companies were either forcefully incorporated into the Nazi war-economy or commanded to operate in accordance with Nazi ideals. In just a few months after the Anschluss, 50% of Jewish businesses were involuntarily dissolved.[14] For the Benbassats this meant that they would lose all five apartment buildings, leaving them with only a small villa on the outskirts of Vienna. The 'Nazi Mortgage Company', as Jacques labelled it, simply revoked their mortgages. Given the ominous political and social climate, and on the advice of Albert Göring, the Benbassats decided to move in the spring of 1938 to Nazi-free Bucharest, Romania.

In Bucharest, the Benbassats also had the added security of knowing that Albert, their guardian, was never too far away; he, too, now lived in Bucharest. As Jacques recalls: "It was mostly moral support and this great solidarity that we knew we had somebody with influence in case." This new-found security allowed young Jacques to regain some semblance of a childhood. He remembers playing on the waterslides and the wave-pool in the local water park that was funnily enough designed by Albert Göring himself — in fact, Albert may have designed the first water park in Europe, if not the world.

Albert also found another way of making Jacques and his family's lives somewhat more tolerable in Bucharest. Prior to the Anschluss, Jacques' stepfather had an extensive collection of very rare and expensive books, "all the classics". Just beginning to read consistently, Jacques took great pleasure in reading these books. This all came to an end when a representative from a large German book dealer paid the Benbassats a visit in Vienna, demanding to buy the whole collection for a fraction of their true value. Since this company was in bed with the local Nazi party and Jacques' stepfather would never jeopardise his family's safety for a collection of books, no matter how cherished they were, he had no choice but to accept the offer.

Months later in Bucharest, Albert Göring became aware of this injustice and took immediate action. He approached the Romanian branch of the German book dealer and casually requested the books back. "Göring says, 'How much did you pay?' 'One hundred [Reichsmarks].' 'I'll buy them from you for one hundred and one.' And they didn't dare say no," Jacques recounts. "Then instantly came a truck full of books in Bucharest. We had a walk-in closet, up to the ceiling full of books. For me it was a real find, I spent hours and days in that closet with my books. It was my first contact with literature!" Jacques reminisces.

Alas, it was only a matter of time before the political environment in Bucharest turned hostile for the Benbassat family. In response to the continued threat of the Red Army, King Carol II of Romania appointed 'The Red Dog' (*Câinele roșu*) General Ion Antonescu in September 1940 as Prime Minister. It took only two days for Antonescu to oust King Carol II and temporarily replace him with a figurehead: Carol's son King Mihai. He was then free to declare himself the supreme *Conducător* (leader) of Romania.

Having allied with Nazi Germany, Antonescu sought to appease and tame the local Fascist and anti-Semitic party, the Iron Guard, by offering them seats in Romania's decorative government. This proved to only temporarily satisfy the extremist party's thirst for power, and on the 21st of January 1941 they attempted an armed coup. Living right in the heart of Bucharest, the Benbassat family were caught in the middle of the gunfight.

"They were shooting in the streets: the Army against the Legionnaires. We had a house with the rear of the house on a plaza. ... And on that plaza there was constant fighting. We could hear them: some shooting and somebody yelling hooray, hooray, hooray," Jacques exclaims. Amid the fighting, their cook, an ethnic German, courageously offered to fetch some food from the plaza for the children. Not too long after, she returned unscathed and bearing food. "And she was our big hero until the Army kicked the heebee geebees out of the Legionnaires. ... I could see them on the roof, across the house ... taking away their wounded," Jacques recounts. The next day the cook told the Benbassats that she needed to immediately leave as her mother had fallen ill. The Benbassats let her go and bade her good luck. Once she had left, though, their Romanian maid walked in to the Benbassat lounge room crying. The maid said that the cook had given them away to the Legionnaires and that "she had told those guys that there were Jews there with nice furniture and so on." The cook even went as far as instructing the Legionnaires: "When you finish here with the Army, come across the mall and help yourselves, and give me a commission." Jacques' voice lowers as he leans over to tell me: "And we would have been dead. These guys didn't care if we were Spanish or Chinese."

Whilst Antonescu helped the Benbassats in ridding them of the threat of the über anti-Semitic Iron Guard, Antonescu was by no means a saviour of the Jewish people. Officialising the country's already long tradition of anti-Semitism, Antonescu's regime began in the summer of 1941 to hunt down and deport 'alien' Jews to various concentration camps in Transnistria, Ukraine — then Romanian occupied territory. By the following summer these camps had swelled to approximately one hundred and eighty thousand inhabitants.[15] Other similar labour camps inside Romania would arise in the ensuing months. Antonescu's Romania was in fact the only other Axis country that matched Germany's resolve to exterminate the Jewish people. The largest massacre occurred on the 24th of October 1941 in Odessa. In response to an explosion destroying the Romanian Military Command in Odessa two days before, twenty-five thousand Jewish men, women and children were slaughtered. As Alexe Neacşu, a Reserve Second Lieutenant of the Twenty-Third Infantry Regiment, testified:

> They proceeded to machine-gun those inside the four sheds .... The sheds were handled one at a time, and the operation lasted until nightfall. ... After having machine gunned those sheds for several hours, the commanders of that operation ... complained that this was the only way that they could liquidate those who were inside; they were visibly annoyed at not having found a faster way to complete these operations. They

resorted to oil and gas and then sprayed and set the sheds ablaze. ... Some of those who had been inside appeared at the windows and, in order to escape the flames, begged with hand signals to be shot and pointed at their head or their heart. ... Some women threw their children through the window.[16]

Indeed, Jacques' stepfather very nearly found himself shipped off to one of Antonescu's concentration camps. On one occasion, a squad of official thugs stormed Jacques' house and attempted to snatch his stepfather away. That was until "some money exchanged hands" and his stepfather was able to buy his freedom. Coupled with this scare and news of the atrocities in the North-East, it became clear that the Benbassats were no longer safe in Romania. It was only for so long that Albert Benbassat's bribes and Albert Göring's protection would hold on. And so the Benbassats were forced to flee yet another city. They chose to swap one dictator for another and travel to Franco's Spain. Franco showed signs of sympathy for Europe's Jews. He instituted a policy that Jews of Spanish origin who could show evidence of their Spanish heritage — such as speak the language — were eligible for Spanish citizenship. Since Jacques' stepfather was of Sephardic Jewish descent (the Spanish-speaking Jews originating from the Iberian Peninsula) and could still speak an old dialect of Spanish, he and his family were granted Spanish citizenship. Before they could travel to Spain they also needed to procure a Romanian exit visa, as well as Hungarian, Croatian, Italian, Swiss and French Vichy Government transit visas. These, according to *The List of Thirty-Four*, were procured by Albert, along with foreign currency for the journey.[17]

During the whole trip they had to act like Spanish citizens, that is, they were meant to speak only Spanish. Jacques had taken Spanish classes at the Spanish consulate in Bucharest and held a sufficient command of the language. But, as Jacques remembers, there were a few times en route when he slipped back into German. Lucky for the Benbassats, the swift arm of his mother was always there to smack the German out of him. Apart from this and some issues concerning his grandma's completely false Chilean passport, their trip to their first port of call, Venice, went relatively smoothly. And who was waiting for the Benbassat family in Venice with a suite at one of the grandest hotels in town? None other than Albert Göring. "He just wanted to make sure that we got there alright," hiccups out Jacques.

From Venice they took the midnight train through Milan into the safe haven of Geneva, Switzerland. They were only supposed to stay in Geneva for a short time, yet an infection to Jacques' stepfather's toe would require that the Benbassats remain in Geneva for a little longer. As Jacques' stepfather received treatment, Hitler decided to invade the semi-sovereign zone of the Vichy Government on the 11th of November 1942. This meant that the Benbassats' visas were suddenly made invalid, stranding them in Switzerland for the remaining years of the war. It was a strange confluence of circumstances in which an initiative from Hitler would actually benefit the family.

The Benbassats were not entirely stranded, though. A friend had left one last gift for them in Switzerland: "Albert Göring helped transfer the currencies for Jews in Romania and other countries under German occupation to Switzerland. And in our particular case that enabled us to have an account in Switzerland when we arrived there."[18]

THE ONCE SLEEPY GREENVILLE airport I had arrived in is

now a madhouse of activity. A queue at the check-in counter winds almost all the way outside the door. The airline staff have one ear on a land-line phone, one on a mobile phone and another to the irate customer in front of them. Despite this confusion, there is apparently nothing wrong, and my flight is scheduled to depart on time. Once I am at the gate, however, the story changes. An electrical storm in Washington DC is apparently at the root of this chaos, and it will inevitably prevent me from catching my connecting flight from there to London.

"When would be the next available flight to London?" I ask an airline representative at the gate. "How does Saturday sound?" she says. It's Tuesday. Okay then, hotel? No, because they are not liable for problems arising from natural forces. Waitlisted flights? No, you must be in DC for that. Any food? No, all the shops have already closed at 9 pm. I am in airport hell!

Pass through those metal detectors and the airport experience tends to be the same the world over: a strange twilight place between the known and yet-to-be known. Like hospitals, they are a crucible of humanity; a forced intersection of people and their journeys. Sometimes they can present a touching scene; the family reunions and tearful goodbyes are better than any Hollywood blockbuster. But stand in the middle of an airport meltdown, complete with condescending staff, heightened security and travellers squabbling amongst themselves, all competing for a way out, and you are sure to behold the worst of human nature. This is Greenville Airport on a bad day. And though it pales in comparison, it seems as good a place as any to contemplate one of man's lowest points of the 20th century.

Watching my fellow travellers unravel with all the confusion, I find myself returning to the narrative that has gripped me for so long: Albert Göring's. Hearing so much of Albert's story recounted by Jacques has my head buzzing. Jacques has had sixty-odd years to contemplate the Nazi legacy and to wonder why Albert fought the regime when so many others remained inert. What pushed Albert to stand in defiance, risking his freedom and even life? And why do this for not only close friends but also complete strangers?

It was on one of the Benbassats' family holidays with Albert in the Alps that Jacques chanced upon the answer. At one point, Albert asked him for his definition of friendship. Jacques, only a naïve teenager at the time, answered: "You know, a friendship is when you enjoy someone's company and you like to hang out." Smiling and shaking his head, Albert whispered into Jacques' ear: "It is much more. A friend is someone who will risk his fortune, his safety, even his life when you need him." Albert apparently saw a friend in everyone.

S I X

É M I G R É

Time runs a lap around the block, but still there is nothing. I try the buzzer again, and finally, after a few more anxious moments, a faint voice responds through the intercom. It belongs to Christine Schöffel, the only daughter of the acclaimed lyricist, script writer, director, producer and witness to Albert's heroism in Vienna, Ernst Neubach. I await Christine outside her lemon-chiffon, terraced apartment, on the rim of the Altstadt in Graz, Austria. The chocolate dome of the Graz Opera House peeks out from the end of the street. The cultural centre of Austria buzzes below. And the remains of the Iron Curtain decay just fifty kilometres down the road.

A large metal double-gate, once the threshold for well-to-do residents arriving home in their horse carriages, laboriously opens, and there to greet me is a picture of European sophistication. Christine is dressed casually in a pair of jeans, a black, long-sleeve top and a pair of trendy, chequered Keds. Her tanned face hints of holidays in the Greek Islands. Her shoulder-length, caramel hair has the sharp finish of an expert — and expensive — friseur. True to her show-business roots, she has an undeniable actress' air to her.

Across the apartment's courtyard to an arched doorway, up a dark, spiralling stairwell with worn wooden steps, we arrive at a high-ceiling apartment. The apartment is an extension of the city of Graz itself, a harmony of antiquity and modernity. There is not a corner of the room or a wall bare of a Picaso-esque painting, a classic stone sculpture, or a piece of furniture, itself a work of art or the result of years of study in furniture design.

Christine whisks off to the kitchen to brew some coffee, and we then settle into the lounge room. She cuts to the chase. She is at a loss as to why someone so young, from a country so far away, would be interested in this period of history and travel all the way to Graz. It is an oft-asked question, and I am able to communicate my intentions effectively. Satisfied with my defence, the intimidating madam seems to relax, and as though a queen on her throne, she flicks her manicured hands, announcing that the interview may begin. "He told me that Albert Göring was a man who helped the people," says Christine, relating the memories of her father. "But not only this, because when he helped the people, it was very dangerous for him. Because you never know if the regime would accept this. How far could he go? He always went to his frontier. And this was a problem for him. But he survived, and that was unbelievable."

"MY FATHER WAS BORN in Vienna, the 3rd of January 1900. … His father worked in the National Railway Authority, and his mother was a housewife. He had one brother," Christine quickly corrects herself, "two brothers." I am puzzled as to why she could have almost forgotten an uncle, but then she reveals: "He had one brother who went to Venezuela in 1938, and the other came to Buchenwald." Buchenwald, said so casually that I almost failed to recognise it as the infamous concentration camp. I would later find out that her uncle Robert was murdered at Birkenau, the largest of the death camps in the Auschwitz network.

Long before losing brothers to death camps and Nazi persecution, Ernst Neubach had a somewhat peaceful life. Upon his birth, Neubach was taken home to the Neubach family apartment in Leopoldstadt, the once predominately Jewish district of Vienna. As Vienna was a unique carnival of cultures, Leopoldstadt was an eclectic *chag* attended by an assortment of Jews. There were the moderate or assimilated Jews of merchants and common workers. And then there were the orthodox Jews with their caftans, untrimmed beards, long *payot* and foreign tongues, who hailed from the eastern lands of the old Habsburg Empire. Generally, the groups did not mix — one group being too 'Jewish' and the other being too 'Austrian'. The Neubachs fell into the latter group, only recognising their heritage on a collection of Jewish holidays.

Indeed, once Neubach had finished his schooling in the Gymnasium, he fought proudly alongside his brother Robert for the Austro-Hungarian Empire in World War I, whilst the eastern Jews, for the most part, stayed behind and ridiculed them for doing so. Neubach saw himself as a proud Habsburger, and after he converted to Christianity to marry his Catholic wife and Vienna became the capital of the new nation of Austria, he considered himself a proud Christian Austrian. A testament to his patriotism, he remained an active member of the Österreichs Bundesheer (Federal Army of Austria) in the postwar years, serving as a lieutenant in the army reserve right up until the day swastikas painted Vienna.

Growing up, Neubach always had the intention of attending university. Yet World War I and the ensuing fall of the Habsburg monarchy would change all this. For when the fatherland succumbed in 1918, so did father Neubach, leaving his family only a meagre pension to survive on. Neubach was forced to abandon any ideas of intellectual enrichment and, instead, don a pair of overalls and put up placards.

With each placard of a new opening play or film that he pasted up, regret cut deeper and deeper into his conscience. He knew that it could have been his name advertised on these placards. He had a talent with prose, and he felt deprived of the chance to demonstrate it. Then one day, when the pain reached such a level that prudence became redundant, he took action. He picked up the pen and proceeded to churn out one hit film script and song after another. In time, he would become the Andrew Lloyd Webber of the day. "He started to write *Trenck* very early. And he made a lot of Evergreens. That means he wrote *I lost my heart in Heidelberg, My song goes around the World* with Josef Schmidt because he did most of the songs of Josef Schmidt," Christine mentions just a handful of her father's triumphs at the box office and on the charts. It was in the middle of filming one of these works at the Tobis-Sascha film studios in Vienna that Albert Göring barged onto Neubach's stage.

"Göring here. I am calling in regards to the bills ... I will regretfully be forced to cut off the power if you don't shortly [pay]," was Neubach's introduction to Albert.[1] As with most filmmakers, Neubach had fallen into the red whilst making his film *Milionäre* at the Tobis-Sascha film studios, of which Albert was now the studio manager.

At that stage, Neubach had only known of Albert through the gossip and rumours that circulated the Austrian film fraternity. He had heard his colleagues developing theories to explain why the brother of Hermann Göring was working as a studio manager, earning him a meagre eight hundred shillings a month, when he could be enjoying a prosperous career in German industry. Nor could he have missed the rumours that the swish, brown Steyr cabriolet, in which Albert regularly flirted around town, was a gift from his brother. For these reasons, no one really knew how to receive and act around Albert. And so, when Neubach went to visit Albert at the film studios in Siebensterngasse, his gait bore a slight tremor.

Albert with his 'oval shaped face, long sideburns and thin moustache' greeted Neubach in his office. He sat at his desk with the rigid, straight-backed posture of a Prussian general. Costs and figures were immediately laid bare, causing a grimace to grow on Neubach's face. Albert took this reaction to be a sign that Neubach would not be able to immediately meet the costs and decided to change tack. He abandoned his stiff manner, moved closer to Neubach and told him that he would give him a three-day extension. Surprised by this bit of generosity, Neubach broke the ice and invited him for coffee. And what an ice-breaker it was, for 'coffee was his chief pleasure'.[2]

After the second cup of coffee, Albert began to chat intimately to Neubach about his lodge in Grinzing and his Austrian naturalisation. After the third cup of coffee, the conversation then jumped to Albert's politics, or rather lack thereof. He revealed that he no longer spoke to Hermann, the Nazi politician, but still considered him as a brother. He fumed at how he could no longer stand the Nazis in Germany, and he 'prophesied a bitter end for Germany'.[3] Here at this Viennese coffee house began a 'little friendship', as Christine put it, between two soon-to-be émigrés.

Half a year later, Neubach was relaxing and listening to jazz music on the radio with his new bride, when the program came to a sudden halt and on came a sombre Dr Kurt von Schuschnigg, the chancellor of Austria: "And so I take leave of the Austrian people with a German word of farewell which I utter from the depths of my heart: Gott schuetze Oesterreich [GOD PROTECT AUSTRIA]!"[4] It was at 7:45pm, Friday the 11th of March 1938 that this broadcast announced Schuschnigg's resignation and ultimately the beginning of the Anschluss. Then as *Die Fahne hoch*, the Horst Wessel song — German Nazism in its musical form — trumpeted through Austrian airways in the early hours of the 12th of March, all of Austria knew it was true: the Germans were here. Mobilised by a Schuschnigg order and stationed at the Franz-Josef Bahnhof, reserve Lieutenant Neubach witnessed his countrymen's reaction to this news. He saw the streets of Vienna swell with people preparing for the arrival. Some did so by packing their bags, whilst others did so by helping them to pack.

That night Neubach received a knock on his door. It was a sympathetic neighbour brandishing an SA list of all the people who were to be arrested first, and on that list was his name. That was it, he had to flee. The next day his wife called an array of consulates to secure an exit visa, only to find out that all of Austria's borders were blocked, except for one: the Swiss border. She found some of her stationery belonging to the firm she was working for at the time and wrote a letter declaring that Neubach was a representative of the firm en route to do business in France. With this flimsy piece of legitimation and nothing but uncertainty ahead, he jumped into a taxi with his wife and mother to the Westbahnhof. As the taxi navigated through a sea of swastikas, they witnessed youths emboldened by hate yelling taunts of 'smoke out the Jewish pest' and brown shirts mocking

'Eastern Jews' forced to dance at their behest. Finally arriving at the train station, they rushed to the platform where the train to Paris filled with other desperate escapees. As that last call whistled out and the train chugged out of the station, Neubach became consumed by thoughts of the life he had left behind: his wife, his mother, his brother, his films, his Vienna. There and then he knew he had just seen his 'beloved mother for the last time in this life'![5]

The day after Neubach fled Vienna, the Gestapo terrorised his wife and ransacked their apartment in search of him. When news of this reached Albert, he visited Neubach's apartment to console his wife. There he reassured her that if called upon, he would do everything in his power to assist in her escape.[6]

CHRISTINE JUMPS FROM HER slouched position in the deep-sunken couch to grab a pair of thick, black square-framed reading glasses from the coffee table. Her dark brown eyes then scan the pages that I have just given her. As she reads, her eyebrows arch with astonishment, and a smile overcomes her face. Behind this excitement is a letter written by her father addressed to the post-war Czechoslovak President Benés — or Monsieur le Président de la République as he referred to him in the letter — sent to aid Albert Göring's defence whilst he was on trial in Prague in 1946 for war crimes against the people of Czechoslovakia. She never knew of the existence of such a letter, let alone laid eyes on this testament of Albert's good deeds. She places the letter down and steps back on stage, narrating Albert and her father's story: "Yes, afterward he told me. He told me that Albert Göring helped a lot of people, a lot of Jewish people, coming out of Germany or France. And he did it like

[this]: he signed a paper or he wrote the paper. He had the letters signed with Hermann Göring and signed with his name. ... And that's what my father told me."

Like a frontline doctor, Albert worked nonstop in the first few months after the Anschluss, healing wounds inflicted by his own brother and his henchmen. One of his first acts was to come to the aid of his Jewish film-industry colleagues. Oskar Pilzer, the man who had given Albert his break in the film industry, ended up himself receiving a break from Albert. "We were terribly frightened. These people came in through the house. They rattled with their guns, and they were in uniform. And they were very menacing. And they took my father, put him in to a corner, put the gun behind his back and stole a number of things in the apartment what they thought was of interest to them. And then they took off with my father. And you can imagine the situation we were in, how we felt," George Pilzer, Oskar's son, recounts the day when the Gestapo wreaked havoc on their lives.[7] Goebbels was apparently not satisfied enough to just pilfer Pilzer's company and livelihood; this time he wanted his life.

An urgent plea was relayed through Albert's busy phone line, and by that afternoon Pilzer was free again. As George Pilzer comments: "Due to his name, he exerted all influence — and I am underlining 'all influence' — to (a) find where they kept my father and to [(b)] obtain his immediate release. And this I owe to Albert Göring, our family owes to Albert Göring!"[8] Albert personally escorted Pilzer to the Italian border and furnished him with foreign currency. Oskar then left Rome to be reunited with the rest of his family in Paris. Sadly, he died shortly thereafter due to complications arising from an operation. But his family would eventually reach the safety of asylum in the USA, via Spain and Morocco. Oskar Pilzer's name is scribbled in at number twenty-four on *The List of Thirty-Four*. In the USA, Oskar's sons George and Herbert carried on their father's tradition: George became the Vice President of 20th Century Fox International for Europe, and Herbert founded Motion Picture Enterprises Publications in New York.

Caught in a whirlwind of panic, many of the Jews of Vienna were desperately trying to find an escape route. With visas hard to procure and the Nazis freezing bank accounts and seizing assets, there was no easy way out. Albert stood at the centre of the mounting hysteria dispatching aid in rapid fire.

Dr William Szekely, a Jewish-American film director and producer, found himself stranded in Vienna and in dire need of help. "All possibilities to obtain the necessary papers to flee proved to be exhausted. Every day a friend of ours was arrested and bank accounts seized. ... Albert Göring, who I had befriended, took us under his care. He secured us exit permits," once recalled Szekely to Ernst Neubach. With these papers, he made it to Switzerland along with some other friends, though he still was not in the clear. In Zürich, he found himself broke with no money to return back to the USA. As Szekely explained: "We had to leave Vienna before I could take any money. Albert withdrew my money from a bank in Vienna and brought it to me in Zürich."[9] At number thirty-three on *The List of Thirty-Four*, Szekely lived to make another film in Hollywood, as did a number of his film colleagues whose names also appear on Albert's list.

The very first slot on the list is allocated to the Jewish-Hungarian director of Intergloria-Film Vienna, Dr Alsegg, and his wife. Albert's protection and financial generosity enabled their escape out of Austria. Following them at number two is Alfred Barbasch, a Tobis-Sascha representative who reached the shores of England with an exit visa obtained by Albert. Joining him in England and number nine on the list, was Dr W. Grüss. Albert provided this Jewish director of Tobis-Sascha with foreign currency and his assistance in fleeing the country.

The calls came day and night, and the danger only heightened with each intervention. Albert's resolve, however, remained ever steadfast. With his usual tenacity and gall, Albert interceded to help his personal physician Dr Max Wolf and his brothers. "He plucked the Wolf brothers out of prison with great danger. Then he had Dr Wolf, who was almost certain to be transported to Dachau, taken to a hospital where he had his appendix operated on. Then he obtained exit permits for him," documents Szekely.[10] A couple of months later Dr Wolf and his wife Margareta sailed pass the Statue of Liberty, no doubt with a whole new appreciation for this landmark. Two other doctors, who could continue to save lives as a result of Albert saving their own, were doctors Bauer and Medvey from the General Hospital in Vienna. They too made it to the USA through visas and currency procured by Albert. They occupy numbers five and eighteen respectively on *The List of Thirty-Four*.

As the horrors of the Anschluss continued, Albert, defender of the persecuted, and Hermann, instigator of the persecution, came together as brothers in May 1938 during a family holiday at Albert's lodge in Grinzing. They were political and ideological rivals on the streets, but in this private world, a sanctum shut to their public lives, they remained devoted brothers. That was one of the most peculiar elements of their relationship: they could somehow detach themselves from their public roles whenever they came together. Even when they drifted apart as Hermann fell deeper into National Socialism and Albert fled to Vienna, they still tacitly loved each other as brothers and no doubt would have received each other amicably had their paths ever crossed during that period.

Yet, on this occasion in Grinzing, both worlds collided when their older sister Olga brought news of Nazi thuggery into the Göring sanctum. Olga related the plight of an old Archduke peacefully living away from the politics of Vienna in Mondsee, who one early morning woke up to the SA banging on his door. The thugs dragged him from his home, humiliated him by shaving his head bald and then carted him off on a transport to Dachau. The victim was Archduke Joseph Ferdinand IV, the last Prince of Tuscany and member of the House of Habsburg-Lorraine.

When Hermann joined the family after 'his parade of triumph' in Vienna, Hermann wanted to share his success with his family by granting each one a wish. Much to the surprise and discomfort of Hermann, Albert and his sister hijacked his offer by bringing up the plight of the Archduke. "My sister and I wished for the immediate release of the old Archduke. Hermann was very embarrassed. But the next day the imprisoned Habsburger was free," Albert revealed to Neubach in Paris.[11] The Archduke holds the number twelve spot on *The List of Thirty-Four*.

It seemed that no one was spared the wrath of the Gestapo. Even the creator of Hitler's favourite operetta, *Die lustige Witwe* (The Merry Widow), endured persecution. The son of a Hungarian bandmaster, Franz Lehár had long been in the hearts of theatre patrons the world over, enamouring them with his sonatas, waltzes, marches, symphonic poems and, most importantly, operettas. *Die lustige Witwe*, undeniably his most lauded work, is still performed in a multitude of countries and languages. Such was his celebrity that Hitler himself had awarded him the prestigious *Goethe-Medaille für Kunst und*

Wissenschaft (Goethe Medal for Art and Science) in 1940.

Yet, when the Austrian master composer married his Jewish wife, Sofie Paschkis, he could never have imagined that this loving union would one day lead to professional excommunication and near disaster. 'One day, two men, who resembled Gestapo policemen, came knocking on my door. They showed their badges and said: "We have come to pick up your wife!"' recounts Lehár. 'My wife, who was present, naturally fell faint. I asked: "What for then?" ... I was in a desperate situation, and then it occurred to me that I could call the former Gauleiter [party leader of Vienna] Bürkel. I got in contact [with him] and ... he said: "Tell one of the men to come to the telephone!" This man spoke for a long time with him and then turned to me and said: "We should go." If I was by some chance not home [then], I would have never seen my wife again!'[12] Not too long after, he received an official letter stating that he was to either divorce his wife or he would be himself classified as non-Aryan, which would result in a total ban on all his works and overseas travel. He needed help.

"In this emergency I turned to ... Dr Nowottny, who then telegraphed the only person who had come to the aid of his friends in every situation ... Albert Göring in Bucharest. Three days later he was with me at the 'Schikaneder-Schlößl' [Lehar's villa] in Vienna, and by the next day he was off to Berlin," Lehár related to Neubach his own account of the events one day on a stroll in Zürich.[13] Once in Berlin, Albert went straight to his brother's office and informed him about Lehár's predicament. Hermann was said to be legitimately concerned and immediately got on the phone with Goebbels, whose ministry was behind the harassment. Hermann reminded Goebbels that Lehár's *Die lustige Witwe* was Hitler's favourite operetta and how much of a disgrace it would be if this absurdity was not immediately rectified. The last thing that Goebbels wanted to do was make his boss angry, so he asked to talk things over with Albert personally in his office. According to a confident of Lehár working at Goebbels' office, Goebbels received Albert as though he was an old friend and told him: "With such a trivial matter you should have come straight to me, my friend, my dear friend. The lower ranks have acted without thinking. Here you have an honorary Aryan certificate for Frau Lehár. Bring this to the maestro with my heartfelt regards."[14]

In actuality Goebbels could not legally hand out 'honorary Aryanship' to Frau Lehár, but he could afford her an exemption or the status of being a member of a 'privileged intermarriage'.[15] Whilst this would save her from deportation, she was forbidden to go out in public unescorted; she had to wear the yellow Star of David; and if Lehár was to ever part with her, she would revert back to her old status. Nevertheless, number fifteen on *The List of Thirty-Four* could live with her husband, free from torment, in their villa in Bad Ischl until she died a natural death in 1947.

'I heard from a German source that German Nazi Extremists have taken complete control in Austria and that all Austrians, even Austrian Nazis, are being pushed into the background,' reported Sir Nevil Henderson, British ambassador to Germany, back to London on the 16th of March 1938. 'There have been numerous arrests all over Austria and it is feared that a policy of vengeance may be pursued against Dr Schuschnigg and his supporters. I am doing all I can privately here both with Baron von Neurath and Field Marshal Goering to whom I wrote [a] personal letter yesterday morning regarding treatment of Schuschnigg etc.'[16] This plea made by Henderson for Schuschnigg's release would go unanswered by his one-time hunting companion, Hermann Göring. Yet on a later occasion Hermann would finally listen to one particular Schuschnigg advocate.

Ever since the beginning of the Anschluss, Schuschnigg and his family had been under house arrest by SA guards. Then, on the 28th May 1938, Schuschnigg was taken away from his family in a curtained car to the Hotel Metropole, the headquarters of the Gestapo in Vienna. As he was introduced to his cell, an old drying room with barred windows on the fifth floor, he was greeted by his new hosts with the house rules: 'Dr Schuschnigg may smoke — for the time being, at any rate. Later on this will come to an end anyway. He can order his food from the hotel kitchen provided he pays for it. A sentry stands in the room at all times. The light has to be on during the night. When a new sentry comes to take over — which is once every hour — firearms have to be ready for firing, safety catches unlocked. Gun-holsters have to remain open. Dr Schuschnigg may not go to or near the window. If he tries to do so he is to be shot at once. The sentry is also ordered to shoot whenever Dr Schuschnigg refuses to obey orders.'[17]

Schuschnigg was broken down through techniques of sleep deprivation, physical and mental abuse, intense interrogation as well as just plain humiliation. 'I have no books, no news — only the company of a fresh S.S. man every hour — and I am not allowed to speak to the sentries. I cannot sleep at nights, because the lights, the changing of the guards every hour, the inspection of my bed, my belongings, e.t.c., which for some reason always takes place in the middle of the night, keep me awake. At 6 a.m. the sentry shouts at me to get up. ... Then my day's work begins,' Schuschnigg recorded in his makeshift prison diary.[18] In solitary confinement, he could not see a lawyer or his fiancée, not least attend his own wedding — a ring in an envelope informed him of his proxy marriage to his wife.

This continued for the next year and a half until Albert Göring had a conversation with a policeman in Vienna. "From a policeman I found out how they were treating Chancellor Schuschnigg. ... When I arrived in Berlin, I talked to Hermann in a small palace and said, 'Is it German to treat a beaten opponent so indecently?' Hermann got on the phone with the Nazi state caretaker Seyß-Inquart and Schuschnigg was finally interned outside Vienna in a villa together with his family," Albert Göring described his side of events to Neubach in a café in Paris.[19]

Although there is a correlation between the supposed time of this intervention and a noticeable improvement in Schuschnigg's conditions, the events did not necessarily transpire as Albert had assumed or was told they had. What may have been the result of Albert's efforts, on the 1st of July 1938 Schuschnigg received a surprise visit from the Austrian State Secretary of Security Ernst Kaltenbrunner and, for the first time since his confinement, his wife. Thereafter he was permitted to see her every week with each visit 'to last eight minutes and take place on Fridays'.[20] Almost six months later, he received another surprise visit but this time from Kaltenbrunner's big boss, Heinrich Himmler. He was actually quite pleasant to him and came bearing gifts, namely new furniture and a radio. After constant promises of being able to live with his wife falling through, a relocation to another Gestapo prison in Munich and the birth of his daughter, the 'villa' that Albert had described evidenced on the 8th of December 1941. Though, it was by no means a 'villa' nor located 'outside Vienna'; it was but a humble wooden shack in the 'special prisoner's colony' of Sachsenhausen concentration camp, just outside Berlin. He was nonetheless able to live there 'together with his family', as Albert mentioned. They would enjoy these living conditions until early 1945 when they were smuggled away from the

encircling Allies to various concentration camps down south, including Dachau. On the 4th of May 1945 Schuschnigg's ordeal ultimately
ended at Hotel Pragser-Wildsee in the mountains in southern Tyrol,
where he and his family were liberated by American troops.

Puzzled by this conflict between Albert's own claims and the
events documented in Schuschnigg's diary, I decided to try to hear
the story as told by Schuschnigg's direct relatives.

In some ways, Schuschnigg was the first of many omens that seemed
to guide me on my journey to unearth Albert's story. Back in Sydney,
working to save for my trip, I was juggling a series of part-time jobs.
For a period of months the corner video store was my second home.

Lulled into a comatose state by the constant loop of '80s slack-
er classics like *Ferris Bueller's Day Off* and the melodious bleep of
each borrowed title, my time at the video store is a blur, save for
one chance encounter. Deep in suburban Sydney, the member card
of a Dr Tschuschnigg bleeped across my register. Before me stood
the nephew of Chancellor von Schuschnigg of Austria — or so he
revealed when I asked jokingly whether he was related.* It's this sort
of random brush with fate that keeps an industry of astrologers and
palm readers in trade. Not prone to superstition or even old-fashioned
ideas of luck and destiny, this chance meeting still managed to work
its way into the recesses of my mind. It would become a little reel
I could play back to dull the sceptics' voices and harden my resolve
to continue my research. It would also prove to be the first stepping
stone in my search for the rest of the Schuschnigg descendents.

I first tracked down Schuschnigg's nephew Heinrich Schuschnigg

---

*After a follow up, it turned out that this particular Dr Tschuschnigg, whose father
had added a 'T' to the surname en route to Australia, was a distant relative of Dr
Kurt von Schuschnigg.

in Vienna and then his son Kurt junior in New York to see if they could verify Albert's account. They could only share with me that Schuschnigg's wife Vera had obtained the help of her obstetrician Dr Rust, who also happened to be Emmy Göring's obstetrician, to recruit Emmy to Schuschnigg's cause. Although Emmy was supposedly concerned, it is impossible to determine whether that had any weight on the issue.[21] Apart from this, both cousins had no recollection of an Albert Göring playing an intervening role on behalf of their uncle and father respectively.

On the other hand, this may be explained by a postwar meeting in Munich between Neubach and Schuschnigg. After both men chatted about their war experiences, Neubach brought up Albert's story with Schuschnigg, only to be met with a blank face. It turned out that Schuschnigg himself was not aware of any actions taken by Albert on his behalf. Yet he did tell him that a sudden improvement in his conditions did take place, and he was not surprised that he had Albert to thank for this.[22]

With Hermann an accomplice in such a major intervention, it is understandable that Schuschnigg was never told of Albert's alleged involvement. Schuschnigg of all people understood this. Albert could not bite the hand that fed him by risking the Göring name being associated with the whole affair and having it come back to Hermann. If it had become publicly known that Hermann, the poster boy of German Nazism, had become soft and helped to undermine the will of some in the Nazi regime, Hermann's head would have been served on a silver platter to his detractors within the party. His power in the Third Reich could have been severely hampered, perhaps precluding him from helping Albert in any future interventions. Secrecy was paramount to all concerned.

IT WAS ANOTHER SURPRISE phone call made in mid November 1938 by Albert that led to the second rendezvous between Albert and Neubach. This time they were both émigrés in Paris, one escaping for his life and the other for his dignity and peace of mind. "Göring here," Albert began the conversation with his usual Prussian directness. Neubach was 'speechless' not only by the fact that Albert was calling out of the blue but that he had tracked him down in Paris. So Neubach responded, "Göring? How the hell did you get to Paris?" "With the train," Albert quipped.[23]

When Neubach arrived in Paris, it did not take long for him to feel at home. At the time of this phone call Neubach had an address on the Champs Elysées and had co-written the screenplay of the film *Pieges* with another émigré, Robert Siodmak. But now, as he made his way to meet Albert, he found himself in a Paris embroiled in turmoil. A couple of days before, a young Polish/German Jewish exile, Herschel Feibel Grynszpan, had shot, in the name of Germany's persecuted Jews, Ernst vom Rath, a German embassy official in Paris. This act launched the merciless pogrom in Germany and Austria known to the world as Kristallnacht, sending shockwaves through Europe.

When Neubach arrived at Café Colisée to meet Albert, he was surprised to be greeted by a melancholy man; not the poised and enigmatic character from his last encounter. It was not necessarily the turn in political events that was behind Albert's depression but the fact that he was being forced to leave yet another country due to the incursion of his Nazi brother and his cronies. The news of Kristallnacht only deepened his depression. "How I envy you that you can stay here," Albert abruptly declared. "What's stopping you from doing the same?" Neubach enquired. "My name!" Albert simply said.[24]

The two men sat in this café drinking wine and swapping stories into the early hours of the morning. One story that Albert told was of an invitation extended to him by Vienna's new Nazi caretakers. They had invited him to join in the pillaging and become the Gauleiter of Austrian film. Albert simply responded to this invitation by saying: "Whoever wants to join in that nonsense, they can go. I'm staying at the office!"[25] Albert then told him that he was fed up with 'working in a business run by pathetic bootlickers and party acrobats sent from Berlin, who turn every classic waltzing melody into a Prussian march'. Albert wanted to escape to a place far from the Nazi creed of thuggery and greed, which, for now, would be Italy. To this revelation Neubach asked: "What will you do in Italy?" Albert then shrugged his shoulders and answered: "Lead the life of the émigré, like you, my dear friend."[26]

After his sojourn in Paris, Albert did in fact leave Tobis-Sascha Wien and settle in Italy at the end of 1938, but he did not entirely break ties with his previous employer. He received a position at Tobis-Sascha's Italian sister company, Tobis-Sascha Italiano in Rome. Accompanying him was his sickly second wife Erna who required the constant attention of a doctor. Unable to find a physician to his liking or one who spoke German, for that matter, Albert got in contact with a friend in Rome and was referred to a Dr Kovács.

Originally from Pápa, Hungary, Kovács had been living in Italy ever since 1930 when a professor in Würzburg, Germany, gave him a friendly warning that he would never wield his stethoscope in either Germany or Austria. Why? Because he was a Jew. After marrying his German refugee wife in 1933, he moved to Rome where he set up a private practice, largely servicing the Hungarian population there.

And now Kovács was on his way to work as usual, making just

another ordinary house call, albeit with some reservations: he had no patient's name, just a warning from this mutual friend to not 'be surprised and to have no fear of the consequences'.[27] Upon arriving at Albert's villa in Frascati, on the outskirts of Rome, and hearing Albert's name, the brother of the man indirectly responsible for his exile, he balked and acted contrary to the advice of his friend. He bluntly told Albert that he would have to find another doctor as there was no way that he would care for a Göring. Catching him at the door, Albert enticed him to stay with the irresistible draw of coffee and an offer of a plain chat. So they talked over coffee, and what Albert had to say or how he delivered it must have been agreeable to Kovács, for he was back at the villa the next day. During this second visit, Albert ranted against Nazism and spat out the blasphemous but welcome statement: "I spit on Hitler, I spit on my brother, on the whole Nazi regime."[28] It was a Franz Lehár operetta to Kovács' ears. He began to treat Frau Göring regularly until he concluded that the sticky climate of Rome was exacerbating her condition and suggested it would be best that she return to Vienna.

Albert had made another friend in Kovács, and as friends do, they helped each other. Albert made the first gesture by inviting Kovács' wife and two children to stay with him at his villa for some respite from the hustle and bustle of city living. Kovács then reciprocated by finding Albert a humble apartment in Rome when Albert declared that he no longer needed a sprawling villa to himself. This exchange of simple, friendly gestures eventually developed into a serious partnership in Nazi subversion. Six months after their first introduction, Albert visited Kovács telling him that he earned a monthly salary of 'approximately 25,000 lire' and of which 'he required much less for his own expenses.' The remainder he would give to Kovács, and he 'requested him to utilise it for the assistance of Jews and other refugees from Nazi tyranny'. And, in typical fashion, he specified that he 'required no receipt nor knowledge of whom was helped'. This arrangement was later refined into a system involving a Swiss bank account opened by Albert at the 'bank Orelli in Berne', where 'it was only necessary for him [Kovács] to write to the bank to obtain money for the assistance of refugees, and for helping them to escape via Lisbon'.[29]

Then the Germans, in response to Mussolini's dethroning, seized Rome for themselves on the 10th of September 1943, and this time Kovács would be the one in need of help. Almost immediately the Gestapo drew up plans to rid Rome of its twelve thousand Jewish residents, who had hitherto been sheltered under Mussolini. On the 16th of October, in the twilight of dawn, their plans went into action. They pounced on a slumbering Jewish ghetto by the old Roman Theatre of Marcellus where they herded over twelve hundred Jews into trucks. In the days to come, the Gestapo, armed with a list of names and addresses, would scour the streets of Rome, rounding up the city's remaining Jews.

Kovács' name and address was no doubt on that list and a visit from the Gestapo looked imminent. But there to preempt the Gestapo was Albert, who bestowed Kovács and his family with Gestapo immunity: 'a statement in writing to the effect that Kovacs was his personal physician, that he, Goering, visited Rome very often, required his regular attention and desired that Kovacs be not molested'. Anxious that the Gestapo would pilfer his furniture, 'Goering gave him a certificate to the effect that all the furniture in the flat belonged to Goering.'[30] Kovács is listed as number fourteen on *The List of Thirty-Four*.

Just after Rome was liberated by the allies on the 5th of June 1944, Kovács was interviewed by a Major A. F. Dunlop of the British

Special Operations Executive (SOE), and at the end of the interview, he included an account of his friend 'Albert Goering' and all his aforementioned acts of defiance and beneficence. The SOE, established in June 1940 with a Churchill directive to "set Europe ablaze", was a clandestine military unit charged with the task of engaging and assisting local partisans in espionage and sabotage in enemy territory. In other words, they were there to make life as hard as possible for Hitler. On this occasion in June 1944 they were interviewing Hungarians living in Rome, who were members of the newly founded association of the Society of Free Hungarians. Hungary had just been fully occupied by German forces in March of that year, and they were looking for people with connections or information to assist them in their efforts there.

Kovács was found to fit this bill when he revealed that he had a radical socialist/anti-fascist brother, who was involved with an underground socialist movement of 'lower grade industrial workers and the intellectual left wing democrats' and suspected, at the time, to have some ties with the Hungarian Resistance.[31] This information must have attracted a raised eyebrow of interest, but it was no doubt that explosive appendix of Kovács' story that caused Major Dunlop to spill his coffee. It must have been hard for him to fathom that the Reichsmarschall's brother could be capable of such humanitarianism. All he could note was that 'this report should be thoroughly investigated'.[32] Had the SOE ever endeavoured to engage in such investigations, they need not have gone too far. They could have slammed the case shut — and perhaps, saved Albert the pain of over two years of American and Czech interrogation and imprisonment — with a simple chat with one of their very own military servicemen.

Major Frank Short, a soon-to-be World War II Royal Engineer in Cairo, lived in Vienna with his Austrian ballerina wife, running the

Austrian wing of Bickford & Co AG, a company owned by Leonard Bickford-Smith. Established in the 1830s and later absorbed into the mega chemical engineering conglomerate of Imperial Chemical Industries, Bickford & Co AG was in the business of manufacturing 'fuse cord and zipper fasteners' used in explosives.[33] It is not known whether Albert became friends with Short through his work at Junkers or his participation in Viennese high society. It is also not known whether it was Albert's seductive personality, work experience or favourable political standing that led to Short offering Albert a sales role with Bickford & Co AG in 1936. What is known, however, is the reason behind Albert's hasty promotion to company president in 1939: it was the Anschluss and the resultant persecution of Short's Jewish wife that called Albert into action.

Albert came to the couple's aid by assisting their flight from Vienna to Cairo and then protecting Short's financial interests by assuming the legal ownership of his company for the duration of the forthcoming war. Albert not only managed to ward off the Nazi hawks of industry from devouring the foreign firm, but at the end of the war, when he handed the business back to Short, he was able to 'show a profit for his six years of management'.[34] At number twenty-nine, Short became the sole Briton on *The List of Thirty-Four*.

Back in Italy, early 1939, Albert was discovering that all Fascist dictatorships were the same in respect to the film industry. Once again he was forced to wear the clown suit, paint on a fake smile and jump through hoops at the behest of another propaganda minister. Despite this, Albert still relished his brief time in Italy. He enjoyed the strong Italian coffee and, not to mention, the wine. And he was not opposed to the siesta-culture. But, most importantly, he could bask in the warm Italian sun that kept the shadow of his brother and all associated Nazi evils at bay … well, at least for now.

Turning the interview over in my mind, I fall upon a final comment made by Christine: "It's like the story from Spielberg. You know the — what was the film? — *Schindler's List*. It's the same story. Because there were a lot of people who helped Jewish [people]. It is not true that nobody helped." But why did these people engage in such activities? Oskar Schindler first entered the game with a profit motive in mind but quickly developed humanitarian intentions and exited as a Jewish saviour. Sophie and her brother Hans Scholl, members of the underground resistance movement the White Rose, were executed for distributing anti war and regime leaflets in Munich. They were guided by religious convictions or the idealistic courage of youth. Raoul Wallenberg, the Swedish interventionist who saved the lives of more than fifteen thousand Hungarian Jews, found himself right at the core of the Holocaust and, perhaps, his Scandinavian, humanitarian roots flung him into action.

In 1973 two Princeton University social psychologists conducted a study investigating the Parable of the Good Samaritan — in other words, altruistic behaviour — in respect to situational variables and religiosity. They found that the most salient factor behind 'Good Samaritan' behaviour was not religiosity or a nominated desire to help fellow man but the perceived personal cost of intervention. The experimental group consisted of theology students, many of whom were studying to become members of the clergy and were thus likely to exhibit altruistic behaviour. The experimenters asked each participant to deliver a speech on various topics relating to the clergy, including the Parable of the Good Samaritan, in a neighbouring lecture hall. En route they were each confronted by an actor feigning to be in distress. Before they had left they were told that they were either running late or had ample amounts of time to reach the lecture hall. Only 10% of the former stopped to help, compared with 63% of the latter. Indeed, many of the participants, who were on their way to deliver a speech on the Parable of the Good Samaritan itself, literally stepped over the man in their haste.[35]

Yet Albert's actions, seemingly devoid of any perception of costs or danger, fall beyond the parameters of experiment. There is scarcely an independent variable that scientists could employ to explain his behaviour. The explanation for his actions lies buried deep in his very being.

Like the Schindlers, Scholls and Wallenbergs, Albert was marked by a rare sense of justice. This was uncomplicated by religious morality and societal norms, or dictated by legal tomes. Albert's innate sense of justice compelled him to act, regardless of the consequences. It was neither rational nor intellectualised: it was the defining principle of his life. To deny this part of him would be to deny his very own existence.

SEVEN

THE KING OF SWEDEN

From Nazi occupation to the dark days of communism, Café Slavia was a hotbed of political dissidents plotting coups d'états, as it was of secret agents trying to dissolve these plots. A lot of the political prominence of this Prague café is largely due to its geography. On the Vltava River side of the café are ceiling-high windows overlooking the Prague Castle, Petřín Tower and Charles Bridge; on the side of the grand Národni třída sit the Czech National Theatre and the Academy of Science; and just behind the café in Bartolomejská ulice stands the former State Secret Police (StB) Headquarters of communist Czechoslovakia.

I am here in this former hub of espionage and resistance to learn more of another coup of sorts. The setting was Nazi-occupied Prague with 'Himmler's evil genius', Reinhard Heydrich, at the helm, and those responsible for the coup were two friends bound by a common repugnance for Nazism: Albert Göring and the grandfather of the man I am soon to meet, Václav Rejholec. Václav's grandfather was once a leading Czech doctor/scientist, head of the Czech Scout Movement, Dachau and Buchenwald concentration camp survivor and number six on *The List of Thirty-Four*. His name was Professor Josef Charvát.

I enter through the café's main doors and find myself in Vienna. With its jade green interior, mahogany furnishings and generous display of marble, Café Slavia is the quintessential Viennese coffee house; a legacy of the days when Prague was the 'Jewel' of the Habsburg Empire. Down a red carpet flanked by two-person marble-top tables, past a collection of framed photographs of erstwhile celebrity guests — from Hillary Clinton to Czech President Václav Havel — I come to the back of the café, swivel around and see a middle-aged man in a grey suit staring at me with a bemused look.

Like his grandfather, Václav is a tall, slender man with a neat business coif of silver hair. He fixes me with a stern handshake and an equally stern look, as though he were the school principal and I the errant pupil. He comments that he was expecting someone a bit different: a grey-haired, American academic in a tweed coat, perhaps. I fret at how the interview will pan out. But, as the interview progresses, his strict business demeanour fades away to reveal a genial man with a penchant for dark humour. He laughs about the absurdity of the Iron Curtain and the bureaucratic restrictions preventing him from visiting his aunt in Germany. Nor can he help but be amused by the irony of his grandfather's countryside retreat remaining untouched by its SS occupants, only to be ransacked by his fellow countrymen at the end of the war.

The waiter places down my coffee, and just as I am about to take my first sip, Václav tells me something that very nearly brings the interview to an abrupt end. "No, no. It was not Albert Göring but the king of Sweden who helped my grandfather because they knew each [other] through this scout movement," was his response to a question about his grandfather's inclusion on the *The List of Thirty-Four*. Cheeks blushing, pores gaping open, oesophagus contracting, I try to digest this revelation. Pages of interrogation transcripts, private interviews, video documentary accounts, the conventional story thus far have all become redundant in a matter of two thickly accented sentences. Václav has effectively called history a liar.

IT WAS A FRIDAY, the 6th of August 1897 to be exact, when Dr Josef Charvát made his first appearance in hospital. He was born into a humble working-class family from the Prague quarter of Královské Vinohrady. His father, a blacksmith and a locksmith by trade, kept the family afloat with his wage earned as a technician at an electric utility station and then later at a transport company. Josef was enrolled at the local Gymnasium, a path which according to the Germanic system of education, was to prepare the student for university education. Whilst he excelled in mathematics and various languages, the laboratory was where he felt most comfortable. For Josef, this laboratory also extended into the nearby forests, lakes and rivers, where instructors did not wear white coats but khaki shorts, shirts with embroidered badges, socks raised to the knees and large brimmed hats. This is where Josef rounded out his education with the instruction of the local scout movement, a movement which he would later lead as well as lead him into trouble.

In 1916 Josef accepted a place at the prestigious Charles University to study medicine.[1] Yet, before Josef could attend his first lecture, he was forced to trade laboratory white for infantry grey and join his fellow Austro-Hungarians in the Great War. Josef's artillery division bombarded the Italians on the icy cliffs of the Dolomites. He endured the lice, the rats, dysentery, mud, trench fever and the hell of the quagmire known as the Western Front. He survived Ludendorff's last-ditch spring offensives. "Yeah, he was lucky to have survived!" Václav delivers this ordinarily serious statement with a chuckle.

Although Josef no doubt received many a medical lesson on the front, the armistice saw the now hardened and mature Josef home and, more importantly, presented him the opportunity to resume his studies in medicine. He made up for lost time, obtaining the title of doctor of medicine in 1923. In February of that year he won a place at the Second Clinic of Internal Medicine in Prague, working under Professor Josef Pelnář whose liberal approach encouraged Josef to venture down untrodden paths. Along with two other young doctors, he brought major advances to the then nascent study of endocrinology. He was often invited to lecture on the subject at a host of major universities around Europe. And in 1933 Josef co-authored, with his mentor Pelnář, the first text-book on endocrinology.[2] "He was quite, I believe quite successful," beginning to list his grandfather's accolades, Václav stalls, looking outside the window as though searching for his words in the congestion of the afternoon traffic. As the traffic lights change and the cars resume their course, so does Václav: "He was one of the first who tried to introduce really scientific principles into medicine. ... He published a lot of scientific papers." Amongst all this, Josef also found time to run a sanatorium in the Prague district of Podolí and since he was such a renowned doctor and was fluent in German, French and English, his services were sought out by a bevy of rich and powerful foreigners. One such person was Albert Göring.

ALBERT WAS NOW IN Prague after fleeing the circus of the Italian (fascist) film industry and accepting a position at the Škoda Works, the mega Czech industrial conglomerate. It had just been incorporated into his big brother's industrial empire, the Reichswerke Hermann Göring AG, which had been swallowing up Czech firms ever since the German annexation of Bohemia and Moravia. Reeking of nepotism, it was an appointment as contentious then as it was after the war when it was called to account by Albert's interrogators at Nuremberg.

"You obtained your job with Skoda through your brother, is that right?" Ensign Jackson prodded during the Nuremberg process. Albert, far too proud of his engineering credentials, refuted: "No, quite the contrary is the case. Several Czech gentlemen asked me to come there and there was a Bruno Soletzky [*sic*], who came to look me up in Vienna and asked me to come to work for the Skoda Works." He then made the point: "I had to ask my brother for permission to go to work there."[3] Whilst Jackson may have tried to implicate Albert with Hermann's criminal and unscrupulous activities, there is some truth behind this.

Less than two months after the first Panzers had rolled over the Czech border on the 15th of March 1939, Bruno Seletzky, Škoda's former representative to the Balkans, fell upon plans in Vienna from the inner sanctum of the Reichswerke Hermann Göring AG. He found out that Škoda's new Nazi owners intended to not only purge its Czech management but also to dissolve the company altogether, reallocating its wealth of industrial capital to other firms within the conglomerate. Drastic action was needed, and what could be more drastic and audacious than to enlist the help of the boss' rebellious brother?

From his dealings with Albert in Vienna, Seletzky was fully aware of Albert's attitude towards the Nazi regime. He knew that Albert, an Austrian citizen, could act as a perfect countermeasure. He knew that Albert would defend Škoda's interests at all costs. So Seletzky immediately travelled to Škoda headquarters in Prague to discuss his plan with Škoda's chairman Vilém Hromrádko and managing director Vilém Vamberský. Both directors loved the idea and agreed to extend Albert an offer to join the Škoda family.

After Seletzky successfully sold the proposal to Albert in San Remo, Italy, both men returned together to Prague where Albert met Hromádko, Vamberský and the other directors. With Albert seeking a change in scenery and Škoda a guardian, Albert signed an employment contract with Škoda on the 4th of May 1939. Later, and at the urging of Albert, Major General Karl von Bodenschatz, Hermann Göring's long time World War I fighter ace comrade and aide-de-camp, was appointed the title of trustee of the Škoda network. His presence would provide Albert a direct line to Berlin.

Upon completing a quasi-trainee year in Prague, Albert effectively replaced Seletzky as Škoda's exports director to the Balkan states (Hungary, Yugoslavia, Romania, Bulgaria and Greece) as well as Italy and Turkey. This position attracted a base annual income of six hundred thousand Czech korunas.[4] This was then augmented with a 4% sales commission.[5]

As soon as Albert had set up office on the 1st of June 1939 at Škoda headquarters, it became clear that Seletzky's piece of ingenious preemptive thinking would pay dividends. For Seletzky himself, number twenty-eight on *The List of Thirty-Four*, Albert's presence secured his safe passage through to Switzerland once SS reports of anti-Reich behaviour mounted against him.[6] As hoped, Albert took every opportunity to uphold the sovereignty of Škoda's Czech management and to undermine its Nazi caretakers' prerogative for exploitation.

By the time Albert had joined the Škoda family, the management structure at Škoda was already subject to strong Reich German influence. At the top was the SS puppet Dr Wilhelm Voss, who, up until Bodenschatz's appointment, held the title of company trustee. Below were the board of directors, comprising seven Reich Germans, including two representatives of the Dresdener Bank and the Economic Minister of the Protectorate of Bohemia and Moravia, Walter Bertsch. The meagre Czech contingent included only Hromádko and Vamberský. In addition, most of the key executive positions in the Škoda network were occupied by Reich German managers.[7] And then there was Albert.

"There were 80 000 Czechs working in the plants, and they wished to work under Czech management, whereas these people [German management] wanted to have the plant run entirely by Germans; and I used to travel to Berlin and talk to my brother, Hermann, and tell him that this was impossible. I told him if he wanted to get any use out of the Skoda Works, it had to be run under Czech direction, because otherwise the workers would not cooperate," Albert, who knew so well how to manipulate his brother, described to Ensign Jackson just one of the many struggles he would have with Škoda's German management.[8]

His habit of causing a stir at Škoda extended beyond defending Czech interests. As Hromádko noted to the 14th Extraordinary People's Court in Prague: "Göring always openly spoke out against Nazism, and often so openly that I preferred to leave his company .... He always protected the interests of the Škoda factories and Czech employees. He never used, as far as I know, the Nazi greeting, nor did he have Hitler's picture in his study, although that was mandatory. In my company, as well as in the company of other Czech directors, he always openly spoke out against Hitler."[9]

[113]

APART FROM CHARVÁT REMEMBERING that Albert was in the company of a beautiful Hungarian woman, Albert and Charvát's first meeting was unmemorable. On the second occasion, though, Albert certainly left an impression. Albert's second wife Erna, to whom he enjoyed the longest stint of matrimony out of his four marriages, was suffering from a form of pulmonary cancer. Upon the recommendation of his new boss Hromrádko, Albert sought out the help of Dr Charvát at his sanatorium. Albert wanted Charvát to provide his wife Erna with a referral to a Swiss sanatorium and the documentation necessary for her to travel through occupied Austria to Switzerland. Charvát was initially somewhat hesitant to offer his services to the brother of Hermann Göring. But when Albert reassured him that he was 'an Austrian citizen and neither a member of the Nazi Party nor interested in politics', Charvát, in the end, willingly obliged.[10]

As they became friends, Albert abandoned all reservation. He told Charvát that 'Hitler and his clique' were '*Lustmörder*' who murdered out of some kind of sadistic fun; that Hitler 'was no German, but an Austrian'; and that he was 'ashamed of Germany'. He also provided Charvát with invaluable information about German troop morale and the progress of the war.[11]

At this juncture in his life, Albert's moral compass seemed, once again, to be disarmed by the advent of a new love interest. Not long after dispatching Erna, his sickly wife of sixteen years, to Switzerland, he filed for divorce. And with Erna out of sight and mind, lying in her sick bed facing the death of her marriage and death itself, he began to woo the former Czech beauty queen, Mila Klazarova. Twenty years Albert's junior and born into the bourgeois elite, Mila was a belle of high society and haute couture. She was Albert's match. "My mother was very, very pretty. My father got in love with her very quickly," Elizabeth Goering*, Albert's only child, reminisces. "And as much as I see from all the papers I can read, all the letters from what he left, they were deeply in love."[12]

A couple of weeks later Erna, broken and abandoned, died.

Albert's soon-to-be third wife was introduced to him by the Swiss Ambassador to Czechoslovakia, Consul Greub, and his fiancée Berta Stranska, at a ball in the Swiss Consulate. Albert and Greub would later collude over a money-smuggling syndicate. Using Greub's connections with the Swiss banking world and his privileges as the Swiss Consul to Czechoslovakia, they managed to channel funds into Swiss bank accounts to assist Jewish refugees.[13] From a *Sicherheitsdienst* (SD)[†] report it is evident that the SD knew all about this financial arrangement, but, fixated by Himmler's constant agenda of undermining Hermann Göring's power, they assumed that the operation was only an attempt to transfer Hermann's assets into the safe haven of Swiss banking.[14]

The love conceived in the ballroom of the Swiss Consulate quickly manifested into an engagement. With her Betty Grable pin-up looks, Mila had a cherub's face with wide-set eyes, blushing cheeks and the curves of a Vogue model. But in the eyes of the Gestapo she was an 'Untermensch', a Slav. Reinhard Heydrich, the Reichsprotektor of Bohemia and Moravia, was outraged by the notion that the brother of an Aryan idol was to wed such a woman. To announce his emphatic disapproval, he sent a posse of Gestapo thugs to Mila's family home, and the house was duly ransacked.

News of this incident sent shock waves through Hermann's offices in Berlin; Hermann had been completely unaware of his

---

*Elizabeth dropped the Germanic spelling of her surname.
†The intelligence gathering division of the SS.

brother's engagement. The man, with all the eyes and ears of the Forschungsamt (FA)* at his disposal, was caught out and immediately demanded that Albert travel to Berlin to explain himself. In Berlin, Albert stood his ground and explained that he was not a member of the Nazi Party and could thus do what he pleased. He was apparently so convincing that Hermann ended up siding with him and sent Bodenschatz, his aide-de-camp, to Prague to smooth things over with Heydrich.[15]

Riled but undeterred, Albert and Mila married on the 23rd of June 1942 in Salzburg, spending their honeymoon at Albert's fairytale, childhood home, Burg Mauterndorf. Notably absent from the festive occasion was big brother Hermann. He may have defended the couple against Heydrich, but he would never accept the union. As Albert later noted: "He did not even give me a present for the wedding, and neither for the baptism of my little daughter."[16]

"EARLY IN THE MORNING at six o'clock, two or even more German soldiers in uniform suddenly came to arrest my father. They told him to get dressed because he wasn't dressed yet. My mother was very, very distressed. She nearly fainted. They took my father away, and nobody knew what was going on or where he was going," Jiřiná Rejholvová, Charvát's daughter and Václav's late mother, recollects.[17] On the day of Poland's invasion, the 1st of September 1939, Charvát was taken, along with a whole list of other prominent Czech intellectuals and politicians, to Pankrác Prison, Heydrich's house of torture.

Charvát was never charged nor did he ever see the inside of a court. He was left in the dark in his dreary cell, clueless as to why he

---

*Hermann Göring's own telephone and radio communications monitoring unit.

was even there. Yet had his warders ever revealed the truth behind his arrest, he would not have believed them. He was arrested for being the leader of a group of children. After the German annexation of Czechoslovakia, the Junák (the Czechoslovakian Boy Scouts), the third largest scout organisation in Europe, was immediately deemed to be in conflict with the Hitler Youth and was consequently outlawed by the German State Secretary of the Protectorate of Bohemia and Moravia, Karl Hermann Frank, on the 28th of October 1940. As the leader of this popular and competitive youth movement, Charvát was therefore outlawed as a 'political threat' to the Third Reich and was arrested accordingly.

Charvát remained in Pankrác for nine days until he was bundled in with a mass of other inmates on a train to Dachau concentration camp.[18] Established in 1933 by the Police President of Munich, Heinrich Himmler, Dachau concentration camp became an important tool in neutralizing anti-Nazi elements and facilitating the total Nazification of German society. As Dachau was designated a camp for mainly political prisoners, conditions were comparatively better than elsewhere in the Nazi concentration camp network. And yet prisoners were still condemned to a life of torture, slave labour, disease, selections, malnutrition and on-the-spot executions. As an ex-Dachau inmate describes his experiences of life there: "During work movements [it] became unsteady, many lost grip of their tools — in our group such things were punished with a blow of the rifle butt. Others fells [sic] from the scaffolding, carrying sleepers they stumbled over the rails and fell under the wheels of the trains."[19] Fortunately, Charvát did not have to endure this life for too long as he was moved to a block for 'special' prisoners, sparing him from the almost certain death of hard labour.

On the 27th of September 1939, Dachau was temporarily converted into a training camp for the *SS Division Totenkopf* (Death's-Head Division), an elite SS combat unit consisting of former camp guards. This meant that all prisoners had to be transferred to either Mauthausen, Flossenbürg or Buchenwald concentration camps. Buchenwald became Charvát's new home.

At the time of Charvát's arrival, Buchenwald was engulfed by epidemics of dysentery and measles. Never one to turn down a chance to alleviate disease, regardless of the patient or circumstance, Charvát and some other Czech doctors prevented medical pandemonium from breaking out by establishing an ordered system of hygiene and treatment. In one instance, he saved a whole trainload of Polish Jews ridden with measles by inoculating them all.[20] "And he told me that even the German doctors appreciated his efforts because it saved them some work and some worries, you know," Václav recalls, breaking into laughter, again seeking solace in his macabre sense of humour. Charvát played the role of camp doctor for the next two months, until he was miraculously released on the 23rd of November 1939, along with another doctor who shared his last name. Sitting on a train from Dresden to Prague, both emaciated Charváts pondered who or what was behind their most bizarre release.

"Suddenly I heard very loud weeping from the corridor. We still had a maid then. I got out of bed and my first thought was, *Daddy is dead!*" Jiřiná Rejholvová recalls. "So I ran barefoot in my pyjamas into the hall. And my mother and the maid were both crying. And the dog was jumping around barking. And my dad was there in borrowed clothes. He was very thin. And our maid, who had been with us for eleven years, couldn't recognise him. When he rang the bell, she opened the door and said: 'What do you want?' And he said: 'Slavka, don't you recognise me?'"[21] By all accounts of Charvát's appearance following the days of his incarceration, the maid could not be blamed for failing to recognise her employer. As Václav illustrates: "I have — how to say — ... kind of sculpture ... small sculpture made by one of his friends, one of [the] inmates .... And this sculpture clearly shows how thin he was. His nose ... no face, you know!" Charvát was free, but why, or rather, who was behind his release still remained a mystery.

I FIRST LEARNT OF the Charvát case through the British documentary based on Albert's life. Through interviews with Jiřiná Rejholvová and Christine Schöffel, the daughter of Albert's good friend Ernst Neubach, the documentary purports that it was Albert Göring who intervened on behalf of Charvát. "He found the letter-head from his brother Hermman Göring, and he wrote a letter with the name of Hermann Göring to the camp commander in Dachau that he had to let free Dr Charvát. The problem was when the camp commander saw this letter he didn't know what to do because there were two Dr Charváts at that time in Dachau, so he let both free," so goes Christine Schöffel's side of events.[22] After Schöffel and some triumphant music, the documentary flashes to Jiřiná Rejholvová describing her father's return, implying the Charvát family is under the same impression.

I had no reason to doubt the story as my visit to the National Archives in Washington DC revealed Dr Charvát's name to be number six on *The List of Thirty-Four*. Then in Germany I managed to get hold of a copy of Ernst Neubach's own magazine article *Mein Freund Göring*. Considering Christine was told the story by her father, it was no surprise that this article corroborated what she had said on the documentary, except for one subtle deviation. Neubach, told the story by Albert himself, suggests that Albert did not commandeer one of Hermann's letterheads or forge his signature. No, he merely used stationery bearing 'the family name and crest' and signed the letter simply with 'Göring'.[23] If this was the case, Albert's cunning verged on genius. He did not technically break any laws of impersonation and so would avoid being incriminated on auxiliary charges had the heist ever been unravelled. Since he was a member of the Göring family, he had every legal right to use the family stationery and sign Göring. It was up to the camp commandant as to how he would interpret the letter, and as the story goes, he chose to interpret the letter as coming from the hand of his daunting superior, not his superior's meddling, younger brother.

Lastly, on my visit to the Czech State Archives I discovered Albert's interrogation report compiled at the Czech Ministry of Interior, dated 17th of December 1946. In it he claimed: "At a certain point in time, which I can no longer recollect precisely, the wife of university professor Josef CHARVÁT and the medical doctor BLAZIL, who also attended to my wife, approached me and asked me to intervene on behalf of her husband …. I wrote to the camp management and obtained professor CHARVÁT's release." In this same testimony and in a similar fashion, Albert claimed that he had also helped the son of another prominent Czech university professor, Dr Diviš. Albert wrote: "The son of university professor DIVIŠ had been arrested during the student unrest in 1939 and then sent to the Buchenwald concentration camp. In this case I also addressed the camp management and obtained his release."[24] Professor Diviš is listed as number seven on *The List of Thirty-Four*.

Considering all this evidence, I expected to hear a similar story going into my interview with the grandson of Charvát …

No, no. It was *not Albert Göring but the King of Sweden who helped my grandfather because they knew each [other] through this scout movement*, Václav catches me off guard. "It was 1939 or 1940. And one of the members of this scout movement was also the King of Sweden who had some contacts in Germany. So through his secret channels he asked some high officials to release Professor Charvát from the concentration camp." After the interview and upon Václav's advice, I managed to find a copy of Charvát's memoirs at a book shop in Prague. It was not until I got back to Freiburg and had key sections translated that I learnt Charvát's own side of the story. On page eighteen of his memoirs *Můj labyrint světa Vzpomínky, zápisky z deníků* (My Labyrinth of Worldly Memories), published nineteen years after his death in 1984, he writes: 'It sounds paradoxical, but my life was saved by scouting. When the Swedish Prince Gustav Adolf (the leader of the Swedish scouts and my friend from many jamborees) heard about my arrest, he intervened by directly contacting Hitler — and that is why I was released from Buchenwald.'[25] Here he not only states that it was Prince Gustav Adolf behind his release but he was released from Buchenwald, not Dachau concentration camp as the story had so far ran.

Upon further reading I learnt that Charvát had befriended the prince through his visits to a number of international scout jamborees in Budapest, Romania, Holland and so on. What would be his last international jamboree as the President of the Junák, Charvát travelled to Stockholm in 1937 for the annual International Scout Jamboree. There he was treated by Prince Gustav Adolph and his wife Princess Sibylla to a royal lunch. This would be the last time that they would see each other as on the 26th of January 1947 the prince and princess were tragically killed in a light-plane accident over the Netherlands.

Referred to at the time by the Swedish public as the *Tyskprins* (German prince), Prince Gustav Adolph had strong ties with many head Nazis through various trips to Germany in the 1930s. There is in fact a famous photo taken in Berlin in 1939 of the prince, his grandfather King Gustav V and none other than Hermann Göring, who also had a connection to the Swedish aristocracy through his first marriage to Carin von Kantzow. According to this story then, the prince had somehow found out about Charvát's predicament and personally spoke to Hitler, requesting Charvát's release. If this story is correct, it was Charvát's involvement with the scout movement that led both to his arrest and release.

The conflicting stories prompted me to search for other evidence backing Charvát's assertions. I made enquiries as to who were the leading historians on this particular period of Swedish royal history and came across the name of Per Svensson. He authored *Han som aldrig fick bli kung - Berättelsen om Carl XVI Gustafs papa*, a book focussed exclusively on the life of Prince Gustav. After tracking him down, I sent him my queries. In his reply, he confirmed that the prince was an avid member of the International Scout Movement, acting as its honorary chairman during World War II. He even mentioned that the prince played an active role in aiding scout organisations banned in various occupied countries. And regarding the Charvát affair, he noted that he had never come across the name of Josef Charvát in his research on the prince, let alone any information suggesting that the prince had intervened on the behalf of the Czech doctor.[26]

Still with no clear answers, I investigated whether there were any records created by his captors at Buchenwald concentration camp. I managed to contact an archivist at the *Gedenkstätte Buchenwald* (Buchenwald Memorial Foundation), but she could only inform me that Charvát had in fact arrived in Buchenwald on a transport of two thousand two hundred inmates from Dachau on the 27th of September 1939; his prisoner number was 35163; and congruent with Charvát's memoirs, he was released that same year from Block 47 on the 23rd of November.[27] Both these sources could therefore neither prove nor disapprove the Swedish prince thesis.

This whole conundrum of what or who to believe left me stumped for some time, until I delved deeper into Charvát's memoirs and chanced upon another key excerpt: 'He [Albert Göring] was an upstanding fellow who I have fond memories of. It was through him that I understood why I had been sent to the concentration camp and how I had so strangely been let out again so quickly.'[28] So it was Albert who led Charvát to the belief that his release was the work of Prince Gustav Adolph. In other words, it was only Albert and, perhaps, the camp commandant who knew the truth behind Charvát's release. But why would Albert tell Charvát one story and then another to everyone else after war?

It could well be that Albert had told his Czech interrogators that he intervened on behalf of a highly prestigious and loved Czech doctor to add some extra weight to his case. Maybe taking a liking to this tale, he then perpetuated it after the war to all his family and friends, who would only contribute to the snowball. But there is no evidence suggesting that this would have been necessary or particularly in character. His was a case rich with testimonies of highly respectable Czech citizens, who repeatedly reported his extensive endeavours on behalf of the Czech people. Work colleagues from Škoda, business associates from his dealings as export director and his friends back from his Tobis-Sascha film days in Austria all supported Albert's claims. Albert, at the time, had also just been exonerated by the Americans, who, wanting his head from the start, took fifteen months of interrogation to find nothing but good against his name. So why would he lie and jeopardise the veracity of his whole case? Surely, the saving of one more prominent Czech citizen would not have afforded his defence with any further great advantage. The cost of being exposed was simply too great compared with the potential benefit of lying.

Rather, it is more likely that Albert had strategically withheld the truth from Charvát himself to protect the welfare of all concerned. Albert did, after all, flout the law in writing a letter of dubious origin that sought to sabotage the will of the Nazi regime. It is also evident that from as early as his first arrest in 1938 Himmler and the SS were hot on his heels, hungry for any excuse to indict Albert and bring down his brother in the process.

By the time Albert had moved to the Škoda Works in 1939 there was already a tall stack of SS reports documenting Albert's 'acts of terrorism' against the Reich. Albert himself knew from Kriegsgerichtsrat Ehrhardt, Hermann's personal counsellor, that he was considered such a headache for the Gestapo that in one report they wrote: 'How long is this public gangster going to be allowed to continue?' He also found out that the Gestapo were somehow privy to a statement that he had made in confidence to friends. Albert had mischievously played with a nuance of the German language by calling Hitler a '*GRÖVAZ*', which is an abbreviation of 'the greatest criminal of all time', instead of Hitler's self-proclaimed epithet of '*GRÖFAZ*', meaning 'the greatest strategist of all time'.[29] Considering this and the fact that Albert had already experienced the wrath of the Gestapo, Albert knew all too well what would happen to him if the SS were to ever fall upon any of his acts of resistance. Prison, torture and even execution were what he, or any accomplices, could look forward to had they been caught out. Silence was thus necessitated, especially in Nazi-occupied Europe. This was Himmler's police state, an Orwellian world operating under a highly sophisticated system of surveillance and denunciation.

Generally, Albert would only reveal his activities during the war to family and friends a long time after Heinrich Himmler took that fatal cyanide capsule. Some beneficiaries of Albert's deeds would in fact never find out who or what came to their aid. This phantom approach is highlighted by an account from Jarmila Modra, the daughter-in-law of former Škoda deputy commercial director, Josef Modrý. Referring to the mass wave of 'revenge' arrests in Škoda that followed Reinhard Heydrich's assassination on the 27th of May 1942, she notes: "He [Josef Modrý] said Albert had helped mainly financially the families of imprisoned Škoda workers. And he helped them in what ever way he could. But nobody knew it was him. Not even those who were receiving the money knew where it came from or who was sending it!"[30] Also noteworthy is that when I interviewed Jarmila she explained that her father-in-law had only told her about Albert and their activities together after the war; it was just too dangerous to "take on board" such information at the time.[31]

A certain level of confidentiality was thus essential if Albert was to remain out of SS custody and continue with his work against the Nazi regime. If Albert's actions were behind Charvát's release, it would have been in the best interests of both parties that Albert dissociate himself from the case altogether, even if it meant fabricating a story of kingly, Swedish benevolence.

THE NEXT DAY, I venture to the site of Charvát's old apartment block on Reslova ulice, just a few blocks away from Café Slavia.

There I find not a grand neo-Gothic, neo-Baroque or Art Nouveau apartment building but a celebration of Modernism. Once again chuckling, Václav had told me that towards the end of the war a misguided American bomb had landed on this building during an unexplained air raid over Prague on the 14th of February 1945. In 1996 the site was given another shake-up, but this time in the name of art and Fred Astaire. Designed by the famous Canadian architect, Frank O. Gehry, this Prague tourist attraction is known as the Dancing House as it resembles two people — Fred Astaire and Ginger Rogers — dancing together.

I walk farther up the street until I come to an Orthodox church. In the lower sections of its grey and weathered sandstone façade is a small horizontal window resembling a gunner's cut-out. Peppered all around this cut-out are bullet holes from seemingly high-calibre machine-gun fire. Above is a plaque commemorating the two British trained Czech agents, Jan Kubiš and Jozef Gabčík, who were involved with the assassination of Reinhard Heydrich. After parachuting into occupied Czechoslovakia, these two men ambushed Heydrich's convertible by the Troja Bridge in Prague, felling Heydrich with an anti-tank mine. A manhunt was immediately launched, which ended here at this very church with a suicidal stand made by these two Czech martyrs.

Prior to this shootout, the Gestapo raided each apartment block in the street in search of the perpetrators. With the barking of Alsatians and Gestapo officers filling the night air, Charvát destroyed all of the notes, lists of contacts, diary entries and various forms of correspondence that he had collected just before and during the war. Embedded in Charvát's mass of paperwork were the machinations of the Czech Resistance. After his release from Buchenwald, Charvát became an active member in the Czech Resistance, helping his fellow countrymen to "disappear from occupied Czechoslovakia".

Number six on *The List of Thirty-Four*, Charvát survived to join Albert in his war against the Nazi regime. As was the case with so many people he saved, Albert's heroism began a chain reaction that would change the fate of so many Europeans. To look into the lives of *The List of Thirty-Four* is to discover a web of survivors; each one an inspiration to others in their efforts to defy the Nazi regime. Albert saved countless people, but he knew it was their survival, not his recognition, that would save countless more.

EIGHT

BARON VON MOSCH

'You've got mail.' It's him. There has been a late change of plans. He wants to meet this Sunday in Paris; it's Friday and I'm in Freiburg. New plan: hire a car today, leave on Saturday night straight after my shift, whisk off to Paris and spend a night in the car, emerging fresh for the interview the next day. Dustin has agreed to tag along again. He used to live in Paris, and I am sure his French will come in handy.

I have served my last pint, cleaned up all the tables and now wait with Dustin for my replacement, the ever-unreliable Moe — a name bestowed on him not by parental volition but rather on account of his uncanny resemblance to a certain *Simpsons* character. Unimpressed by the inflationary effects of the new 'Celtic Tiger', Moe dragged all fifty-five kilos of himself from Tipperary to Freiburg. Moe is a somewhat puzzling character. He loves his new home, especially for its cheap yet delectable beer; but he is not terribly fond of its natives — with their obsession for *Ordentlichkeit* (orderliness) and strict attitude towards *Spaß* (fun). He is convinced that without certified permission *Spaß* is generally *verboten* by Germans. Yet, for all Moe's whinging about the Germans as a people, he has in many ways become one of them. Watch him at a set of traffic lights and you know he has crossed over, physically and metaphorically, to the other side.

Traffic lights serve not only to separate pedestrians from auto traffic but also foreigners from Germans. Germans normally wait patiently at the lights, whilst the unruly '*verdammte Ausländer*' (damn foreigners) stroll nonchalantly across on a red signal. I used to be that '*verdammter Ausländer*'. It always amused me to see someone at midnight on a deserted street contentedly awaiting their flashing licence to cross. But as time went on those scorning looks from older folk and parents gnawed away at my conscience, and a sense of guilt overcame me. I was a child murderer. I was Judas. Even worse, I was an outsider. Finally an unconscious sense of wanting to fit in took over, and I began to wait for that green man. I would not, however, dare submit to the lights in the presence of a fellow expat. That was until last week in the company of Moe.

As usual, I disregarded the red signal and proceeded across to the other side, only to realise that I was alone. Moe was still on the other side, doing what the Germans do. He just stood there, albeit sheepishly. He had been caught out. As he (legally) made his way over I gave him a smile, not a mocking smile but a reassuring smile, letting him know that I, too, had succumbed and become one of them. Could it be that the stick of German social order is so strong that even the most anti-German or anti-establishment could be brought into line?

Moe finally stumbles through the door, and the root of his tardiness is revealed. He looks like death on a pair of chicken legs and reeks of Jägermeister. Apparently he has just woken up after a bender that bent into the morning. I throw him my apron, along with the responsibility of the pub, and head for the car with Dustin.

We wake to tourists jostling past our car, some peering curiously through the windows as though we were from Mars. The fact that we parked 400m away from the Sacré-Cœur may have something to do with it. After a spot of *petit déjeuner* at a Montmartre café we descend into Paris' underworld, the Métro. Down the tunnel we pass a man playing the saxophone to an '80s back-up beat, an old drunk screaming out profanities and a suit publicly urinating against the tiled walls. Public transport always gives you a glimpse of the underbelly of a city. Paris is the only city that can somehow carry the mantle of the most romantic city in the world whilst grown men in suits can be found urinating on Métro platforms. Above ground the city of lights shimmers and seduces; underground it festers and revolts — the unsavoury elements unwelcome at the show above.

"École Militaire", our stop is announced. As the tunnel brightens towards the Métro exit so does Paris. It is a clear, late-winter's day, and the Parisians are out at play, posing out on café terraces in this swank *arrondissement* shadowed by the Eiffel Tower. The École Militaire owes its name to the renowned military school housed here in a grand 18th century building. It is where France's favourite pint-sized Corsican honed his military skills in 1784. Opposite École Militaire is the café Le Tourville where I am to meet Jorge Sobota, the son of Karel Sobota, Albert Göring's former personal assistant at the Škoda Works in Brno.

It is more a bustling bar than a chilled café. Waiters, trays in hands, dodge through a clutter of tables and bodies as they try their best to ignore the barrage of '*pardon*'s and '*s'il vous plait*'s thrown their way; the roar of conversation and 'foreground' music is just too loud. Overwhelmed by this bustle, I look around and inadvertently say out loud: "Where's my man?" A voice from below surprises me by saying: "I am your man."

Jorge is casually dressed in a black Levi's T-shirt and light blue jeans. He shares the tall frame of his Czech father and the vivacity of his South American homeland. He is never shy to show his infectious smile, especially when he recounts his father's stories from the three years he called Albert boss and friend.

"My father told me the story [of Albert Göring] but he changed the name," Jorge says. "Maybe he was afraid when I was a kid to tell me the real name …. If I started telling my small friends there, and then it would go around. You know that kind of information … could bring him some problems. So he called him Baron von Mosch."

YOUNG KAREL SOBOTA HARDLY knew his father. He was only five years old when his family, just a few weeks into World War I, received word of his father's death. Without a breadwinner, Mrs Sobota was forced to leave their home in Jinonice — then a small rural town located on the outskirts of Prague — and seek refuge at Karel's paternal grandparents' home in the centre of Prague. From then on, his grandparents provided for Karel and his mother, brother and sister. This was no easy task for his elderly grandparents. Grandfather Sobota was a skilled stonemason, but he no longer had the help of his trusted apprentice and son. His two ageing and worn hands could only provide the food on the dinner table.

This did not, however, prevent Karel from pursuing his life-long passion for linguistics. "When he was a child, maybe seven years old ... his grandparents would give him now and then some pocket money, some pennies. They were not so rich; they were poor. So when his friends took the money and ran to buy candy and things like that, he just saved the money," Jorge says. Each time he saved enough money he would pass his friends at the sweet shop and head for the local book shop where he would indulge his sweet tooth for foreign dictionaries and grammar books. Karel's zeal for linguistics served him well in school, earning him a scholarship at the prestigious Edvard Beneš Commercial Academy in Prague. There he studied international business and linguistics.

After graduating in 1928 and working as a translator at a local firm in Prague for eight years, he became employed by Československá Zbrojovka Brno, an arms manufacturer famous for its collaboration with Enfield British Royal Small Arms Factory in the development of the Bren light machine-gun. Established in 1918, and with the major German firearms manufacturers disabled by the Treaty of Versailles, the company flourished and quickly became one of the world's leading producers of Mauser rifles. It later joined the Škoda consortium in December 1938 when it bought out a major share of its arms division for nine-and-a-half million US dollars from the world-renowned French arms producer, Schneider et Cié in Creusot. Then, in the summer following the German annexation of Bohemia and Moravia on the 15th of March 1939, it became the first subsidiary of the Škoda network to be forcefully acquired by Reichswerke Hermann Göring AG.[1]

With his expertise in languages and technical terminology, Karel worked in the export division of Československá Zbrojovka. He interpreted for his senior managers and entertained foreign military attachés, chaperoning them to test sites or just out to dinner. His position afforded him many close and important contacts, namely the British Ambassador to Iran, the exiled King of Afghanistan, and one mysterious German count.

Baron von Mosch, or Albert Göring as we now know him to be, had just taken over the role of export director of the Škoda Works (including Československá Zbrojovka Brno) and was in need of a personal assistant for his office in Brno. Impressed with Karel's credentials and good standing at the company, Albert offered this job to Karel sometime in 1940. Karel accepted, though not without reservations. Karel, like most other employees at Škoda, was very suspicious of his new boss. He knew all about Albert's initial stirrings at Škoda: his refusals to salute Nazi officials with 'Heil Hitler'; his failure to display a picture of Hitler in his office; and his efforts to protect Czech workers from the two key Nazi managers, Dr Wilhelm Voss and Herr Lüdinghausen. He also enjoyed Albert's company in the office. Yet Albert remained, undeniably, Hermann Göring's brother. It was not until witnessing an incident in 1942 that Karel began to truly trust Albert.

"There came — I do not know how to say it in German — but he was a kind of general in the SS. And the guy came all in black and with insignia. He just passed by my father and entered into Albert Göring's [office] without knocking," Jorge sets the scene. This rude intrusion was immediately met by a barrage of heated words, and the general was banished out of the office. Albert then opened his door and invited Karel, a Czech, into his office to browse through his photo albums. This impromptu 'happy snaps' session lasted for around a half hour until Albert finally said to Karel: "Okay Herr Sobota, thank you very much. You can let the gentleman go in [now]." "My father gets up, and then the general was there, sitting

[133]

there; he was red in the face. ... And so the joke around in Škoda [was] that he was the first red Nazi that they had ever seen!" Jorge, at this stage in full laughter, is barely able to finish the story until he says: "So this kind of showed that there was some kind of link, some kind of appreciation."

This was not the only time that Karel was audience to Albert's daring insolence. "Yes I remember another thing. ... This was a very subtle insult. Because when you meet at that time [a Nazi official] and if you forgot to raise your hand high, depending on the situation, you could be arrested," Jorge explains. "So there came, I think a colonel, or something like that. Normally, they [firstly] talk with my father and [then] have a meeting with Albert. And my father introduced him and entered into the room: 'Here is Herr bla bla, ober', something like that. The colonel clicked his heels and [gave a] Heil Hitler. And Albert, my father told me, [just said] 'Hello Herr Colonel, how are you?', and he didn't even raise his arm!" With anecdotes such as these circulating through the factory, Albert was beginning to gain somewhat of a cult following amongst the workers. He became their Scarlet Pimpernel.

BY 1940 ALBERT HAD found his niche in life, and what a comfortable niche it was. He retired each night to the embrace of a Czech beauty queen. Exempt from war rationing, he indulged in an extravagance and excess enjoyed only by (Nazi) royalty: free-flowing Champagne, smoke-filled cabaret dens and authentic coffee, not the crude *Eichelkaffee* (acorn coffee) allotted to the masses. He was a thorn in the backside of Škoda's Nazi management and a hero to his Czech colleagues. He was in his element; a man rolling in style, quite literally. If he was not cruising through Eastern Europe in his luxury cabriolet donated by the Mlada Boleslav Škoda factory, he was in his head-turning Steyr-Daimler-Puch auto.

The latter owed its impressive, hyphenated name to a merger in 1934 between three leading Austrian auto manufacturers: Steyr-Werke AG, Austro-Daimler and Puch-Werke. Like most other leading Austrian manufacturing firms, this company was incorporated into Reichswerke Hermann Göring AG after the Anschluss in 1938. With Škoda adopted by the empire roughly a year later, Steyr-Daimler-Puch and Škoda became sister-companies in Hermann's industrial empire. Through a business arrangement between the two subsidiaries, Steyr-Daimler-Puch's interests in the Balkans were assumed by Škoda's export department, which, of course, was directed by Albert. One of the perks of the job was a Steyr-Daimler-Puch car.

In this Steyr-Daimler-Puch Albert travelled through the Balkan countries as well as Italy and Turkey, securing contracts from these governments for what he would personally claim in Nuremberg after the war as 'peace-time goods'. According to Albert's definition, these peace-time goods included locomotives, cranes, diesel motors, various machine tools and even tobacco-processing machines. This begs the question, how peaceful were these peace-time goods? Did Albert exclusively deal in these goods or did he also dabble in the armament industry? Was Albert a war criminal in facilitating the production of goods that served to prolong the war? These were among the questions that Ensign Jackson had in mind when he interrogated Albert at Nuremberg.

The term peace-time goods was always going to be a point of contention for Ensign Jackson. Albert was, after all, not only the younger brother of the man behind the Four Year Plan but also employed by a firm integral to this plan. During his interrogation

Albert, nevertheless, held his ground. Both accuser and accused squared off in a stuffy interrogation room in Nuremberg. Although Albert admitted that artillery was produced by Škoda, he ardently denied that he had anything to do with this division and defended his role at Škoda as a peddler of benign wares. Albert retorted:

> No, no; this couldn't have been the case, because I had nothing to do with all that. I was responsible for the export of peacetime goods in order to insure that Skoda would not lose their market for the postwar times. It is a fact that artillery was produced there, but I had nothing whatever to do with it. This is also evident from the fact that to those countries for which I was responsible, exports of armament were made ....However, this was fixed up between Prague [Škoda's head office] and Berlin, and I had no more to do with it than to collect payment for it.[2]

Albert continued:

> I collected all kinds of documentary evidence that further production of these goods was necessary, first of all, for export, so that foreign currency could be had with which the Czechs could buy food. ...One day an order came in from the Economy Group (Transportation), and the order was to stop at once the further production of automobiles. I intervened at once, and I went all the way up to see Neurath, who was then the Protector of the country; and I told him it was impossible to stop the export of automobiles to Hungary and Rumania; and he granted this; and they continued producing these automobiles.[3]

It was not only automobiles that Albert reallocated resources to: "Once, King Boris of Bulgaria, who is a trained locomotive engineer, asked me for six locomotives for Bulgaria; and I succeeded in getting him them; and he was very happy with them. But you really couldn't say that such a poor country as Bulgaria was enabled to stay in the war by something like giving them six locomotives."[4] Suffice to say, Albert's efforts would have diverted resources to non-armament production, thereby limiting the potential supply of munitions to the German cause — not aiding it, as Ensign Jackson implied.

Once Albert had exonerated himself at Nuremberg, he was extradited to Czechoslovakia to face further war crimes charges, and his role at Škoda, once again, came into question. Here his former colleagues from Škoda came to his aid. Josef Modrý, the former deputy commercial director at Škoda, testified during Albert's trial overseen by the postwar Czechoslovak Government: "Göring was a really good man who also benefited the interests of our enterprise economically, namely by the fact that according to an agreement of the Czech management of Škoda before the war, who wanted to limit armament deliveries to Germany as much as possible and orient its exports to the South East and to Russia, and Göring supported this attempt as the export manager. He thus indirectly supported the war effort of the Allies."[5]

FROM 1940 TO 1945, Albert was a busy man. In addition to his involvement in the industrial engineering and auto industries, he dabbled in finance and foreign trade. In 1940 Albert assumed the position of representative and supervisor of the Anglo-Prager Credit Bank's branches in Bucharest, Belgrade and Sofia. Although the position may have topped up his already more than comfortable salary, Albert used it as just another tool to protect Czech interests at the expense of the Nazi regime.

Not long after the Wehrmacht (German Army) had stormed Prague, Albert managed to foil a takeover attempt by a Nazi consortium of major German banks. In a detailed twelve-point letter to Reichsprotektor Neurath, he argued that such a move would be adverse to all parties. Namely, he noted that it would create unnecessary and costly business transactions, hindering an already smoothly running and profitable Czech operation.[6] Since the dreaded word 'inefficiency' had been invoked, they had to listen. And they listened for at least a year until another bid was made, and this time even Albert could not prevent the total dissolution of the bank.

Albert also held ties with the multinational, import firm Omnipol. This firm was essentially a bartering apparatus that acted on behalf of Škoda, securing payment of tradable commodities from other firms based in countries with unfavourable currencies. These commodities were then exported back to Czechoslovakia and converted into cash. Operating primarily in the economically volatile Balkan countries, Albert regularly utilised this service, but come October 1941 their roles would reverse.

In 1941 a Nazi-appointed director, Herr Febranz, began to share control of Omnipol with the incumbent Czech director František Zrno. Febranz immediately conducted a bit of spring cleaning, replacing forty Czech managers with forty German counterparts. On the 25th of September 1940 Josef Modrý, Škoda's deputy commercial director, released a report criticising Febranz's methods. "Febranz must have felt that the basis for this report was given to Modrý by us, the Czech directors," František Zrno later testified. "He must have reported us to the Gestapo, namely me, Alfons Pler, Josef Schwarz, Jaroslav Vanek and František Dolensky, who were also Omnipol directors."[7]

At the time, Febranz had ideas of lining his own pockets and needed to dispense with any opponents, namely Czechs, who might call his actions into question. So he concocted an accusation of espionage against the five Czech directors. He backed the allegation with a collection of photographs taken from a Prague trade fair which seemingly depicted the accused conspiring with a member of the British Army, General Spears, and a German Jewish émigré, Herr Kalman. They were promptly arrested by the SS, despite the fact that these photographs were taken before the war in 1938. With the accusation of treason on their heads, the directors waited in their Prague gaol cells for their inevitable executions. That was until Albert came to Prague from Bucharest and was asked to intervene by Josef Modrý.

'He [Albert] wrote a letter to [SS Grupenführer] K.H. Frank, where he pointed out that the meeting took place in 1938 and rejected all the high treason accusations against director Zrno,' Dr Vladislav Krátký, Škoda's archive director, begins to describe Albert's involvement in the affair. 'He also involved general Bodenschatz, the head of administration for the Reichsmarschall. When in December 1941 he found out that this intervention did not help, he came back to Prague and along with Bodenschatz, addressed the deputy Reichsprotektor Reinhard Heydrich. He referred to his brother's order requiring the arraignments to be sent to Berlin or for the arrested to be released.' Bodenschatz's intimidating presence and the Reichsmarschall's stern words must have caused Heydrich to baulk as 'after several weeks, in January 1942, all Omnipol employees were released'.[8]

Albert also managed to have most of the Omnipol directors

reappointed in various areas within the Škoda network. 'After a month-long recovery holiday, Zrno became the director of the building society of Škoda factories, and his colleagues were placed in other management functions in the syndicate,' writes Krátký.[9] As Zrno, the last name on *The List of Thirty-Four*, accredits: "I would also like to recall that I found out from directors Modrý, Hromádko and Skřivánek about the eager and earnest efforts that [Albert] Göring made for my liberation and the liberation of the other prisoners, and I am personally convinced that it was only thanks to Göring that we were freed. It was also thanks to Göring that we were released so quickly, since I found out from deputy Hladky that the Gestapo was still investigating me in another matter."[10]

No sooner had Albert freed the Omnipol directors than he found himself in another battle with the SS. As of March 1939, all citizens in the protectorate of Bohemia and Moravia were ordered by the authorities to hand over all rifles and pistols. If anyone was found thereafter with such a weapon, they were liable to the death penalty. The pistols and ammunition belonging to Škoda's directors and armoured guards were, however, exempted from this decree. Under the direction of a Herr Weber — a 'Prague police officer and German counterintelligence representative' — they were permitted to store them in a secure warehouse in Prague.[11] This arrangement functioned smoothly until Škoda's Nazi management began to hatch new plans to rid Škoda of its Czech directors. The directors were accused of concealing illegal weapons by the very man who had permitted them to store such weapons in the first place: Herr Weber.

As part of a greater plan to find other more incriminating evidence on Škoda's upper management, a search warrant was issued by SS Grupenführer Karl Hermann Frank, the then Secretary of State of the Protectorate of Bohemia and Moravia. The residences of Škoda's managing director Adolf Vamberský and directors Modrý and Benés were swooped upon by Gestapo agents. The agents did not centre their attentions on the basements or any gun cabinets but in the libraries of the directors' homes. They were in search of hidden files. Although no truly incriminating documents were found, the bogus charge of concealing illegal weapons was maintained.

Urgent calls were made and pleas dispatched. With time against the directors, Albert rushed to Berlin to beseech his brother to quash the charges. Once in the capital he convinced Hermann to send a letter to his subordinates in Prague, outlining the groundless nature of their accusations and the importance of the directors to the German war effort.[12] The arrests were thus averted, and Albert galvanised his guardian title within Škoda circles.

LIKE A TRUE PARISIAN, Jorge flings his arm up, clicks his fingers and grabs the attention of a passing waiter — he has lived in Paris on and off for some time now. In fluent 'Parisian', pausing with 'uhs' and all, he orders another round of beers. With our pallets whetted by a sip from another nine euro beer, Jorge begins to tell me about the resistance movement amongst Škoda's shop-floor employees.

The shop-floor workers, constantly observed, rarely engaged in any overt acts of resistance but still caused havoc through a passive resistance campaign. They were masters in subtle sabotage. Such tactics might include producing dud rounds by minimising the amount of gunpowder in each cartridge or prolonging projects right up until a German supervisor would be forced to personally oversee the project to its completion. "Albert never bothered about the resistance activities at Škoda; he looked the other side," says Jorge.

On one occasion, Karel and his cousin in Prague almost over-stepped the passive resistance line through a little bit of creativity in wine production. "One day they took some herbs … and they managed to put this in … a big depository of wine for the German troops," Jorge says with his usual chuckle. "And the next day all who had drunk the wine were [ill] with diarrhoea. People rushing." Jorge's laughter slowly fades away as he reveals the identity of the man behind all these wickedly mischievous acts of sabotage in Škoda: "Jan Moravek was the top [resistance] man in Škoda."

The top man in Škoda's resistance cell also just happened to be a very good friend of Albert Göring. Jan Moravek was the export director of Česká Zbrojovka Brno — and also Karel Sobota's former boss. It was in this capacity that he first met Albert — the then Junker's representative to Austria, Hungary and Czechoslovakia — in 1933 at a trade fair in São Paulo, Brazil. The two engineers instantly hit it off. After the merger between Československá Zbrojovka Brno and Škoda, their acquaintance evolved into a long and fruitful friendship.

Along with his brother Breta, Jan was a key member in the Czech Resistance, a fact that Albert was well aware of. Heavily involved in conveying strategic information, Jan's most notable and daring act for the Resistance was his involvement in 'Operation Crossbow', the British bombing mission on Germany's secret V-1 and V-2 ballistic missile plant at Peenemünde. After finding out the location and purpose of the plant from a scientist friend working there, Jan sent word along the Czech Resistance lines to London on the 15th of August 1943.[13] Forty-eight hours later the RAF launched into action, dropping a barrage of bombs on the infamous missile plant off the Baltic coast.

Operating amongst a web of Gestapo agents and informers, Jan never breathed easily under Nazi occupation. Yet the daily threat of arrest stayed just that until 1941.

'One early morning in June, while still asleep, she [Mrs Moravek] received a call from my Aunt Libuse asking her to come over to my uncle's place, without giving any further explanation over the phone,' writes Elsa Moravek Perou de Wagner, Jan's daughter, in her memoirs *My Roots Continents Apart: A Tale of Courage and Survival.* 'By the sound of my Aunt's voice, my mother expected that something was wrong!'[14] When Elsa's mother reached her brother in-law's home, she was told that her husband was in grave danger; the Gestapo were on the hunt for him with a warrant for his arrest.

The day before this phone call the Gestapo had pounced on Jan's parents' country home at Starý Ples. They were supposedly there in search of an unregistered pig — a serious violation then — but coincidently ended up uncovering a folder containing receipts of undeclared overseas funds and assets. For the Moraveks this came as something of a relief; had the Gestapo applied their normal diligence they would have discovered a suitcase of files clearly documenting Jan and his brother's involvement with the Czech Resistance. As Moravek Perou de Wagner writes: 'Both my father and my uncle, and perhaps our whole family would not have survived had the officers not gone without it.'[15]

With Jan away in Yugoslavia on business, Mrs Moravek received a call from a Škoda secretary requesting her to attend a meeting the next day at the Škoda headquarters. Who she would meet, the secretary did not say. With grave reservation, she attended the meeting. At the headquarters she was led by a secretary to an office and 'introduced to a tall handsome man smoking a cigar behind an imposing desk. His looks didn't match the image of other Nazis she had met. On the contrary, he had a gypsy type of look.' It was her husband's friend, Albert Göring. After greeting her in French, he told her 'in German, and in a few concise sentences' that she would soon leave for Romania where she would be reunited with her husband.[16]

At first, Mrs Moravek was naturally wary of this generosity extended by a German, not to mention the brother of Hermann Göring. Mrs Moravek's unease lifted to some extent when Škoda's chairman Hromádko reassured her that 'Herr Göring' was an anti-Nazi, a man to be trusted and who would arrange everything for the family.

Albert contacted Jan in Yugoslavia first and directed him to not return to Prague at any cost but instead travel to Bucharest where a managerial position overseeing Škoda's Romanian factories awaited him. The position came with a more than comfortable salary that would be needed to pay the fine arising from his accountancy transgression. Once a new life for the Moraveks was arranged, Albert then sought to reunite the family. Operating under a veil of secrecy and outsmarting the local Gestapo, Albert spent the next year plotting their escape. By now he had become deft at securing travel papers, foreign currency and counterfeit passports.

'An unknown person' visited the Moraveks' home and supplied the family with tickets and German passports. The person then told Mrs Moravek that 'she would leave that same evening at 10pm with the night train, alone with the children and with no more than two suitcases'.[17] En route, a 'young man with dark hair' appeared at the Moraveks' train compartment and told them that he had been sent to make sure that they would safely reach Romania.[18] On the morning of the second day of travel, in Romanian territory, the train stopped at a town called Braşov, 166km outside of Bucharest. And there, calling out the children's names, was their papa. 'Overwhelmed with joy and happiness, we all wanted to embrace and hug him at the same time,' recounts Moravek Perou de Wagner.[19] The Moraveks are listed as number twenty on *The List of Thirty-Four*.

Despite his having sprung them out of their Gestapo squeeze, Mrs Moravek still held that scepticism she felt on her initial encounter with Albert. She loathed his presence and tried to avoid him. She challenged him at every chance. At one dinner party Albert proclaimed, "I am not really a German, I am an Austrian." This caused Mrs Moravek's blood to boil, and she responded: "How strange. It has to be a German miracle that you, being a German, are really an Austrian, and I, being Bolivian, have now become a German." Albert took this comment in his stride. He told her that he admired her candidness, a virtue he seldom saw since most people feared him because of his brother.[20] She was taken aback, and from then on a platonic love began between these two like-minded individuals. Albert became a most welcome and cherished guest in the Moravek family home.

On one evening Albert turned up uninvited to one of the Moravek's many dinner parties in Bucharest at his favourite time of the evening: when the cigars rolled out, the liquor cabinet opened and his favourite topic of Nazi bashing made its rounds. 'He knew how to hold interesting conversations, which were always very animated, and his views regarding the war were truthful and sincere, even though coming from a German, very sad and gloomy. He was almost sure that Germany would lose the war, and was very concerned about the repercussions that the imminent debacle would have for his fatherland and the rest of Europe,' writes Moravek Perou de Wagner.[21] At these parties it was not just this ideological wedge between the two Göring brothers that drew attention but also their stark physical differences. Albert usually deflected such prying questions by jesting that his real mother was a Bohemian gypsy.

This conviviality extended to the Moraveks' ski lodge in the resort town of Poiana, nestled in the Southern Carpathian Mountains. 'As soon as he arrived he would ask for a glass of Fernet Branca and coffee …. He enjoyed life to the utmost. … He was amiable, lively and amusing. Later on, I heard that most ladies had a crush on him,' remembers Moravek Perou de Wagner. Albert also considered himself something of a chef, collecting fresh mushrooms from the neighbouring woods, creatively preparing them and treating his hosts to an appetizing meal. After meal time he would then entertain the children, taking them for moonlit sleigh rides or skiing outings. As Moravek Perou de Wagner notes: 'Albert was again the perfect companion, because he loved children, and playing in the snow was his favorite [*sic*] amusement.'[22]

Despite Jan's forced exile, the resistance movement within Škoda marched on, in time discarding passiveness for direct action. Up until 1944, Karel Sobota's plant in Brno remained unscathed by any allied bombing raids. The air-raid sirens always rang, the planes always flew overhead, and the employees always evacuated the plant, but not one bomb was released over the plant. "So everybody would go out of the factory and go to a small forest that was a little bit out of the factory, and they stayed there until there was a sign that they could go back into the factory," Jorge explains.

These false alarms became such a normal and predictable fixture at the Brno plant that the German high command began to take note. "Then it was interesting because the Germans, they think well the Americans do not bomb the factory so we are wise men, we will build a centre of command inside the factory," Jorge comments as he creeps to the edge of his seat, becoming more involved in the story. To house this military command post, the Germans immediately began construction of a concrete bunker, an impregnable fortress — well, almost impregnable.

Jan Moravek's former protégés of resistance at Brno discovered the bunker's Achilles heel. They noticed that the entrance was not reinforced and that a lateral strike could take out the whole complex. This information was then relayed secretly through the Czech Resistance network to the Allies, and, sure enough, a couple of months later the US Fifteenth Air Force happened to be on a bombing mission over Brno. Whilst it is not clear whether the Fifteenth were drawn to Brno on account of this intelligence or they were just on a mission for 'targets of opportunity', the bunker was destroyed, as well as most of the plant and surrounding areas. One of the casualties of this surprise raid was Karel Sobota. After all the false alarms, Karel and the rest of his colleagues decided, this time, to ignore the sirens and remain inside the factory, only to find themselves caught in a hail of debris. The next thing Karel knew, he was in hospital with two broken ribs.

The Germans were full of rancour and did not believe that the bombing was a coincidence. They deduced that such a precision hit could have only resulted from inside information coming from someone very familiar with the plant's layout. With no lead as to the culprit, the Gestapo swarmed the factory in a torrent of barked orders and heavy boots. They carefully placed the cold metal of their Lugers to the temple of the nearest employees and waited for someone to step forward with a confession. "Pa! Pa! Pa! And they killed," Jorge says, voice wavering. With men slumped and bleeding at their very workstations, the stifled cries of those surrounding them, the Gestapo moved on from one group to the another, trying to force out an informer. "I don't know how many persons were killed by the Gestapo," Jorge continues. "So he [Jorge's father] told me that 'I was lucky because I was in the hospital. Because maybe if I was there ..."'

BEFORE THE JEWISH QUESTION was met by a clinical answer; before the ghettos in the East were brutally disbanded, and their inhabitants transported to the various death camps; and before Reinhard Heydrich and a collection of top Nazi officials met in Wannsee on the 20th of January 1942 to conceive the the Final Solution, the Third Reich's war against European Jewry bore a far more primitive and blunt shape. The perpetrators were members of the infamous Einsatzgruppen or action squads. Trailing behind the steamrolling Wehrmacht on the Eastern Front, these death squads, made up of members of the *Ordnungspolizei* (Order Police), SS, Gestapo, SD, *Kripo* (*Kriminalpolizei*: Criminal Detective Service) and local volunteers, swept through towns, singled out local Jews, Communists and potential political agitators, and murdered them. Their preferred method of murder involved marching their victims out of town into the woods, forcing them to dig their own graves and then executing them with a spray of machine gunfire. And when that later proved too costly, they lined them up one behind the other and shot them down the line with a single high-calibre round.

Such was the brutal efficiency and veil of secrecy of these squads that Albert Göring, a man privy to most of the activities of the Third Reich, was unaware of their actions until some years after their first murderous campaign in 1939. It was from a somewhat unlikely source that Albert first learnt of these atrocities. It came in the summer of 1942 from Dr Max Winkler, the secretary of Albert's arch-opponent within Škoda's German management, Dr Wilhelm Voss. Winkler had just come back from Poland and requested an audience with Albert in Vienna, knowing that he would be very interested to hear such news and most likely act upon it. He proceeded to tell Albert how he had heard of "whole trainloads of Jews, men, women and children, old and young" being led up into the mountains and massacred by machine-gun fire.[23] Albert had already witnessed his share of the barbarism of his countrymen in Vienna and Prague, but when he heard this story, he became physically sick to think that these cultured, educated and once rational people could commit such atrocities.

Haunted by this glimpse of the Holocaust, Albert burst with rage. He instantly compiled a report for his brother detailing all that he had heard, albeit keeping his source anonymous. "I could not reach my brother on that day, and it so happened that I had to return to Bucharest via Prague," Albert tells his interrogators in Nuremberg. "However, I filed a report with the Ministry of Air, and requested that it be given to my brother. Then when I came back sometime later, I asked what had happened to the report, and I received the answer that it had been transmitted to the competent department, which in my mind could only mean Himmler, and thus the vicious circle was completed. In other words, the thing ended where the murder had started."[24] Apart from giving invaluable ammunition to Himmler to use against Hermann in their power struggle, this report culminated with Albert's second Gestapo arrest warrant. At this time Hitler's confidence in Hermann was waning with each Luftwaffe debacle, yet the ever-loyal Hermann came to his younger brother's aid and dismissed the arrest warrant.

If Albert was before considered an annoyance by the Gestapo, he was now reviled as a 'public enemy' of the Reich, an enemy worthy of constant surveillance. Every move he made was documented, and every step out of line was met with attempts to punish him. It was well-known by the local Gestapo in Prague that Albert Göring was the first name on every person's lips when they found themselves in trouble with the Gestapo. This became apparent to Albert once Hermann showed him a report produced by the local Gestapo in Prague. It claimed that 'the office of Oberdirektor Göring in the Škoda factories is a real intervention centre for 'poor' Czechs.'[25] Considering the list of all the smaller interventions that Albert made on behalf of the citizens of Prague, this colourful language does not seem at all unwarranted.

In one instance, Albert helped a Prague dentist, Dr Engelmayer, who had found himself in hot water for employing an assistant of full Jewish blood. Albert cooled things down and managed to maintain the jobs of both dentist and assistant.[26] Albert had another opportunity to help the dentistry fraternity in Prague when a Czech female dentist, Dr Duchkova, was suddenly evicted from her premises and livelihood. Upon hearing of this, Albert protested with "the corresponding German authorities" and had the eviction overturned.[27]

Concerning himself with the plight of so many, Albert's reputation as the good German spread. His office and home phones buzzed with requests for help. "In 1943, during the closing of businesses, the glass shop PENKAVA in Vodickova Street in Prague was also shut," claimed Albert at the Czechoslovak Ministry of Interior. "The owner and his wife, both elderly people, came to see me at the Škoda factories and asked me to intervene on their behalf. I addressed Mr. VEDESTÄDT at the office of the Reichsprotektor and managed for the shop to remain in their hands and to be reopened." In similar circumstances, Albert answered the calls of Frantisek Šimonek — number thirty on *The List of Thirty-Four* — whose sizeable family plot, including the 16th-century Castle Stránov, came under the scrutiny of the Land Authority in Prague. By the time Albert was called for help most of the holding had already been possessed, but he at least managed to save Castle Stránov.[28] To this day the castle remains in the Šimoneks' hands.

Though Albert developed a reputation as the man to seek out for help, he did not always wait to be asked. On a train journey Albert struck up a conversation with a young couple, Karel and Hana Schön. Marked by the Star of David, Hana listed the daily persecution she faced, and after learning of Albert's own disposition towards the Nazi regime, she confided their plans to try and flee Nazi-occupied Europe. Upon hearing of their intentions, Albert provided them with a sizeable amount of Swiss francs and Italian lira to use as bribes or simply to survive. Albert would later find out from the couple's parents, who could not thank him enough, that they had safely reached Buenos Aires.[29]

This sort of generosity seems like a tiny footnote to Albert's heroic tale, but its impact should not be underestimated. Alexandra Otzoup — her family listed as number twenty-two on *The List of Thirty-Four* — provides another story of Albert's timely heroism: "In the autumn of 1939, my husband and his son from his first marriage were persecuted. Mr Göring managed to transmute a sentence of incarceration in a concentration camp into an expulsion from the country and organise their departure."[30] These are just a handful of stories of Albert's good deeds for the Czech people. No doubt there are a whole host of other undocumented stories out there, told around Czech dinner tables, except the name of the protagonist may be unknown or at least given an alias: Baron von Mosch, perhaps?

THE CAFÉ TERRACE IS emptying. The sun retreats below the Parisian skyline. As our Paris excursion comes to a close, Jorge reveals the last chapter of Albert and his father's narrative. By 1943, it had become increasingly evident to Karel that the Germans were beginning to lose their grip on the war. The Russians were on the front foot, and Czechoslovakia was in their sights. All of a sudden being the secretary of the brother of Hermann Göring was not all that appealing. So one day Karel met with Albert to discuss his future and asked to be transferred. "And my father told me that Albert was very surprised," Jorge says. "And [then Albert asked], 'But why Herr Sobota do you want to be transferred? Are you not well? Are you not being paid here [enough]? Are you not doing what you like to do?'" Karel then simply responded to Albert's pleas for clarity by telling him: "Yes, everything is okay but you know I cannot stay."

Despite trusting Albert and knowing how understanding he was, that was all Karel felt comfortable enough to tell him. Karel would not dare to tell Albert the true reason. The last thing he wanted was to tell the man, who had been so good to him and helped so many other people, that his own welfare might be in jeopardy through mere association with him. As Jorge explains: "So my father told me like this: he explained me, 'Jorge, I could never tell him. Even if being a man like he was that I think that Germany would lose the war.'" Albert felt he was losing not just a close and competent ally but a friend. He was, however, savvy enough to read Karel's body signals. He weighed up all the other variables and promptly changed his tone. "And then Albert immediately understood. ... 'Ah I understand; No problem!' And then my father told me, 'Yes my son, do you see that if I stayed there with the Russians coming in they would not ask questions. I was working for the brother of the Reichsmarschall!'" Jorge says.

Albert had himself always predicted that the war would end with a German defeat and Germany would be, one day, held accountable for its crimes. He was also well aware of the power of his last name.

Whilst his brother Hermann remained in power, it could be manipulated to effect good. But if circumstances were to ever change in the future, it could prove to be the ultimate liability, not just for him but for anyone aligned with him. This was a liability that the Russians would no doubt pursue with vengeful vigour. So Albert arranged for Karel to see out the rest of the war in another position in Česká Zbrojovka.

Karel remained there until 1947 when the plant became a victim of the Czechoslovak Government's policy of nationalising industry. By the year of 1949, the year of the communist takeover, Karel had already grown tired of the stifling red and grey of communism and decided to flee his homeland for a more colourful life. He ultimately found this new existence in Brazil in 1955, via a stopover in Tehran in 1949, a wait as a displaced person in Cairo in 1950 and a five year period of employment in La Paz, Bolivia.

As hard as it was to make that decision back in 1943 and break ties with Albert, hindsight provided Karel with ultimate vindication. As Jorge is readying to leave, he leans over and whispers: "The guy, a Czech guy who took [my father's] place, was shot by the Russians."

NINE

BREDOW STRAßE

On the 20th of July 1944, the one-eyed Count von Stauffenberg and his briefcase attended a military conference held at the *Wolfsschanze* (wolf's entrenchment) near Rastenburg in East Prussia. All the top military brass were there, as was their commander-in-chief, Adolf Hitler. In the middle of the proceedings, at around 12:30pm, the count excused himself to go to the bathroom, leaving his briefcase laden with plastic explosives by Hitler's feet. Ten minutes later the conference room was engulfed by flames, killing a major-general, a colonel, a general and a stenographer, yet sparing the commander-in-chief. The briefcase had seemingly grown legs. That very night the count was hastily ordered before a firing squad by General Fromm, who, as an abetter to the plot, was attempting to save his own skin. He was, nevertheless, executed eight months later.

In the wake of the assassination attempt, around five thousand other alleged co-conspirators were incarcerated, two hundred of whom were consigned to a slow and excruciating death: hanged by piano wire.

When news of the assassination attempt reached Dr Josef Charvát, Albert Göring's Czech friend and member of the Resistance in Prague, he was struck by disbelief, not only because of the momentous nature of the event but because one of Albert's tips, told to him months prior, had been realised. 'In the beginning of 1944' Albert had told Charvát 'something very intriguing about Hitler': a plot to assassinate him. 'Although I didn't suspect that an assassination on Hitler would ever occur, I sent a message to London,' so Charvát wrote in his memoirs. Interestingly, he added: 'Also, when I learnt in a timely manner of the V-1 [ballistic missile] and its attempted launch, I accordingly sent another message to London.'[1]

Such was Albert's privileged status and knack of being around the right people at the right time that Albert was privy to information that even, at times, the SS remained unaware of. His name and role at Škoda gave him a golden passport; there was almost nowhere in Nazi-occupied Europe he could not travel to. He held entrée into the inner sanctum of the highest military circles. Highly confidential information was just a trip to Hermann's Berlin headquarters or a phone call away. And, more importantly, he was not afraid to share this information with his friends and confidants, knowing very well that they were involved with the Resistance. Yet it was always done with subtlety and tact, for he was committing treason, a charge not even his brother could dismiss. The piano wire would await him, too, should he ever be caught.

Karel Staller was one man in particular who received more than conviviality from his friendship with Albert. Known as 'Whizz Staller' due to his technical prowess as an engineer, Staller became the general director of the Škoda subsidiary Československá Zbrojovka Brno in 1939. He was not only the brains behind the Bren machine-gun but also a number of Czech Resistance activities. Radomír Luža, a Resistance agent who often worked alongside Staller, offers insight into his character: 'He was as excessive in his resistance efforts as he was in everything else, willing to do anything to damage the Nazis, even though he worked under their noses as one of their essential technical experts.' Staller was a chief financier to the movement, either supplying funds from his own purse or by siphoning 'funds from the Small Arms Factory part of Hermann Göring Konzern'.[2]

He also established and led an intricate system of expediting secret information to the Czechoslovak Government-in-Exile in London, headed by President Beneš. Due to a clearance allowing Staller to travel to Slovakia, he would travel to Bratislava where his son lived, linking up with a Slovak exporter who 'was allowed to travel to Switzerland five times a year'. The Slovak sugar exporter, Rudolf Frastacký, would then smuggle the information, usually in the form of microfilm, in the heels of his shoes until he could safely deliver it to the former Czechoslovak envoy to Switzerland, Jaromir Kopecký, in Switzerland.[3] From Switzerland, Kopecký sent the information to London.

It was a crude joke that would set the tone for Staller and Albert's friendship. It was told flippantly by Albert, Staller's new Škoda colleague, only ten minutes after their first meeting in 1939. It went: a dentist's assistant is carrying a ladies' hat box and someone asks her what type of hat is inside. She answers, "that's a Prussian's dentures!"[4] The comparison between the jaw structures of those in power in the

Third Reich and a horse immediately and loudly announced to Staller Albert's surprising condemnation of the regime spearheaded by his very own brother. For that, Staller realised where Albert's loyalties lay and that he could be very useful to his cause.

As Staller would later testify in a letter dated the 6th of December 1946 to the 14th Extraordinary People's Court in Prague: 'He [Albert] was a good barometer of the situation and knew some rumours that he heard from his brother. I did this with a view to be able to pass on the information that I got from him abroad. Once this worked out. It was the warning about the attack on France, which I managed to send in time to the British intelligence service in London through Dr Novotný at the British Embassy in Bucharest. The information was very detailed and provoked interest. Göring told me about the preparations for the invasion around three weeks before its start, and within four days Bucharest already had the exact data.'[5]

Albert also managed to prevent the termination of Staller's position at Československá Zbrojovka after his suspicious and erratic behaviour had come to the attention of Škoda's Nazi management.[6] Staller occupies number thirty-two on *The List of Thirty-Four*.

On other occasions Albert aided and abetted the Resistance by offering indifference to covert operations occurring under his nose, gifting them carte blanche to carry out their work. This simple and yet perilous arrangement was one that his Czech boss at Škoda, Dr Vilém Hromádko, took full advantage of. Through his close connections in Russia and position of influence in occupied Czechoslovakia, Hromádko was a natural choice for the Soviets in becoming one of their informants. Since he was a director of a major military munitions factory operating in occupied Czechoslovakia, Hromádko's main role was to supply the Soviets with prototypes and plans of the latest advances in Škoda's weapons program. He achieved this through various business trips to Belgrade where he would meet with local Soviet agents.

After Germany's occupation of Czechoslovakia and Škoda's absorption into the Reichswerke Hermann Göring AG in 1938, his movements in Yugoslavia became increasingly scrutinised by Škoda's Nazi management. Their suspicion led them to assign a Nazi supervisor, Herr Schmidt, to monitor his activities on these trips. This naturally restricted Hromádko's ability to conduct his 'extracurricular activities'. As fate would have it, Herr Schmidt conveniently broke his leg, requiring the Nazi management to find a replacement. They decided to elect someone who would surely always have the best interests of the Third Reich in mind by diligently reporting any suspicious behaviour. They chose a brother of an old boy of the Munich Beer Hall Putsch days, Albert Göring. They obviously did not have access to the Gestapo's thick file on Albert's past insurgent activities.

And so, beginning in May 1940, Hromádko and Albert began to travel to the Balkans together. Albert did fulfil his job, at least by definition, in meeting Hromádko at the train station, though from there his responsibilities would end, with both men parting ways. Whilst Albert would retreat to some Bohemian café sipping coffee and catching up on some of his own work, Hromádko would pass crucial information to his Soviet contacts and assist his compatriots marooned in the area. As Hromádko later testified at the 14th Extraordinary People's Court in Prague: "Göring gave me complete freedom of movement abroad, i.e. in the Balkans, thereby enabling me to financially support our émigrés and to arrange for our people in Yugoslavia to obtain Yugoslav passports." He went even further to state: "Göring evidently knew about my contacts and activities, as well as Staller's contacts; he tolerated this and even warned me to be careful. It was also Göring who tolerated my trip to Moscow."[7] The trip to Moscow that Hrodmádko refers to here was prompted by a piece of highly-sensitive information given to him by Albert.

Along with information regarding the location of a German submarine engine factory, Albert had told Hromádko about Germany's plans of breaking the 1939 Molotov-Ribbentrop Pact about four months before Operation Barbarossa (Germany's invasion of Russia) sprung into action on the 22nd of June 1941. "I handed over this report to London as well as to Moscow," Hromádko reveals, "and this information was very important for the Russians as well as for the West since factories were bombed accordingly, and the Russians were informed [of the invasion] on time."[8]

BY THE TIME HITLER's last would-be assassin hung from the rafters, his war, his Reich was nearing its own death. At home, morale had reached nadir as the Allies stepped up their bombing campaign over Germany (over five thousand bombers a day), and more and more mothers were forced to dig their limp children out of debris. To the east, the rapidly thinning German lines were crumbling under the pressure of the Red Army's sheer numbers and superior T-34 tanks. Whole garrisons of emaciated German POWs had already begun their death march to awaiting labour camps in Siberia. And if any disbanded troop did manage to evade the Soviets and was devoid of the necessary marching papers, the German military police, the 'bloodhounds', were there to 'assert order' with their noose. To the south, German and Italian forces were pushed farther and farther north; thrown out of Rome on the 4th of June 1944 and

Florence two months later. To the west, the Allies were taking one French and Belgium town after another; one last major battle, the Battle of the Bulge, was all that stood in their way to Germany proper. The Wehrmacht was in disarray. An end to Germany's campaign looked inevitable.

But for Albert and his perennial offensive against Hitler, the war kept rolling on, much to the ire of the SS. In one 1944 SD report, the SD red-marked Albert, listing a number of his 'crimes' against the Reich. The first of which involved the 'politically objectionable' representative of Československá Zbrojovka in Brno, Herr Novotný. Albert had, this time, subverted the will of the Reich by taking Novotný and his family under his wing and arranging their flight to Bucharest and then ultimately the USA.[9]

Albert also came to the aid of the wife of the Greek Škoda manager, Michail Kopelianos, when she was denounced for expressing 'derogative' comments about Hitler during a 'hostile outburst' at Škoda's Bucharest offices.[10] On a different occasion, Kopelianos himself attracted the attention of the SS when his Aryan papers were found to be lacking the appropriate amount of Aryanism. Albert was there again to mend things. "When I found out about that, I used a pretext to send him to Budapest and then to Bucharest, where he then worked until the end of the war, without anyone causing any difficulties to him," Albert claimed in his personal defence during his postwar stint in Czech custody.[11]

Like Albert, Vilém Mašek, a Škoda manager, had chosen an unacceptable bride, only his wife was not just Slavic but also Jewish. For this 'misalignment', Mašek not only lost his job at Škoda but he and his wife were also forced to flee the Gestapo. Before the Gestapo could catch up with the couple, Albert intercepted them and hid them in Bucharest for the entire duration of the war. Jirí Kantor*, a Škoda engineer and Hungarian Jew, also saw his contract in jeopardy at Škoda due to his genes. Albert 'prevented that by transferring him to the branch of our company in Budapest'.[12] Jiri remained in Budapest untouched until German perfectionism demanded the last piece of their deranged puzzle and the ultimate perfectionist SS Obersturmbahnführer Karl Adolf Eichman — 'the architect of the Holocaust' — was sent to Hotel Majestic in Budapest. From there he would 'process' Europe's last remaining Jews. Jiri, however, was transported to Buchenwald concentration camp, not to his death at Auschwitz like four hundred thousand of his Jewish-Hungarian compatriots. At Buchenwald, he received some respite as Albert 'Göring sent him money and food'.[13] He takes up number thirteen on *The List of Thirty-Four*.

Seeing hundreds of thousands of people being sent to their deaths with ruthless efficiency and knowing there was little he could do about it, Albert was hit by an acute feeling of helplessness in the latter stages of the war. Even Albert, who had already helped so many others, began to break down and, perhaps, question whether he could have done more. Elsa Moravek de Wagner describes one occasion when Albert fell apart in front of her mother: 'once he became very emotional while talking about the suffering of the prisoners, children in particular. With tears in his eyes, he would talk about the horrible ordeal of the victims of the concentration camps.'[14] Spurred on, Albert became bolder in his subversive actions, desperate to make a greater dent on the Nazi's plans of the eradication of Europe's Jews. He began to hatch plans for his own version of the 1943 'Great Escape' at Stalag Luft III.

---

*Also known to use the German equivalent of his name: Georg Kantor.

Given its close proximity to the Škoda Works in Plzen and Prague (only 60km away), the site of Albert's most daring heist was most likely Theresienstadt concentration camp, or otherwise known as the 'Paradeisghetto'. This camp is most famous for the fact that it was the only concentration camp that was visited by the International (Swiss) Red Cross, even though the whole visit was nothing but one big propaganda farce. Once the Red Cross had left, the façade of propriety quickly dissolved, exposing the camp as an overcrowded cesspit of disease and a holding-bay for the extermination camps. Thirty-three thousand inmates died at the camp and eighty-eight thousand more were deported, mainly to Auschwitz.

Commandeering a convoy of trucks and drivers, Albert had planned to present himself to the camp unannounced and then, under the guise of a labour detachment or through the sheer power of his last name, fill up the trucks with as many inmates as possible. A somewhat simplistic and brazen plan, yet one that, according to Jacques Benbassat, was successfully executed: "He said, 'I am Albert Göring, Škoda Works. I need workers.' He filled up the trucks with these workers. The head of the concentration camp agreed because it was Albert Göring. He took them into the woods and let them out. And in that way, he probably saved quite a few lives!"[15]

This credulous, or incredibly prudent, commandant was most likely Theresienstadt's last commandant, Karl Rahm. Aware of the increasing advancement of the Red Army and fearing the red hangman's noose, he reportedly procrastinated in implementing Heinrich Himmler's orders to gas the final inhabitants of the camp. He was hanged on the 30th of April 1947 by the postwar Czechoslovak Government for crimes against humanity.

This would be Albert's last intervention during the war. His audacious behaviour was beginning to catch up with him.

AT TEN O'CLOCK IN the evening of the 23rd of August 1944, Dr Joseph Charvát was rattled awake by the shrilling of his door bell. Fear and panic immediately crowded Charvát's thoughts, for such a sound at such an hour usually meant only one thing: a visit from the Gestapo. *They have come again to take me away.* 'I went to the door alone, opened it and standing there was Albert in a miserable state, filthy, tired, and he said: "I'm running for my life!", 'Charvát recounts.[16]

A few weeks before, Albert had attended a banquet in Bucharest where he met a German Consulate official. After chatting for a while, the official asked Albert why he constantly refused to accept Manfred von Killinger's, the German consul to Romania, invitations to attend various functions in Bucharest. To this enquiry, Albert replied: "I would rather sit down with a chauffeur of a taxi than sit down with a murderer!"[17]

As an ex-torpedo boat commander in World War I, and like so many other disenchanted World War I veterans, Killinger joined the ranks of the Freikorps in an attempt to crush the new — and very foreign — democratically elected Weimar Government. His association with the Freikorps ended with the failed 1920 Kap Putsch. After licking his wounds, he later became involved with the Organisation Consul (OC), a right wing, anti-Semitic and pro-monarchy terrorist organization. In the years of 1921 and 1922 the OC engaged in a number of assassinations of several high profile Weimar politicians, including the Reich Finance Minister Mathias Erzberger as well as Walther Rathenau, a former Jewish industrialist, a so-called 'November Criminal' and, at the time, the Reich Foreign Minister. Due to Rathenau's willingness to comply with the conditions of the Treaty of Versailles, he became a target of the OC and was ultimately assassinated by a hail of OC machine-gun fire and grenades in Berlin on the 1ˢᵗ of February 1922. Armed with inside information, Albert had always maintained that it was Killinger who was behind Rathenau's assassination. Albert considered him a murderer, plain and simple. Once Albert's 'murderer' comment came to the attention of Killinger, he immediately sought revenge through the Gestapo.

Killinger's calls were answered by the newly-promoted General of Police in Prague, SS Obergruppenführer Karl Hermann Frank. Towering in height, his face leathery, gaunt and weasel-like, his leather SS uniform weighed down by a booty of medals, this Sudeten German, who once proclaimed that in "the whole Czech nation there is not a person who would not hate me or be my enemy", was a man to be reckoned with.[18] Albert knew all about the brutal efficacy of Frank's whip — how he had ordered, as retribution for Reinhard Heydrich's assassination in May 1942, the liquidation of the Czech village of Lidiče, the home to Heydrich's assassins. Every male and a third of the female inhabitants were executed on-site, and the rest, along with all their children, were deported to Ravensbrück concentration camp. Over three-hundred residents were ultimately murdered as a result of Frank's reprisal. Albert was also well aware that Frank, seething with frustration at seeing him slip one Gestapo noose after another, wanted his blood even more than Killinger. Frank was a man that even Albert feared.

Frank made an immediate request to Himmler for Albert's arrest on charges of defeatism and anti-National Socialist behaviour. In a wire to Himmler dated the 24ᵗʰ of August 1944, Frank wrote:

Mr Albert Göring, who I personally consider as at the very least a defeatist of the worst kind, arrived in Prague yesterday from Bucharest with abhorrent news and is staying with his Czech mother-in-law. Since he has support through his connections with a number of untrustworthy Czech industrialists, I consider his freedom of movement as being politically dangerous and thereby request him to be seized by the Gestapo and permission to send him to Berlin for interrogation and clarification of these grave, suspicious facts at the Reich Security Headquarters.[19]

Even before this wire was sent, Albert had found out that 'the war intelligence department had acquired information that Ambassador Killinger had an order from Berlin to shoot him'.[20] On top of this threat, he also had to contend with the rapid advancement of the Red Army into Romania. The Soviets had already taken the first major Romanian city of Iaşi with relative ease and were gaining momentum. All that lay in their way was a German/Romanian force with half their number of troops and artillery. The longtime imploding Antonescu government was all but dead, and murmurs of a royal coup were already beginning. Romania was aflame with hysteria and anarchy of Hobbesian proportions. The whole country lay in wait for the Soviets. 'When we reached Brasov the streets were dead empty,' Elsa Perou, the wife of Albert's close friend Jan Moravek, begins to capture the mood of a terrified Romania. 'At first I assumed there had been another bomb attack. As we got closer to the town center, the emptiness became terrifying. ... At last we realized that most of the stores were doing business, but behind half closed doors; shopkeepers were gazing at the street, armed with whatever weapons they had. We saw rifles, pistols and even machine guns. Stores belonging to Germans were the most heavily armed. The whole town was ready for combat.'[21]

Killinger, Frank, the Gestapo, the Soviets, all baying for his blood, Albert needed to flee Bucharest, his erstwhile sanctuary. Yet he had no means of escape; he could not use his passport and risk being seized by Gestapo agents with a warrant for his arrest in hand. He, nevertheless, made his way to Bucharest central train station, armed with only his famous last name and charm. There he managed to win over some sympathetic German soldiers, who arranged counterfeit travel documents and smuggled him on board a freight-train to Berlin, which was to stop in Prague.

And so on this evening of the 23rd of August Albert stood a ragged mess, unshaven, unwashed for days and quaking with fear, at the door of Charvát's apartment, mustering enough energy to utter: *I'm running for my life!* Charvát hastily ushered Albert inside and sent him to the bathroom to wash and shave, whilst his wife prepared some dinner. Once settled, Albert began to tell Charvát all about his ordeal. "God willing, why didn't you travel to the Alps like I advised you?" Charvát interjected.[22] Here Charvát was referring to a contingency plan that he and Albert had previously agreed upon. In such circumstances, Albert was supposed to travel to the Austrian Alps and hide out in a mountain hut until things cooled down.

A new plan was concocted; Albert was to immediately leave for the train station and catch the midnight express train to Linz, Austria. Though before the Charváts could fix Albert a travel bag, the phone rang. "Bredow Straße.* Is the engineer Göring still with you?" a chill ran down Charvát's spine as he heard the voice of the omnipresent and efficient Gestapo. "No, he just left," he hastily answered. The call was a flex of Frank's muscle, a message to Albert that he could run but not hide. Then 'Bertl', as Charvát affectionately called Albert, disappeared.[23]

---

*The address of the Gestapo headquarters in Prague.

But Albert did not board that train. He went instead, as Frank had reported, to his mother-in-law's home where he shortly received a visit by his own guardian angel, General Bodenschatz. After Frank's request for Albert's arrest had sent waves through the German intelligence community, Hermann, as usual, initiated damage control. He sent his aide-de-camp, Bodenschatz, to Prague to retrieve Albert so that he could personally plead his own case in front of him in Berlin. "When I arrived he showed me documents that made it clear that the German secret police had issued two arrest warrants for me, one of which was for anti national socialist activity and defeatism," Albert recounts his meeting with his brother in Berlin.[24] Once Hermann was satisfied with Albert's explanation and assessed the situation, he managed to dismiss this arrest warrant and reinstate his travel privileges. Before he let Albert leave, he warned him that this would be the very last time that he could ever come to his aid.

Livid that his attempts to root out this extremely large and aggravating thorn in his side were once again averted by 'big brother' in Berlin, Frank did not relent and organised another series of accusations in October 1944. This time one of the accusations threatened Hermann himself. In a Gestapo document dispatched from the Gestapo headquarters in Prague, four main accusations against Albert were purported. They included:

1. Albert Göring intends to flee to Switzerland
2. A substantial money withdrawal [774,000 Reich marks] made by Albert Göring
3. Anti-National Socialist remarks by Albert Göring
4. Intended attack on Herr Reichsmarschall by Albert Göring[25]

These accusations were largely sourced from one of Albert's secretaries in Prague, a Fräulein Hertha Auer von Randenstein. Auer von Randenstein, a reportedly die-hard National Socialist, was a Gestapo informant who over the years had collected evidence of Albert's various misdemeanours, even secretly procuring his private correspondence. As Albert notes: "The reason for these warrants was a denouncement against me by my secretary, Ms. Von AUER, who had been assigned to me, but in reality was a Gestapo informant and regularly submitted reports about me, among other things stating that I had expressed myself negatively about the party, that I had helped Jews and so on."[26]

The whole affair was settled on the 13th of October 1944 by a meeting in the Adlon Hotel in Berlin between Škoda's German Chairman Dr Voss — Albert's perpetual opponent in Škoda who would later be arrested himself by the Gestapo for unscrupulous business activities — and Hermann's men: Kriegsgerichtsrat (Judge Advocate) Ehrhardt and SS Obersturmbahnnführer Alfred Baubin, Albert's long-time ally in the SS. After intense debate and demonstrations of power, Hermann Göring's will won through, with the charges against Albert being deemed unfounded.

What is more, Ehrhardt sent a wire on the 30th of December 1944 to the Gestapo headquarters in Prague, in which he relayed a General Bodenschatz order stating that Fräulein Auer von Randenstein was to be immediately arrested for 'false allegations and defamation' against Albert Göring's name.[27] Already having suffered from the embarrassment arising from their last efforts to lay charges against Albert, the Gestapo in Prague back-pedalled. They denounced Fräulein Auer von Randenstein as one of their informants and gave the assurance that Albert's private correspondence would be returned to him promptly. Frank was once again forced to admit defeat, confirming Bodenschatz's order in a memorandum dated the 2nd of February 1945: 'Through telephone notification from officials at the Reich Justice Ministry, Obergruppenführer Dr Kaltenbrunner [and] Dr Thierack requested in writing, in accordance with the Reichmarschall's wishes, for Hertha Auer von Randenstein's arrest due to false allegations causing detriment to Albert Göring.'[28]

This would be the very last time that Hermann would have to shield Albert from the Gestapo. Hermann's clout in the Third Reich had by this stage taken a nose dive, along with each Luftwaffe plane and Allied bomb over Berlin. He was also a sleep-deprived mess, haunted day and night by his workload and his quest for that war turning and reputation-salvaging wonder weapon. And yet Hermann still put all these issues aside and defended his little brother one last time; but not before laying down the law. "My brother told me then that it was the last time that he could help me, that his position has also been shaken, and that he had to ask HIMMLER personally to smooth over the entire matter, and he ordered me to move to Salzburg, where my wife was already staying, and not to return to Prague."[29] Albert dutifully obeyed this order and returned to Salzburg to be reunited with his family.

Despite being withered and shell-shocked, Albert sat content with his young family in their home in Salzburg, for he knew that he had survived the war and cheated death. But his contentment lay much deeper than that. From his outpost in Austria he began to hear the creak and then crash of the Third Reich toppling over. The chimneys of the death camps no longer puffed out Jew or gentile, priest or thief, communist or capitalist, geriatric or infant, heterosexual or homosexual, Pole or German. Hitler's ardent followers booked tickets to South America. Hitler himself had already retreated to his concrete grave. Germany, that great nation Albert's father had helped to forge, his Fatherland, was free to return from exile … and so was Albert.

TEN

'REASON FOR ARREST: SUBJECT IS BROTHER OF REICHSFELDMARSCHAL GOERING'

I t was the 20th of April 1945, and Hitler was 'acknowledging' his fifty-sixth birthday, but the mood in Hitler's bunker in Berlin was anything but jovial. Himmler, Goebbels, Göring, Speer and a handful of newly decorated members of the Hitler youth were there, but nobody wanted to celebrate, except for the dreamy Eva Braun. Berlin crumbled around them, both in concrete and spirit. Radio reports and telegrams piled in, documenting one German defeat after another. The pimple-faced and grey-haired alike swung from lamp posts; signs hung from their necks declaring that 'he who was not brave enough to fight had to die.' Boys as young as twelve, recruited from the Hitler Youth, in oversized uniforms with Mauser rifles, offered the last resistance to the encircling Russians. Amidst this chaos, Hermann would bid his beloved Führer 'auf

Wiedersehen', although knowing he would never see him again.

Hermann left the bunker and hurried off to the safety of Berchtesgaden, far away from 'Ivan' and his noose. Three days passed, and Hermann, upon seeing the dire circumstances in Berlin, decided that his chance to seize the leadership of Germany and bring an end to the war had finally arrived. And so he sent that infamous telegram to Hitler's bunker, delicately enquiring whether it was a pertinent moment to implement the Führer's succession decree of the 29th of June 1941. This decree stated that Hermann Göring would succeed the leadership of the Third Reich if Hitler was to be ever incapacitated in any way. The 'polite' enquiry, however, was accompanied by a not-so-polite statement of intent, whereby Hermann Göring declared that if he did not receive a reply by ten o'clock that evening, he would assume that Hitler was in fact in an incapacitated state and would therefore actualise the edict. He finished the telegram: 'What I feel for you in these hardest hours of my life, as you know, I can not express through words. May God protect you and let you in spite of everything come here as soon as possible. Yours faithfully, Hermann Göring.'[1]

Hitler, at first, was surprisingly calm upon receiving this telegram, but upon the arrival of a second telegram later at around six in the evening, he fell into a fit of rage. He decried it as an ultimatum and a treasonous act, calling Hermann a 'morphine addict', before weeping 'like a child'.[2] Hitler then brushed the tears away, fixed his hair and signed a radio message composed by Martin Bormann, his private secretary and confident. Bormann also happened to be one of Hermann's staunchest opponents. The radio message accused Hermann of high treason warranting the death penalty, although, in Hermann's case, it would be downgraded to a dismissal of all his offices.[3] Hitler lastly guillotined all association with Hermann by writing on the 29th of April 1945 in the second part of his political testament: 'Before my death I expel the former Reichsmarschall Hermann Göring from the party and deprive him of all rights which he may enjoy by virtue of the decree of June 29th, 1941; and also by virtue of my statement in the Reichstag on September 1st, 1939, I appoint in his place Großadmiral Dönitz, President of the Reich and Supreme Commander of the Armed Forces.'[4]

In the mean time, Martin Bormann contrived to eliminate his competition for good. Circumventing Hitler, Bormann sent an order in the evening of the 23rd to SS Führers Frank and Bredow demanding that Hermann and his family, servants and adjutants all be arrested at Hermann's residence at Berchtesgaden. After a heavy RAF air raid on the Eagle's Nest and the Görings' residence, Frank received another telegram, which was supposedly from Hitler but was most probably the work of Bormann, that declared that Hermann Göring was to be shot upon the capitulation of Berlin.[5]

Yet Frank had the foresight to deduce that with Hitler and Bormann out of the equation, a man like Hermann Göring, one of the last surviving high-ranking officials, would have to negotiate an armistice with the Allies. So when the news came of Berlin and Hitler's downfall, Frank left his Luger in his holster and ordered Hermann and his entourage to be escorted to the nearest safe haven. This happened to be Hermann's Austrian manor, Burg Mauterndorf. During the thirty-six-hour trip Hermann received one last slap to the face when he heard over the radio that he had supposedly "suffered a heart attack" and "the Führer had named Generaloberst Ritter von Greim as the new commander-in-chief of the Luftwaffe and at the same time promoted him to Field Marshal."[6]

Not too long after the party had arrived at Burg Mauterndorf, they were liberated from their SS captors by loyal Luftwaffe airmen.

"And suddenly the SS were gone. Suddenly there were no SS people around anymore. And then Hermann Göring said goodbye to the people of Mauterndorf. He invited my father and the mayor and everyone. And then he drove off to the Americans. Because the Russians were already at Scheifling. That was only 80km from here, and he didn't want to fall in the hands of the Russians," Dr Lielotte Schroth, a relative of the Epensteins, offers her personal eyewitness account of Hermann's final days as a free man.[7]

In his bulging white Mercedes-Benz, wearing his bulging dove-blue Reichsmarschall's uniform, Hermann set off with his entourage to Castle Fischorn in Bruck, near Zell am See, to await the Americans. From Castle Fischorn he sent his first Luftwaffe adjutant Colonel Bernd von Brauchitsch to the American lines at Kufstein with a sealed letter addressed to General Eisenhower, in which Hermann formally recognised Germany's defeat and requested an audience with Eisenhower to broker an armistice. At Kufstein, von Brauchtisch was presented to US Brigadier General Robert Stack of the 36th Infantry Division, who immediately demanded to be taken to Hermann. After finding Castle Fischhorn empty, the hunting party began chase and finally ran into Hermann's procession just out of the town of Radstaat on the 7th of May. As Stack recounts: 'We finally came to a detachment of about 25 vehicles, halted on the road and facing the direction from which we were coming. This was Goering's personal convoy. He had with him his wife, his sister-in-law, his daughter, General von Epp (the Gauleiter of Bavaria), his chef, valet, aides, headquarters commandant, guards, etc — altogether 75 persons. He and I got out of our vehicles and von Brauschitz [sic] introduced us. Goering gave me the old German Army salute, not the "Heil Hitler", and I returned it.'[8]

Although Hermann may have expected to be whisked off in

a plane to meet Eisenhower, it was never to be. In the eyes of the Americans, Hermann was no longer seen as a statesman or someone they could negotiate with but already a prize war criminal. He was flown in a Cub plane to the 7th Army Interrogation Center in Augsburg, where he was ordered by Eisenhower to receive the same treatment as any other POW. Any fantasies of meeting with Eisenhower were quashed when he was formally stripped bare of his power, that is, his Grand Cross of the Iron Cross (Großkreuz des Eisernen Kreuzes), golden Marshal's Staff, Pour le Mérite and even his diamond ring.[9] Naked and humiliated, Hermann the Reichsmarschall became Hermann the defendant.

As HERMANN MADE HIS first complaint about the food at the 7th Army Interrogation Center (SAIC) in Augsburg, another Göring, also fearing the Russians, presented himself in Salzburg to the American Intelligence Service on the 9th of May 1945. After a brief interview with Counter Intelligence Corps (CIC) Agent B.F. Egenberger, it was 'recommended that GOERING, Albert, be forwarded to 7th Army Headquarters CIC Detachment for further interrogation and proper dispositions. It is felt that subject has on hand vaious [sic] important information that would interest the proper authorities in a higher echelon.'[10] Albert was subsequently arrested on the 13th of May and taken to the SAIC in Augsburg for initial interrogation, where, for one last time, he would be reunited with his big brother.

As Hermann marched down the courtyard and Albert stared out from his gaol cell, the brothers caught a glimpse of each other. Albert obtained permission to join his brother for a stroll and after they embraced and took a few steps, big brother Hermann tried to reassure his little brother: "I am very sorry Albert that it is you who has to suffer so much for me. You will be free soon. Then take my wife and child under your care. Farewell!"[11] Intuition told Albert otherwise. He sensed he would not be 'free soon' and that he had to take action into his own hands by building up his own case. Titled *Menschen, denen ich bei eigener Gefahr (dreimal Gestapo-Haftbefehle!) Leben oder Existenz rettete**, Albert began to draft *The List of Thirty-Four*. Despite his efforts to meticulously and clearly direct his interrogators to potential witnesses who could testify on his behalf, it is doubtful that they even bothered to investigate a single name on the list.

This dismissive attitude was especially evident in Albert's first real interrogation with a Major Paul Kubala. Loudly announcing the type of treatment that Albert would receive for the duration of his stay in US custody, Kubala wrote: 'Albert GOERING claims that his life was nothing but one continual battle with the GESTAPO. It seemed that the REICHSMARSCHALL had nothing else to do except extricate his brother from scrapes where Albert protected old Jewish women, refused to give the "Heil Hitler", and made politely disparaging remarks about the Party.'[12] With the rest of his report tainted with similar sarcastic and coloured language, it is quite clear that Kubala had already made his mind up before he had interrogated Albert. For him, Albert was always going to be guilty, just for the simple fact that he shared the same last name as Hermann.

What may have especially irritated Kubala could have been Albert's comments describing Hermann in human terms, not as the gluttonous fiend portrayed by the media and propaganda reports. Albert told Kubala that 'Hermann GOERING often saved his life

---

**People whose lives or existence I saved at my own peril (three Gestapo arrest warrants)*

and never tried to curtail his Samaritan activities, only cautioning him to have some consideration for his position' and that 'he is firmly convinced that the war would have ended much sooner if HITLER had abdicated, or died, and brother Hermann GOERING had become FUEHRER as it had been previously planned.'[13]

GROWING SICKLIER AND MORE frustrated by the day, Albert was sent on the 17th of August 1945 from the recently-relocated SAIC headquarters in Seckenheim to warm up the benches in Nuremberg for his brother and all the other high profile defendants. After a brief spar on the 3rd of September with Colonel John H. Amen, Albert was put in the ring with Ensign William (Bill) Jackson, a New York lawyer and the son of Hermann's principal prosecutor in the Nuremberg Trials, US Chief of Counsel Robert H. Jackson. There as ringside commentator was a young interpreter named Richard W. Sonnenfeldt, a Jewish émigré from the north German town of Gardelegen.

As a fifteen-year-old, Sonnenfeldt took flight from Germany to England in 1938, where he was erroneously interned as an enemy alien in 1940 and was sent, just like those bread and apple thieves in 1788, to Australia. The seventeen-year-old did not warm to the heat in Australia and longed to be involved in all the action in Europe. He thus began a colossal journey, taking him through India, South Africa, South America, to a citizenship ceremony in Baltimore and then around the corner to a US Army enrolment office. He then proudly flew his fresh set of stars and stripes at the Battle of the Bulge and finally here in Nuremberg as the chief interpreter of prosecution of the American council, fighting the likes of Hermann Göring. "Yeah, I was 22 years old. Here I was face-to-face with people who

[177]

destroyed the world" says Sonnenfeldt.[14]

But now Sonnenfeldt found himself struggling to fathom these two brothers; one who, as he said, 'destroyed the world', and the other who bettered it. Just as the legacies of each brother would have their own unique character, Sonnefeldt found their demeanour and physical appearances were also night and day, almost as if they were not related at all. As Sonnenfeldt noted in his memoirs *Mehr als ein Leben* (More Than One Life) : 'The contrast between the two men could not have been bigger: Hermann was short, plump and authoritarian and grandiose; Albert was tall, thin and obsequious.'[15]

Riddled with anxiety, the 'obsequious' Albert spluttered out one story after another of his various interventions, but it was to no avail as his desperate and nervous demeanour was only interpreted by the interrogation team as the symptoms of a man lying. "He was a hand-wringing type of witness who talked too much, volunteered information that no one had asked him. He was highly nervous. He would tell an amazing story that I found hard to believe at the time because he was just not a convincing witness," Sonnenfeldt recounts. They suspected that he was lying so that "he wouldn't get tarred with the same brush as his brother" or if he actually carried out these acts, it was only done for personal financial gains.[16] But what became clear to Sonnenfeldt was the method that Albert may have applied to secure Hermann's acquiescence. Sonnenfeldt, who had witnessed the scale of Hermann's ego, commented: 'Albert knew that Hermann was a braggart and disapproved of his politics. [He] used his vanity to help his friends: "Hermann you have the power!"'[17]

Whilst Albert was not given his liberty back as a result of the interrogation, the spectators of the bout in Nuremberg were at least given a thrilling show dictated by character-revealing rallies of 'whys' and 'becauses'. After the last 'why' was backhanded with the last 'because', the spectators had in front of them an all-explaining epilogue of Albert and Hermann's story, revealing the ins and outs of their peculiar relationship and individual characters. The first glimpse of ink of their epilogue evidenced with Jackson opening the interrogation with a harmless, straightforward question about Albert's relations with his brother. To this straightforward question Albert offered a detailed definition of their relationship:

> You must differentiate here between two things when you speak of "relations". The first thing is my relations to him as a private person, as my brother; and the second point is my relations to him as a statesman. In his capacity as a brother, he was good to me and also helpful, as you already know from previous interrogations. As brothers, we were very close together, and we had the usual relationship as brothers would have inside a family. I have had no relations with him as a statesman. I want to say here, that from 1923 on, that is, from the date when the Party was founded, I was one of the strongest opponents and an active opponent against the Party, and I had no contact with him in this capacity.[18]

A few more sentences were added to the epilogue when Jackson threw in a question which he thought would be surely answered by an agreeable response. "Your brother was quite a hard man, wasn't he?" he simply asked. Showing that strange sense of loyalty underpinning their relationship, Albert countered: "No, on the contrary he was very soft. He did everything for my sisters and cousins, and he spoiled them. However, he knew that I didn't like things like that, and I went my own way, and there was nothing between us."[19]

To the same question posited a couple of weeks earlier by another incredulous interrogator, Albert delivered another 'on the contrary' response when he replied: "As far as he could he helped me .... At the beginning he had the power to do so; later he did not because Himmler was so powerful. He always had a warm heart and when he heard of something that was unjust and I called it vehemently to his attention, he always tried to right things."[20] Indeed, this fraternal loyalty appeared to linger even when Hermann had his hands tied in Nuremberg. Asked about his siblings and their whereabouts during a preliminary interrogation, Hermann mentioned that he had a brother called Albert who "is in a camp" but made a point to note that he "never was a party member".[21]

Midway through the fracas the epilogue received a radical twist. The cause behind this shift: the Jewish question. Once that explosive question came up, all of a sudden the rosy, brotherly picture that Albert had hitherto painted combusted. Through the sparks and smoke appeared the other side of Albert and Hermann's relationship, the darker half he had alluded to in his previous definition. "What did your brother say when you told him about the terrible things that were being done to the Jews?" asked Jackson. Albert replied:

Well, his reaction was always that these things were exaggerated, because he had exact reports on them. He said for me not to mix into affairs of state, and affairs of history, because I had no political knowledge whatever. His very words were: "You are a political idiot!" I made many difficulties for him, because I always did mix into these things, well, you know, he is over there in Cell#5, and he can tell you about it. I also know, with another interrogation report, he called me the "Black-sheep of the family". He called me an "Outsider".[22]

[180]

Pressing for the answer he wanted, Jackson continued: "But he never denied knowing that those things were going on, did he?"

"No, he never denied them. He only made them seem less strong, so to speak. He always said that those things were exaggerated. I suppose that the underlying motive of all this was that he did not wish to exhibit his weakness towards Himmler."[23]

As Sonnenfeldt had observed, Albert went on to provide unsolicited information: "Just to give you an idea of how little actual power my brother really had in these matters, I want to give you another example: One day we were talking about the general subject of Jews, Gestapo, and so on, at dinner."

"That is, you and your brother?" clarified Jackson.

"Yes, and I asked him what his plans were, or what he knew about the Jewish question, and he said that personally he had a plan whereby a large area of Poland, with Warsaw as the capital, should be given to the Jews, who were to be collected there from Germany, Austria, and Czechoslovakia; and that they would be autonomous in that area, in other words, they could handle their affairs as ever they saw fit. This was really a huge ghetto, but nevertheless it was a much more humanitarian idea. Of course, this thing never came into reality, because the 'Lustmerder' Himmler prevented any such plan. This word means somebody who likes to murder for fun."[24]

I am sure Jackson and his team, like any other outsider to the Göring family, were secretly laughing at the absurdity of such a story. For they only knew a very different Göring: Göring the public figure, not the caring and loyal brother who Albert and his family knew. They also had access to a pile of transcripts of various speeches and meetings that were conducted by Hermann, which told a much more sinister story. A story, which history knows so well, of Hermann the racist, 'Jew-baiter', hate-inciter and facilitator of the Holocaust.

They only needed to look at Reichstag President Göring's speech in 1935, formed to urge the assembly to pass the notorious Nuremberg Laws, in which he proudly proclaimed: "God has created the races. He did not want equality and therefore we energetically reject any attempt to falsify the concept of race purity by making it equivalent with racial equality. ... This equality does not exist. We have never accepted such an idea and therefore we must reject it in our laws likewise and must accept that purity of race which nature and providence have destined for us."[25]

They could have also browsed through the text of another Hermann Göring speech made to the people of recently annexed Vienna on the 26th of March 1938. Seizing the historical moment, he announced that he "must direct a serious word to the City of Vienna. Today Vienna cannot rightly claim to be a German City. One cannot speak of a German City in which 300,000 Jews live. This city has an important German mission in the field of culture as well as in economics. For neither of these can we make use of the Jews."[26]

If that was not incriminating enough, they could have drawn on a stenographic report of a meeting chaired by Hermann in the aftermath of Kristallnacht. Charged with the Four Year Plan, Hermann crudely saw the costs stemming from the destruction of Jewish property only in monetary terms or as an inconvenience to his wider plans, blindly ignoring the true costs of the heinous acts. In a meeting on the 12th of November 1938 he therefore said: "I have received a letter written on the Fuehrer's orders by the Stabsleiter [Chief of Staff] of the Fuehrer's deputy Bormann, requesting that the Jewish question be now, once and for all, coordinated and solved one way or another. ... Since the problem is mainly an economic one, it is from the economic angle that it shall have to be tackled. ... Because, gentlemen, I have [had] enough of these demonstrations!

They don't harm the Jew but me, who is the last authority for coordinating the German economy. ... I should not want to leave any doubt, gentlemen, as to the aim of today's meeting. We have not come together merely to talk again, but to make decisions, and I implore the competent agencies to take all measures for the elimination of the Jew from German economy and to submit them to me, as far as it is necessary."[27] He then closed the same meeting with some chilling and mocking lines: "I shall close the wording this way; that German Jewry shall, as punishment for their abominable crimes etc., etc., have to make a contribution of 1 billion. That'll work. The pigs won't commit another murder. Incidentally, I'd like to say again that I would not like to be a Jew in Germany."[28]

And finally, Jackson and his team could not have possibly overlooked that infamous 'Final Solution' memorandum bearing Hermann's signature. As history shows, this memo dated the 31st of July 1941 gave Reinhard Heydrich a free hand to initiate the total extermination of Europe's Jews. It read: 'Supplementary to the task entrusted to you by the decree of January 24, 1939, to solve the Jewish question under the prevailing circumstances by emigration or evacuation in the most favorable [*sic*] way possible, I herewith commission you to carry out all necessary preparations in regard to organizational, practical and material matters for a total solution of the Jewish question [Gesamtloesung der Judenfrage] in the German sphere of influence within Europe. ... I further commission you to submit to my office in the near future an overall plan that shows the preliminary organizational, practical and material measures requisite for the implementation of the projected final solution of the Jewish question [Endloesung der Judenfrage].'[29]

Although Heydrich and Hermann may have held different interpretations on what 'the most favorable way possible' was and other considerations may be at play behind his other public announcements, it is evident that Hermann the statesman, political opportunist and power addict publicly espoused a different view of Europe's Jews than did brother, father, husband or uncle Hermann.

"To go back to your conversations with your brother about the Jews, did you ever protest to him about the treatment they were receiving? Did you ever ask him to do something about it, to stop it? What did he reply to you, and what did he do if anything?" Jackson put Albert back on track. "Well, this was really the main conversation which I had with him on that point. That is, when I told him about the atrocities committed in Vienna, which I saw with my own eyes; and also in Trieste, where I once saw some Jews who had emigrated there from Vienna; and I gave them some money; and he told me that if I wanted to protect the Jews and wanted to help them, that was my affair, but I would have to be more careful and more tactful about it, because I made endless difficulties for him in his position," Albert answered.[30]

After Albert had entertained the interrogation team with the story of his interventions on behalf of the former Austrian Chancellor Dr Kurt von Schuschnigg and Archduke Joseph Ferdinand, Jackson, sensing a crack in Albert's case, prodded: "Why were you interested in the case of the Archduke and that of Schuschnigg, if your activity in Czechoslovakia was solely in connection with commercial matters in the Skoda Works?"

"When the affair with Schuschnigg and Joseph Ferdinand happened, I don't believe that I was even with the Skoda Works at that time," Albert corrected. "It has been the tendency all my life to help whomever I could, without looking at their nationality, their country, their age, or whether they were Jews or Christians. I have helped people from Rumania, Bulgaria, Hungary, Czechoslovakia, and Germany, whenever I could, whether they were poor or whether they wanted to emigrate, or what, and I never expected or received any compensation for it, because I did this for religious reasons."

"What is your religion?" Jackson humoured Albert's response.

"I am a Protestant by confession, but I have been in the Orthodox churches, in synagogues. I have been to Buddhist and Brahmin services, and it doesn't make any difference to me. There is only one God, but I am a Protestant by confession."[31]

Jackson did not, however, accept this. He hit at what he thought could be the only true motive behind Albert's actions and Hermann's cooperation: money. Hearing how Hermann had always come to Albert's aid when he was either in trouble or needed a favour in order to fulfil his 'religious work', Jackson asked: "And after all he did for you, do you mean to tell us that you did nothing in return for him?"

"What was there that I could do for him? The only thing I ever did for him was one [sic] I made him a present of a picture. What could I do for him? He was a great man, and what could the little 'black sheep' do for him?" Albert replied.

"But you never handled any funds for him?" Jackson pushed further.

"No, I never made him any such presents; I never handled any money for him ...," Albert said.[32]

Jackson may have been in fact on the right track as there is evidence from at least one source that Albert may have used gifts, such as artwork given to him from his benefactors, to secure Hermann's assistance. As Elsa Moravek Perou de Wagner, the daughter of Albert's close friend Jan Moravek, remembers: 'We also learned that he accepted gifts from rich Jews, especially important paintings and art works. Looking back, I now understand why he did it. His brother became famous for amassing a [*sic*] extensive art collection, most likely not acquired with his military salary. Albert probably used those "gifts" to reward his brother; each time he averted his arrest.'[33]

JUST BEFORE HIS INTERROGATION with Colonel Amen, Albert had written a letter to Colonel Burton C. Andrus, the no-nonsense warden of Albert's Nuremberg Prison quarters. In it he detailed his worsening kidney condition and asked for answers about his unwarranted and, what seemed to be, endless detention. Andrus must have not been in the mood to act upon a plea for help from a Göring, for Albert neither received a reply nor the much-needed medical care.

His temperature creeping up each day, Albert decided to send a follow-up letter to Andrus on the 10th of September 1945. He wrote: 'I take the liberty of making the polite request to ask the Colonel, whether he has also received my second letter from the 26th of August and forwarded it. Above all I would like to know, whether any news has arrived from the competent authority. Now it has been four months since I have been deprived of my liberty and soon it will be four weeks for me in this prison, without knowing 'why'.'[34] This letter, too, was to never to reach 'the competent authority'.

In the meantime, whilst Albert lay in limbo, there was at least one agency from across the Channel which held some concern about Albert's welfare. The Section V, the offensive counterintelligence department of the British Secret Intelligence Service (SIS), were so anxious to know how Albert was doing that they contacted their US counterparts on the 8th of October with an urgent request for his whereabouts. This arose due to a little piece of misinformation which alerted the pride of British intelligence that 'Major Albert GOERING formerly Reichsverteidingungs [Reich Defence] Chief in the R.A.M. [Reich Air Ministry]', as they called him, 'had succeeded in getting away to Portugal by plane.'[35] As the Americans dutifully informed Section V a little more than a week later, this of course was far from the case as Albert was still sweating away in his Nuremberg gaol cell.

This piece of less than diligent intelligence work did at least force someone to retrieve his case file and reassess his status. This someone was Lieutenant Colonel Arthur A. Kimbal who, although he knew that Albert had been recently exonerated after interrogation, was unsure on how to proceed, and so he sought help up the chain of command. He wrote on the 24th of October: '1. Albert Goering is now being held by this office in confinement in Nurnberg [*sic*]. His record shows no connection with his cousin [*sic*], Hermann Goering, or reason for his continued detention. He is of no further use to this office. 2. Request instructions to be forwarded with reference to release or disposition of Albert Goering.'[36] An answer came back down the line with a large, heartbreaking stamp of 'disposition', and Albert was moved to another form of internment, albeit a somewhat more hospitable form.

He was moved to the Civilian Internment Camp No. 4 at Hersbruck, where he was told he would only remain until the Nuremberg Process was completed. Within a year, on the 17th of June 1946, he was then shuffled off again to another civilian internment camp in Darmstadt. After more than a year of confinement and without ever being indicted, Albert began to see freedom as a state he would never attain again, all for the fact that on each arrest report the reason for arrest was stated as being: 'brother of Reichsfeldmarshal Goering'.

Albert, nevertheless, filed an application for release on the 5th of July 1946. With his conduct during his period of incarceration being rated as 'Good' and Albert stating that he 'was not a party member and politically active', Albert received his chance to plead his case again, and this time fate would be in a far more charitable mood.[37] Fate presented a Major Victor Parker, Albert's new interrogator. "One night he [Parker] came and said, 'Guess who I met, who I interrogated today: Albert Göring,'" recollects the major's wife, Getrude Parker. "I had no idea who Albert Göring was, so he explained [to] me that he was the brother of Hermann Göring. During the interrogation he mentioned the name Lehár. That he found out that Albert Göring helped Lehár with his wife Sophie Paschkis."[38] This stopped Parker short. Paschkis was his christened name.

Parker, who had anglicised his name in America, shared more than a surname with Sophie Paschkis. Parker was in fact Sophie's nephew. Sophie, the wife of Austrian-maestro Franz Lehár, owed her life to Albert. After coming under Gestapo scrutiny for her Jewish ancestry, Albert interceded on her behalf; travelling to Berlin to secure her 'honorary Aryanship' from Goebbels himself. Her name was carefully written down at number fifteen on *The List of Thirty-Four*.

There are only thirty-four names on the list, and the probability of a direct relative of one of these people being a U.S Army interrogator in Germany, let alone assigned to this particular case, in this particular civilian internment camp, on this particular day, is beyond calculation. It was a mathematical anomaly that verged on providence.

Face to face with the man who had saved his aunt from certain death, Parker wrote in his interrogation report:

Subject was arrested as brother of Hermann Goering. Subject was never a member of the Party or any affiliated organizations and was known as an antifascist all over Germany and mostly Austria as Subject resided there for the last 15 years. Subject became Austrian as opposition to the Third Reich in 1933 and stayed in Austria with the hope to live like a free man in a democratic country. After the occupation of Austria subject [*sic*] used his influence on his brother and helped various people, which he mentioned on enclosed chart. Most of those people could be reached very easily if needed as witnesses. The above mentioned story is believed to be the truth because this interrogator knows personally that Subject had helped Franz Lehar who is the uncle of this interrogator. Subject's release is recommended.[39]

ALL OF A SUDDEN that once-distant memory of freedom became a not-so-foreign concept for Albert. All signs were pointing towards an imminent release. Yet those in Washington and Wiesbaden had other ideas. As early as the 25th of November 1945 there was already correspondence regarding a request by the postwar Czechoslovak Government for Albert's extradition; it was the Czechs' turn to grill Albert over his so-called war crimes. After a series of telegrams were sent between the Secretary State office in Washington and the office of the Deputy Theater Judge Advocate in Wiesbaden, it was finally agreed on the 15th March 1946 that 'GOERING, Albert, Chief Director of SKODA works, CIC#4, Hersbruck, Germany, be delivered to General B. BOER, the duly authorised representative of Czechoslovakia.'[40] So through these taps and buzzers Albert's hopes for release were quickly quashed. He was forced, once again, to pack his belongings.

In August 1946, Albert was transferred to an intermediary prison in Plzen, where he received a little taste of the hospitality of his new hosts. "In my whole life I had never copped so many slaps to my face as in Plzen!" Albert later commented to his friend Josef Charvát.[41] After Plzen he was carted off to a far more brutal environment at Pankrác Prison in Prague, the very site where, not too long before, the local Gestapo had overseen wholesale torture and carried out more than a thousand executions. Though by the time Albert had been squeezed into his cell, the gaol was overflowing with the perpetrators of these barbarous acts and the people who Albert had fought so hard against. Only two months prior to Albert's arrival, SS Obergruppenführer Karl Hermann Frank, the postwar Czechoslovak Government's big catch and Albert's old nemesis, was housed under this very roof. If this was not disheartening enough for Albert, he also had to contend with living conditions rivalling that of the former concentration camps and Czech guards seething with five years of pent-up hatred for any and all Germans.

Albert then endured a period of gruelling interrogation, and as he had done a little more than a year before in Augsburg, he wrote up his own defence testimony, documenting each Czech he had intervened on behalf of and how he had benefited the Czechs in general. On the 6th of November it was finally time for Albert's day in court before Judge Dr Fryc. His case was heard at the 14th Extraordinary People's Court in Prague, one of twenty-four Extraordinary People's Courts established by President Edvard Beneš' — the former leader and hero of the Czech Resistance — postwar government. Luckily, news about Albert's predicament had spread through the old Škoda fraternity and his fellow colleagues came en masse to his aid. It was now their time to repay the generosity that Albert had shown to them ever since he began his employment at Škoda.

His old friends and beneficiaries of his deeds from the upper echelons of the Škoda network — the former Chairman Vilém Hromádko, the former deputy commercial director Josef Modrý, the deputy managing director Vaclav Skřivánek, and the director of Omnipol František Zrno — all gave testimonies in Albert's defence. Even the Factory Council of the Nationalised Škoda Factories, who did not believe that there was such thing as a good German, testified that "it is out of the question that he should have harmed Czechs. There are no reasons to initiate criminal procedures, and he should be handed over to Austria."[42]

The glowing testimonies did not stop with Škoda's upper management. Lower tier employees also did their bit. Frau Alexandra Otzoup, a Škoda employee, issued a statement outlining Albert's efforts to liberate countless Škoda employees who were arrested by the Gestapo as a reprisal of Heydrich's assassination: 'Albert Göring ensured that the families of those arrested would receive their full salaries, even though this was forbidden. By supplying funds and dealing with the authorities, he helped several Jews to flee and emigrate out of Czechoslovakia. Through his aid many human lives were saved.'[43]

Such was the extent of Albert's good will and celebrity that news had managed to reach Western Europe. Ernst Neubach, Albert's friend from his film days in Vienna, sent a letter in French to President Beneš himself, outlining not only Albert's role as a saviour of Czechs but also other citizens of Europe. He concluded the letter with this statement: 'I will no longer bother you by citing similar examples since there would be far too many of them. I know, Monsieur le Président de la République, that this special case is very delicate and painful, but I think that, at a time when it is all too unfortunate to realise that there are thousands of assassins and Nazis happily and freely walking around in Germany and Austria without being punished, there is no need that a man who fought for years against the Nazis, who saved the lives of the persecuted, should be condemned because he carries a burden like the name of a criminal that he tried to escape from for years.'[44] From Austria, the former SS Obersturmbahnnführer and Albert's guardian in the SS, Alfred Baubin, wrote a letter of endorsement to the court, testifying Albert's role in freeing the Omnipol directors and that 'he was Czech friendly and was always ready to intervene on the behalf of Czechs.'[45]

Albert's already sound case then received a final impetus from a very unlikely source: the Americans. After the liberation of Prague, the Americans acquired the help of a former SS officer, who in turn led them to a series of tunnels just outside the village of Štechovice in central Bohemia. They burrowed their way through a rubble of concrete and steel — the SS' last-ditch attempts to hide their crimes — and uncovered the state archives of the Third Reich. It was said to contain the regime's looted treasures, but, more importantly, it housed aisle upon aisle of confidential files: a library of Nazi crimes. Amongst these files was Albert's Gestapo case file, which detailed all of Albert's 'crimes' against the Third Reich and interventions made on behalf of the people of Czechoslovakia. Once these documents surfaced into court and the overwhelming amount of evidence was considered, Judge Dr Fryc had no choice but to let his gavel announce a not-guilty verdict and order Albert Göring free.

ON THE 16TH OF October 1946, Hermann secured his own release with the use of a fatal cyanide capsule. Five months later, Albert, aged and frail from two years in prison, was set free on the 14th of March 1947. He was released back into a world that had already begun to forget him. Though bars no longer obscured his view, he still felt caged, alone in a Prague he no longer recognised. He knew that he had to get back to his wife and daughter in Austria, but how? He had neither a cent to his name nor any travel documents. All he had was the wretched convict clothes on his back. He also knew that he was in the Russian occupied zone and if he was to be caught by them, they would not even bother to give him the luxury of a trial. He did not know where to turn, until he thought of his old friend Josef Charvát.

He firstly tried Charvát's old address at Reslova Street, but all that was waiting for him there was a heap of debris. He persisted and somehow, as he had done once before, found Charvát's new address. 'I opened the door, and there stood a grotesquely dressed Albert,' recounts Charvát in his memoirs. 'He wore a green shirt with a bow which was worn during the First World War by a few Bavarian regiments. On the elbows were sewn on parts of linen. On the back was a large P. He wore unbelievably bad pants and shoes which were totally deteriorated and wilted. I ushered him to the bathroom, threw out his clothes into the rubbish and gave him some clothes of mine. Since we had a similar figure, everything fitted him, only my hat was a little too big. He shaved and then met me in the library. He could hardly hold a cigarette, and he didn't want to look into my eyes whilst I gave him a whole pack's worth of American cigarettes. After a snack he started to tell me about his ordeal.'[46]

Although his state said it all, Albert told Charvát a story of starvation, brutality, ignorance, frustration and alienation, which ended in a mixture of relief and almost disbelief: "As they were bringing me in an armoured car to the Inner Ministry, you know, it seemed odd when they offered me a cigarette. Then they said to me, 'Herr Engineer, we have nothing to show against your name, you are free!'"[47]

The next day Charvát gave Albert some money and pushed him back out into the wild to buy a hat. This ordinarily simple task turned out to be somewhat of an ordeal for Albert as he quickly found out that it was no longer all that pleasant to be a German in Prague. "Rarely will I speak German and cop a hit to the mouth," said Albert to Charvát. "Who said that you have to speak German? If you speak French, they will answer you in German, and then you will select a hat in broken German."[48] The next task was to find a way back to Austria through the soviet lines.

They visited the Austrian consulate in Prague who shared the same concern about the Russians as Albert did and told him they could repatriate him back to Austria, but it would take some time. Charvát, however, struck upon another solution. Charvát's youngest daughter, a passionate horse enthusiast, had an Austrian friend from the equestrian circuit who was a travelling sales representative at the time and regularly travelled between Austria and Czechoslovakia. With a means of transport secured, they had to now arrange a means of deception. They fabricated false travel documents 'with large seals and stamps and in more languages'. The Charváts then furnished Albert with 'clothes and a few dresses for his daughter and more importantly, a pack of sugar cubes, which were not only a rarity but could also be used as currency'.[49] And so with fake documents and sugar cubes in hand, Albert left Prague in the summer of 1947 for the Austrian border with the sales representative and his 'Russki-friendly' vehicle.

Before leaving, Albert scribbled a telegram to his wife Mila: 'My only and beloved Mila! I am free at last. I am sure this news will have brought you great joy. ... Now I have to be very patient and a lot of time may pass until I will be with you again, at last, at last, dearest.'[50]

ELEVEN

SCHWARZ, ROT UND GELB

"*B*erlin, Berlin, wir fahren nach Berlin!*" the hoarse voices chant into the balmy night. Freiburg is swimming in the Black, Red and Gold. It hangs from street lights. It is wrapped around torsos. It glares in their eyes. Swarms of silly hats and Michael Ballack jerseys migrate up Bertoldstraße. A procession of cars crawls along the Werderring, tooting horns to the proverbial 'O-lay'. Some, a little overzealous, rock and heave at the side of busses, trying, in vein, to topple them over. Germany has just made it through to the 2006 World Cup semi-finals. 'Berlin, Berlin, we're heading to Berlin' is a declaration that the German fans have been singing ever since their first group stage victory. The final in Berlin may still be one game and a staunch Italian side away, but, at this moment, in the eyes of this revived nation, they are already in Berlin lifting up the cup.

At first, the sight is a little overwhelming. Germans chanting en masse tends to evoke images of the Nuremberg Rallies and the like. But this is a new Germany. A unified Germany that has had a little over sixty-five years to reconcile its collective conscience and heal its deep wounds. It is a day that Germans can roar in unison to the world that they are proud to be German.

Yet I have already heard this sentiment for some time now. I hear it in the conversations that I have with my German friends. They are the grandchildren of the Third Reich. They are no longer restricted from discussing this period, as was the case with their parents. But then again, it is not a topic they necessarily welcome. For them, it is a subject that has been discussed to the point of cliché. Many loathe how it is often the first question that foreigners fire at them: 'So, what did your grandparents do during the war?' I can understand their irritation. They have no responsibility for what their grandparents did, except for the role of educating others on their mistakes and promptly extinguishing any hint of resurgence. They are their own people whose makeup is more than Hitler, Auschwitz, Lebensraum, Panzers and Swastikas. And so with Germany breathing close to a World Cup victory and a renewed sense of national identity, I join my friends in the chant … "Berlin, Berlin, we're heading to Berlin!"

THE NEXT DAY, BLEARY-EYED and a little worse for wear, I need a kebab. The streets look, well, how they always look: pristine and orderly. There is not a beer bottle — or toppled bus, for that matter — to be seen. The little German elves of *Ordnung* (order) have been hard at work in the early hours of the morning. What has hung over from last night, however, is the city's glow, albeit a more sober version. Down Goethestraße I pass a mother on her bicycle making silly faces to a chariot of toddlers clad in German football team paraphernalia. A student couple, he bare-chested and dreadlocked, she wearing a loose-fit, purple dress, stroll under an arch of acorn trees, sharing gelati and giggles. Besotted with the idea of victory and a new found nationalism, Germany is on honeymoon.

I cross the tram tracks and rest my bike by the kebab shop's window. Emre is working today. At two euros a kebab I have come to know Emre and this haunt well. He arrived in Germany at the age of twelve, when family duty required his labour in his uncle's shop. Now sixteen, he spends most of his afternoons and weekends at the shop, rolling fresh döner and flirting with the female clientele. We tend to educate one another on our respective homelands. He always reminisces about his old life in Istanbul: about the cat-eyed beauties, the azure of the Marmara Sea and, of course, the progress of the Turkish national football team. And I in return play around with my own country's stereotypes: the bronzed blondes, *our* Kylie, and, of course, the kangaroos — he can't get enough of this bounding anomaly. In a way, we can empathise with each other. We are both foreigners uttering out a primitive German lumbered by foreign accents — although his German is somewhat more sophisticated than mine. Somehow our mutual linguistic shortcomings make for a freer, less self-conscious conversation.

Emre has the same bags under his eyes as me, and so I ask him what he got up to last night. "The game!" he says, as though I were an alien. "Yeah, it was definitely a good night, maybe too good," I add as a taste of last night rises into my throat. It turns out that Emre was up until the early hours joining in the mass street party that was Freiburg. As Turkey failed to make it through to the World Cup finals, I have been trying to determine where his allegiances lie ever since the draw was announced. Each time I ask he remains ever coy and always denies me an answer. But today, when I push again, he answers: "Germany, of course!"

THE TRAIN IS LATE. A whole five minutes late. "*Scheissse*", a businessman to my right exhales. He bears the face of a man staring down the Apocalypse. In my world, a late train is a major bonus: a five-minute delay means complimentary coffee, orange juice and snacks. The Deutsche Bahn employee wheels around her cart of contrition, her eyes fixed upon her wares, refusing to look the disgruntled passengers in the eye. Many ignore her, as though in protest to the insolence. The slick ICE train finally arrives and the hostility lifts from the train platform.

I am on my way to Berlin; though, not to attend a World Cup final featuring Germany but to meet an old friend. Indeed, Germany's party ended months earlier in Dortmund where they lost to Italy in the semi-final. Their attacking flair, fluid formation and heart lost out to the Italians' no-nonsense defence and highly structured attack; a painful irony. It was a fizzer of a night. Stuck at the pub on the evening shift, I had a front-row seat to the crowd's hopeful faces. But by the time the Azzuri had kicked two goals in extra time, they had disintegrated into funeral mode. The Black, Red and Gold ran down their faces; grown men were in tears. They wept not so much out of sadness but shock; they wept in silence. Such was their optimism and the rapture of the moment that they never stopped to consider an end other than victory in Berlin.

For two weeks after Germany remained in mourning. But now, just three months hence, all the emotion, both the joy and pain, evoked by the World Cup seems to have been buried by apathy and normalcy. It is as though the World Cup was just a summer fling.

[198]

As the train pulls into the Berlin Hauptbahnhof (central station), a cathedral of glass greets me. A testament to modernism and that shiny, happy look that outsized shopping malls seem to specialise in, the station is a sunlit opus to transportation. Outside is much the same. The gritty and retro Berlin that I saw only five years ago has been glossed over by a luminous veneer. The Marie-Elisabeth-Lüders-Haus, Kanzleramtsgebäude and Paul-Löbe-Haus, all constructed in the years leading to the World Cup, combine in one loud and glaring aesthetic of glass, irregular shapes and soaring white walls. Timelessness was obviously not the brief handed to the architects. Bold and dynamic, rather, was what Germany wanted to present to the world. The new landscape is certainly fresh and enlivening but somewhat faddish.

It reminds me of my home city of Sydney where the landscape is constantly undergoing a facelift. Each new look sees her beauty celebrated as the pinnacle of all that is modern and dazzling. Yet in a few short years she is reduced to a faded relic in search of yet another makeover. Nothing lasts. I fear the same for Berlin's latest architectural triumph. This attempt at reinvention seems as ephemeral as all the energy, hope and national pride that the World Cup promised. Did Germany's Zeitgeist yo-yo reach its peak this summer and now is beginning to spiral back down towards the ground, just as it did in the '70s and '90s?

The 1972 Munich Summer Olympics, 'the Happy Games', was meant to be the moment the country (West Germany) and its people broke free from the past. Security was light with the two thousand-strong security force unarmed and dressed in mellow, dove-coloured uniforms. The world became enamoured by the Games' mascot 'Waldi', the rainbow-coloured dachshund. Peace in institutional form was in town and Germany hoped to hitch a ride on the dove's back to international acceptance. Alas, a group of Palestinian terrorists, Black September, thought otherwise and the Games ended with more Jewish blood spilt on German soil. Perhaps, it was premature in the first place. Perhaps, the Games was just a façade masking deepseated problems.

Whilst the world fixed their eyes on Munich, the long-brewing discontent in Germany's student fraternity reached a crescendo. Anarchy and revolution were the words on their lips. They called for a national discourse on the inconvenient truths of the past that their parents refused to recognise.

It's this generation, the Baby Boomers of Germany, that are perhaps the most complex generation to understand. Growing up in the wake of the war, they were raised with great deprivation and hardship. Worse, they were given no collective identity and only a history to be ashamed of. The student revolutions were their chance to address this pain and forge a new Germany. Yet, unlike Woodstock or the '68 Paris Student Uprising, the German equivalent has not been wrapped up in the same level of folkloric romanticism. A lot of this has to do with the delivery of their message. Frustrated that their voices were being ignored, some within their ranks, namely the Red Army Faction, began to speak with Kalashnikovs and dynamite. Such was the violence and barbarism that their message was not only lost but abhorred, even by their student brethren. In the end, the Baby Boomers found themselves still alienated from society and Germany remained as fractured as ever.

Around twenty years later came a renewed thrust for national identity and international redemption. On the 9th of November 1989 the Berlin Wall was torn down by both East and West German hands. Images of East and West Germans linking arms and doing the can-can on top of the crumbling wall beamed across the world. West

German deutsche marks flooded into the decrepit, former Soviet satellite. Potholes were filled and new schools built. Supermarket shelves brimmed with choice. The football greats Matthias Sammer of the East and Jürgen Klinsman of the West joined together under the same strip. Germany looked set to merge and, more importantly, address its issues as one.

Yet there is a big difference between a unified country and a unified nation. When the realities of capitalism stormed into the East along with the Coca-Cola trucks, many began to question the virtues of such a life. It was, and still is, a shock for East Germans to adapt to such a foreign system. Gone was the job for life, the crime-free streets, the crèche-to-university education system, the planned economy, the stability and Spreewald gherkins. And in its place stood a cloud of uncertainty and a lesson in realpolitik.

A movement of GDR (German Democratic Republic) nostalgia, 'Ostalgie', has since emerged to tap into this sentiment. Ostalgie bars, adorned with portraits of Lenin, the hammer and compass and time-warped '60s interiors, have sprung up. Old Scout organisations of the defunct nation-state, such as the Free German Youth (FDJ), are singing *Bau Auf, Bau Auf* and other GDR anthems again. Shops offering the wares of the 'good ol' days', such as Zetti chocolate flakes, Werder Ketchup and Vita Cola, have appeared. One producer has even released a product, Eau de Trabant, that consists of a tin of exhaust fumes coughed out by the Trabant, the former spluttering pride of GDR auto engineering. It is, of course, a selective nostalgia. They forget the darker elements of the GDR: the police state and its brutal enforcers the Stasi, the constrictions on travel, the antagonism towards the church, the censorship, the fifteen-year wait for the delivery of their Trabant cars …

A divisive discourse has also crept into German conversation.

West Germans have become '*Wessis*' (Westies) or '*Besser-Wessis*' — a pun on the German word for know-it-all, '*Besserwisser*'. And East Germans have become '*Ossis*' (Easties) or, more derogatorily, '*Scheiß Ossis*' (Shit/Damn Easties). Those in the West opting for the latter, tend to see these sixteen million new citizens, scarcely educated in ECON101, as 'economic liabilities' or 'deficits' on their erstwhile impeccable ledger. Such a sentiment has grown louder as Germany's economy quietens. Germany has been battered by high unemployment, and it is no more acute than in the East. Energy and living costs have skyrocketed. Worse still, their welfare system struggles to meet the demands of an ageing population.

JACK FINALLY ARRIVES AT the hostel. He is an old school friend from Sydney taking a little European sojourn from the dizzy pace of investment banking. It's already ten in the evening, but he insists we explore Berlin's Bohemian substratum. And Kunsthaus Tacheles, he assures me, is the place to start.

Situated in the old Jewish quarter, 'Tacheles' was born out of a clash between an unforgiving censorship regime in the GDR and a thespian community yearning for 'true' and unbridled artistic expression. It takes its name from the Yiddish word for 'plain, honest talking'. It has been a Weimar shopping centre, the central office of the SS and a gaol for French war prisoners during the Third Reich, and under the GDR, the headquarters of the omnipotent *Freier Deutscher Gewerkschaftsbund* (Free German Trade Union Federation). But since the wall came down, it has evolved from a squatters' colony to a (legitimate) complex comprising art galleries and open studios, an indoor and outdoor cinema, and four bars. Home to subversion, warehouse parties and the sort of artistic freedom that illegality tends to encourage, the squat has been at the avant-garde of Berlin's counterculture, both pre and post wall.

And now Jack and I are in the thick of it as we scale the graffiti-coated staircase to the top-floor bar. The beat is thumping, the funk of weed is in the air, anti-Bush posters and political statements are sprayed on every surface. It has the feel of a student house on acid. Anything goes. We manage to find the bar through the haze of smoke, pick up a couple of beers and find a free corner. We need a breather just to orientate ourselves. But, as we take our first sip and exchange what-have-we-got-ourselves-into looks, a dark figure approaches us. In at least his late thirties, his ear lobes gaping open with eyelets and his grey dreads done up like a pineapple, he bears a 'Big Lebowski' look: the older dude at the party. He asks us in English, although with a thick German accent, whether we would like to buy anything, patting his pocket. "No, thanks. The atmosphere is enough for us," we stammer out like true freshmen. As though feeling a bit guilty about his proposition, he feels obliged to inform us that he isn't really a drug dealer — okay, maybe a part-time one — but a struggling artist. He comes here to tempt the backpacker crowd with his portfolio of hallucinogens. "Easy pickings," he says.

An alarm bell goes off in my head. Tacheles, for all its Bohemian reverie, seems dangerously close to a tourist trap, or worse, the frame-work for a gentrification in the manner of the Meatpacking District in New York. The real subculture seems to have moved on.

Our Big Lebowski friend seems set to take us under his wing and asks us what we are doing in Germany. I tell him how I live here and about my experiences of Germany's roller-coaster bid for the World Cup, making a note of the sudden dampening of public mood. "Do not worry, we will bounce back!" he says. "Look at this place. It has been all kinds of things. It has made many roller-coaster rides, as you say. *Aber weißt du,*" he slips to German before catching himself, "it has always been the same building, same foundations, same geist. They tried to tear it down in the '90s, saying it was a danger or some kaka like that. But the artists made a new survey and you know what? It is as solid as a rock." I guess it depends on how you see it.

TWELVE

THE CONTENTED PARIAH

S ummer 1947, Salzburg. Most of the head Nazis have met a common criminal's death in Nuremberg. The second Nuremberg trials are under way. Poland has just received a new coat of red paint. Truman is developing a paint-thinner to prevent this red 'menace' from spreading. And Albert Göring is finally reunited with his wife and child. The baby, who he only briefly glimpsed before he gave himself up to the Allies, is now a bubbly two-and-a-half-year-old girl. His beauty queen wife looks more radiant than ever. Austria may still carry the scars of war but for her adopted son Albert and his young family, life is blissfully peaceful.

Immediately after his return, Albert spent most of his time reuniting with old friends; some of whom came to heap praise on their saviour. One such person was Franz Lehár who, due to the grace of

Albert Göring, was still able to share a few last compositions with his sweetheart before she passed away later that year in September. He thanked Albert by dedicating a stellar performance to him and agreeing to become the godfather of his only child.

With bills to pay and an identity to resurrect, Albert decided to enter the job market. A man of his experience, a man who gave so much to his inherited Austria would have surely had no troubles in finding employment in the finest of engineering firms. But Albert now lived in a very different Austria. Like Germany, Austria was engulfed in the hysteria of the de-Nazification movement, exorcising its Nazi demons, not just from official posts but its collective memory. And for Austria, Albert was an inconvenient reminder of that pain. They did not bother to consider his credentials and good deeds of the past; all they saw was one cruel truth — that he shared the same last name of a man largely responsible for their current despair and humiliation.

Each job interview was thus cut short with an excuse that they could not afford to take on another employee or with the plain truth that his association might alienate their firm. Albert, with a degree and more than thirty years in engineering, could not find work rebuilding Europe. "After the war things changed dramatically for them. And everything what they possessed was taken by the government or by the Allies. And the hard times started for every one of them," Elizabeth Goering, Albert's only child, recollects.[1] The same name that, mentioned only once, could cause the most hardened SA thugs to disperse like rabbits; that could dictate life or death for hundreds of victims of Nazism; that gave Albert carte blanche to subvert the will of the Nazi regime; this name of Göring, in a world rid of Nazism and Hermann Göring, was now at the root of Albert's demise.

Despite this stark reality, Albert stubbornly refused to change his name; perhaps he still clung to a sense of familial pride or a naïve notion that it is a man's personal actions not another's that should dictate how he is received. This stand for his beliefs provided Albert with some comfort for a short while, but with each rejection and condemning look his resolve began to falter. And soon that same feeling of helplessness that afflicted him during his incarceration would return but only this time magnified tenfold. His sharp appearance became neglected. His tall, Prussian posture relaxed to a slouch. His charismatic smile turned to a scowl of anger, then a grimace of dejection and then a smirk of abnegation. Like his father who found himself in a similar predicament at his age, he turned to the bottle. "I remember he was sort of angry at the time. But I guess he had his reasons. … He felt it was unfair because he was a very good engineer," Jacques Benbassat, Albert's close family-friend, comments.[2]

Fuelled by alcohol and desolation, Albert began to self destruct. His eyes began to wander. He plunged into adultery. He was caught out. Mila Göring announced her emphatic disapproval by splitting with him in 1948 and later taking her child and mother in 1951 to begin a new life in Lima, Peru. As Elizabeth adds: "She was very, very disappointed. She gave him her whole life and allusions and everything. And then suddenly she sees and discovers that she's not the only one!"[3]

This was, of course, not the first time that Albert was guilty of such a transgression. His sudden divorce from his first wife, Maria von Ummon, and his abandonment of his sickly second wife, Erna von Miltner, show a pattern of disregard. It is baffling to think that this was the same man who dedicated his life to defend humanity. Conversely, his brother Hermann, whose legacy has been made synonymous with all that is evil in humanity, was ever loyal to his family.

When I looked for an explanation for this anomaly in Albert's character, I asked Jacques Benbassat, who was close to Albert at the time, for his own opinion on the matter, and he answered: "No idea, except that he felt very, very hurt by his wife. Whatever affair he had — whatever, you know broke it up — he felt it shouldn't have happened. You know, Middle European morality."⁴ Perhaps, Albert in his self-pity saw himself as the victim. He may have felt that his wife had abandoned him at a time when he most needed her, or that his philandering did not warrant such a drastic response as dragging his only daughter to the other side of the world. He may have maintained that his behaviour was nothing out of the ordinary for the day. This was still very much a chauvinistic age, an age before the Women's Liberation movement. Wives were almost expected to turn a blind eye to their husbands' frivolous behaviour. Having a mistress was fashion in high society. Indeed, Albert's birth may well have been a product of such an arrangement.

Yet this explanation or any other attempt at reasoning cannot account for his behaviour, or lack thereof, towards his only daughter, Elizabeth. Shunning his daughter after the estrangement, he refused to acknowledge her, either in person or through correspondence.

During my interview with Elizabeth I tried to broach this subject and gain her perspective. Now in her late sixties, a successful businesswoman, mother of two talented sons and leading a comfortable life in Lima, Elizabeth seemed to be resigned to her fatherless childhood. But her wavering voice and nervous laugh spoke of a tacit and lumbering pain that she carries with her to this day. "Well, I was not angry: I was nothing. Because you see … you have a father who doesn't answer," Elizabeth said. "My mother forced me to write until I was about 10. And she always said, 'Your father is going to have his birthday … so you have to write him a letter, you have to make him some drawings.' So I had to prepare everything for my father, year after year! Then for Christmas, for I don't know what, for Easter and for everything possible. ... So she sent the letters over there, but he never answered, you see, he never, never answered! ... So why should I keep writing to someone who doesn't want me; that was very clear to me, he doesn't want me! ... I told my mother, 'Well, you do it by yourself. Don't use me as an excuse!'"[5]

For all the pain and hurt that Albert visited upon her, Elizabeth's mother, Mila, still seemed to maintain her respect and, perhaps, love for Albert. "One thing I have to say," Elizabeth added. "I don't know what happened between them and how long it took my mother to decide the divorce or whatever, but ... [my mother and grandmother] never, even after, said a word against him; they always spoke for him."[6] According to Elizabeth, Albert was the only German her Czech grandmother respected. It was a respect that lasted through divorce, abandonment and the distance of time and geography.

ALL ALONE NOW AND still jobless, Albert moped around until his former housekeeper, Brunhilde Seiwaldstätter, opened her doors to him. A war widow, she was by no means a beauty queen, but at least, she had all the attributes that Albert usually looked for in a woman: considerably younger and plumper than him. In years to come, Brunhilde would become Albert's fourth and last wife.

He now had a new address and bed partner, but he was still harassed. "The Americans came, knocked on the door and shouted: 'Where is Göring?'" recounts Brunhilde Löhner-Fischer, the daughter of Brunhilde Seiwaldstätter. "The apartment was in my mother's name, and she immediately blocked the door and said: 'No Göring here. I'm Seiwaldstätter. There is no Göring living here.' And he was in the bedroom, hiding under the bed, quaking. They wanted to take him away. That's what it was like then."[7]

Broke, now with another two mouths to feed and with no real prospects of gaining employment, Albert, the once millionaire and ultimate philanthropist, now desperately needed some philanthropy himself. Luckily, there were some out there who did associate the name Göring with good. "He had help of course from those he got out from the camps and from the Jews he had helped. We got food parcels, and he got a bit of support, you could say. Otherwise he couldn't have survived," Brunhilde Löhner-Fischer explains.[8] One of these families was the Benbassats.

The Benbassats would invite Albert to join them on vacation in the Austrian Alps to go skiing or to just enjoy the company of their dear friend. Jacques Benbassat, their son, was especially spoilt by Albert's congenial presence. As Jacques Benbassat once shared with me: 'I really came to know Albert in Bad Gastein and Innsbruck, Austria, on the occasion of a few vacations spent there with my parents after the war. My father had each time invited Albert to spend these vacations with us and we were pretty much constantly together. I came to like him on a personal level as he seemed to enjoy my company, in spite of my young age.' As hard as the adult world punished Albert, Albert managed to momentarily forget his troubles and extract some enjoyment from being in the company of youth: 'We used to sit in the comfortable hotel lobby, drinking coffee together, just Albert and I, and I confess that I was much less interested in history at the time than in observing the ladies passing through the lobby. Fortunately, Albert shared this interest most intensely, even though our tastes diverged somewhat. He definitely preferred the better nourished beauties and once startled me with the statement: "A woman cannot be too fat!"'[9]

If Europe no longer welcomed Albert Göring, perhaps the anonymity on offer in South America would provide him a new chance at life. Surely South America, renowned for harbouring wanted Nazis, would accept the brother of one. This was the idea that Albert flirted with when he travelled to Argentina in the mid '50s.

News of Albert's travel plans quickly reached his ex-wife Mila via Albert's sisters in Austria and sent the house into abuzz of talk that perhaps Albert would also make the trip to Lima. "So we expected him to come over here to Lima, and I was very happy to finally meet my father," Elizabeth Goering said, before breaking into a nervous chuckle and concluding, "but he didn't come. He didn't come. He never said anything!"[10]

Instead, Albert remained in Buenos Aires and met up with his old friend Jan Moravek and other old business associates. He hoped that Jan and his friends would assist him in finding employment and forging a new life. It is not clear whether Albert managed to attain this new life or even went to one job interview, but we do know that it did not take long before he was on that long boat ride back to Europe, back into uncertain waters.

It seemed for a while that this change of plans would pay dividends. In 1955, Albert received a big break when a construction company in Munich offered him a permanent engineering position. Albert took it with both hands and moved back to Munich with Brunhilde and her daughter. All of sudden he found himself doing what he had longed to do for ten years: making a contribution. He had an obligation to fulfil. Someone would notice if he was away sick from work or did not show up on time. He had rekindled a sense of self-worth. That was until someone read his name-tag.

Gripped by the fervour of the *Wirtschaftswunder* (Economic Miracle), Germany had already begun to move on from her dark past.

All was focussed on the *now*. There was no time or room for retrospection; that would have to wait for later. Germany was in denial and had a bad case of post-traumatic stress disorder. The German people did not need someone like Albert to crash the party and remind them of their own guilt. And so once the employees of the firm learnt of Albert's true identity they let their protests be heard. "There were four hundred people employed there at the time," says Brunhilde Löhner-Fischer, "and they found out that he was Hermann's brother, and so he was sacked. The head of the company called him into his office and said, 'I'm sorry but they all said, 'It's either him or all of us!'' And because he was on his own he had to go."[11]

This type of resistance was not new to Albert. In his prime, he would have exercised a bit of charm, offered a witty comment here and there and won over the most obstinate to his side. In other words, this would have never happened had the old Albert Göring turned up to work at that company. But that Albert Göring was long dead, and in his place stood a shell: a passive, battle-weary Albert Göring. As Brunhilde Löhner-Fischer opines: "The man was embittered. He was not happy with his life. He was in turmoil. It was a result of the war. Perhaps he compared what he was before with what he had now: having to beg to do a translation job to get a few pennies to rub together. For someone like that to fall so far, it makes you think."[12]

IN THE EARLY '60s, in a Munich restaurant, a young Christine Schöffel, the daughter of Ernst Neubach, bore witness to a transformation in Albert Göring — although she would not have known it at the time. It appeared that he had, by the '60s, resigned himself to his predicament and ceased his brooding. Gone was the self-pity and mantle of pariah. He began to appreciate life as it was, not what it should be. He cherished his strolls in the Englischer Garten, freshly made coffee in the morning ... freedom and peace. He was quietly content with his life shared with both Brunhildes in their humble apartment in the suburbs of Munich. He was at peace with providence.

"My father took my mother and me to Albert," Christine said. "We met him in a restaurant, and we had a little walk. ... And I remember that my father was very proud about it. It was something [that] gave him: I know Albert Göring, not because it was Albert Göring but because he was proud to know a man who helped other people at the time. And he — I have to say it in German — *Er hat ihn sehr geschätzt. Eine große Achtung für ihn gehabt*: Respect!"[13]

One part of the meeting that she still so vividly remembers was his eyes: "very strong but soft eyes not as his brother. There are two different eyes: his brother had cold eyes. Ching, ching, ching. Like that," she poked her fingers as though she had two daggers in her hand, "and that was not Albert Göring". She then added: "For me it seemed that he was very quiet, nice and *bescheiden* [humble]. ... You would never think that he came from such a family, from such a history!"[15] Just as the group were about to part ways, Albert imparted to the young Christine some timeless advice: "You will always on Earth meet good people and bad people, and [that's] everywhere in the world. So I'm educated. I'm not educated with the terrible Germans and the terrible Russians, or something else. I'm really educated in good and bad, and that's what you have to learn in life. And it never changes."[14]

Around this time, Christine's father wrote an article about Albert

---

*He really admired him. He had huge respect for him.

in the *Aktuell: deutsches Wochenmagazin*, and in its conclusion he tried to tackle the psyche of the Albert Göring he last saw. He wrote: 'He could be now leading a rich and unmolested life somewhere in South America if only he had chosen so. Instead he lives in Munich off an extremely humble pension, drinks a lot of coffee and enjoys a good glass of wine. He never sold his memories, let alone accepted a plump offer from an American film studio.' When Ernst asked Albert why he would choose to forfeit a potentially more comfortable life, he just answered by reciting the wise words of Schopenhauer: "In this world nothing becomes lost; it just passes from one to another."[15]

Only a couple of years after the Neubachs had shared this meal with Albert in Munich, Dr Josef Charvát, his old Czech friend, received two letters from Albert's address in Munich. As Charvát wrote in his memoirs: 'For a long time I didn't hear anything from him until suddenly I received a letter from Munich, in which Albert talked about his problems with indigestion. The letter was very philosophically stoic in nature. It hinted that he was either married again or at least was living with another woman, who was also caring for him. He also sent me a magazine, which had a story about me. Then came a letter from that aforementioned lady that ....'[16] Albert Göring, at the age of seventy-one, died of pancreatic cancer on the 20th of December 1966.

THIRTEEN

FROM ONE TO ANOTHER

Off the bus steps an elderly lady dressed in her Sunday best, carrying a bouquet of wildflowers. She makes her way through the gates of the Waldfriedhof cemetery with slow resignation. I look down to my map and then up again. She is gone, lost to the depths of the forest. I begin to follow the path, but, as soon as I break stride, the heavens open up. I seek cover under the umbrella of a red oak as the pit and pat grows into a pitterpatter. The tired oak creaks and groans under the weight of the wind; its leaves rustling the dark current of the imagination.

I'm stuck in this ghoulish scene for what seems an eternity, until a break in the weather finally ushers me back on track. As I walk deeper into the wood, under its green blanket, a sense of security and tranquillity begins to quell my initial apprehension. The faint melody of birdsong reassures. Every step is observed by sculptured angels. I begin to appreciate the beauty of such a cemetery.

One of the first of its kind in the world, the Waldfriedhof, in Munich's outer suburbs, is not based on the standard design. There is no grid system efficiently accommodating corpses but, instead, maze-like paths and points of meditation. The flora merges organically with grave plots and tombs, as nature and death are inexorably entwined. It is as much dedicated to the living as it is to the dead.

Following the pebble path, I come to a small grave plot marked out with a sandstone edifice with a fence of cloves and lanterns, a weathered, grey roof and, like most homes in Bavaria, a crucifix of Christ inside. In old German fraktur script the name of Dr Heinrich Ernst Göring, the former *kaiserlich deutscher Ministerresident* (the German Imperial Minister Resident) is inscribed and directly below is his wife Franziska Göring, née Tiefenbrunn. And at the foot of the headstone I see him: Albert Göring, engineer, born on the 9th of March 1895, deceased on the 20th of December 1966. This is the closest I will ever be to the man I have never met but have grown to know so well.

I have made the pilgrimage to pay homage and bid one last farewell. I have been travelling with Albert for the last three years; he the guide and I the student. He took me into smoky cabaret dens and Bohemian cafés. He threw me into the centre of an angry Viennese mob. I knelt down with him and old Jewish ladies forced to scrub the cobblestones of a Viennese street. I heard his cries of disbelief and rage after he saw the civility of his people being reduced to thuggery and then criminality. I was there at Hermann's Berlin office as he pleaded the case of a colleague. The Gestapo hot on his heels and his fear-struck face. His cigarette holder and Carey Grant air. And the coffee; the aroma of good, strong coffee will ever evoke an image of

Albert in my mind.

Yet, as I reflect upon Albert's life by his grave, it strikes me as odd and unjust that it is only here that I can engage in such retrospection. Unlike Oskar Schindler and Raoul Wallenberg, there is no tree planted in his name along the Avenue of the Righteous at the Yad Vashem memorial site. Nor is there a museum that we can visit and learn about his heroics. This patch of moss-covered sandstone is all the masonry that has been allocated to his legacy.

THE STORM CLOUDS HAVE now left the wood, marching on to harass the city centre. All that is left is a pink and blue marbled sky, the sweet scent of fresh rain, myself and the Görings. My feet squish over brown pine needles and cones as I try to take a closer look at the grave. There is something missing. There is no mention of the most recorded Göring of them all, Hermann Göring.

On the 15th of September 1946, Hermann's body was found in his Nuremberg cell, limp and filled with potassium cyanide. Some argue he had the cyanide capsule hidden in a jar of skin cream all along, whilst others claim it was a guard under the spell of a young Fräulein who unwittingly handed him his suicide. When Hermann was sentenced to death he requested a soldier's death by firing squad. This was denied. Faced with a common criminal's hanging, he played his last card to taunt his adversaries. His lifeless body, one eye open in a frozen wink, was taken to the execution hall. There it was met by many baffled and red faces — and no redder was Colonel Burton C. Andrus' face, the commandant who had meticulously employed every conceivable measure against prisoner suicide. Even in death, Hermann could strike a blow. Then, just after midnight, Hermann's corpse was dispatched, along with the corpses of his ten former Nazi colleagues, to a US crematorium in Munich. His ashes were tossed later that day into the barely three-meter-wide Conwentzbach creek.[1] There they were left to drift down into the Isar River and then through Munich, the Englischer Garten and rural Bavaria, until they were, perhaps, swept up by the current of the mighty Danube, dropping by the cities of Vienna, Bratislava, Budapest, Belgrade and finally released into the Black Sea. There is no gravestone or official marking of his death.

I look down to the grave's copper base, green from oxidation and fastened down by brass bolts with Iron Crosses for washers, and scrape away a layer of dirt. I gradually uncover an etching of a soldier with a safari hat and a rifle at his side. This must be an image of *Reichkommissar* Heinrich Göring conquering the new frontiers of South-West Africa in the name of the Kaiser. Flanking this imposing image on both sides, in old German fraktur script, almost indecipherable from old age and weather, is a small eulogy championing the core values of the Göring family. Beginning on the left flank it writes: *Wir sind nicht von denen die da weichen*; and on the right flank it continues with: *sondern von denen die da glauben*. 'We are not among those who yield but among those who believe.'

Staring at this sight, it is easy to see why, when young Hermann and Albert Göring looked upon this very grave on the day of their father's funeral, tears of guilt and regret filled their eyes. Only then did they truly realise what a great man their father was and what it meant to be bearers of the Göring name. They, too, wanted to extend the great traditions of their forefathers. They wanted to make their father and family proud. Yet what different paths: Hermann's led to the muddy waters of a small creek in Munich, whilst Albert's ended fixed in stone and, more importantly, in the lives of those he touched — including mine.

Albert's selfless bravery during this dark period of history has gone unacknowledged; no medals or formal accolades are pinned to his legacy. Worse still, his life has been relegated to a footnote of his brother's brutal history. But journey along the many paths Albert lit for us, trace the narratives of those he saved and inspired, and you behold the silhouette of a spectacular, if unconventional, family tree. It is a genealogy not bound by bloodlines but by the single architect of their collective families' survival: Albert Göring. Through my journey I have come across doctors and movie makers, statesmen and scientists, musicians and businessmen, royals and professors; all of whom can link their very breath back to the heroism of Albert.

Though history has labelled him rogue, Nazi, cad, hedonist and criminal, posterity has bestowed him his final epitaph. He is patriarch of an enduring family of hundreds of survivors and their descendents scattered across the globe. It is then, looking at his gravestone, that I realise this isn't really the end.

In this world nothing becomes lost; it just passes from one to another.

NOTES

ONE: THE COMPASS

1. Major Paul Kubala, *Final Interrogation Report: Albert Goering, Brother of the Reichsmarschall and Agent of the Skoda and Brno Works*, Seventh Army Interrogation Center (SAIC), Augsburg, 19th September 1945.(File Number: XE002282); Personal Name File (PNF) 1939-1976, Goering, Albert; Investigative Records Repository (IRR); Records of the Army Staff, Record Group (RG) 319; National Archives at College Park (NACP), MD.

1. Frischauer, W. (1950) *Goering*, (London: Odhams Press LTD), p. 15.

2. Dungern, O. (1936) 'Uhnentafel des Ministerpräsisdenten und Reichsluftfahrtministers Generalobersten Hermann Göring' IN: *Ahnentafeln berühmter Deutscher: Herausgegeben von der Zentralstelle für Deutsche Personen und Familiengeschichte*, (Leipzig: Zentralstelle für Deutsche Personen und Familiengeschichte).

3. Butler, E. & Young, G. (1989) *The Life and Death of Hermann Goering*, (Newton Abbot, UK: David & Charles Publishers plc), p. 12.

4. Singer, K. (1940) *Göring: Germany's most dangerous man*, (Melbourne, Australia: Hutchinson & C0. LTD,), p. 17.

5. Frischauer, W. (1950) *Goering*, (London: Odhams Press LTD), p. 16.

6. Ibid, p.15.

7. Gewald, J.B. (1999) *Herero Heroes: a socio-political history of the Herero of Namibia, 1890-1923*, (Oxford: James Currey LTD), p. 31.

8. Mosley, L. (1974) *The Reich Marshal: a biography of Hermann Goering*, (London: Weidenfeld and Nicolson), p.2.

9. Ibid, p. 4.

10. Frischauer, W. (1950) *Goering*, (London: Odhams Press LTD), pp. 17-18.

11. Gewald, J.B. (1999) *Herero Heroes: a socio-political history of the Herero of Namibia, 1890-1923*, (Oxford: James Currey LTD), p. 31-32.

12. Mosley, L. (1974) *The Reich Marshal: a biography of Hermann*

Goering, (London: Weidenfeld and Nicolson), p.4.

13. Ibid.

14. Frischauer, W. (1950) Goering, (London: Odhams Press LTD), p. 20.

15. Mosley, L. (1974) The Reich Marshal: a biography of Hermann Goering, (London: Weidenfeld and Nicolson), pp. 4-5.

16. Ibid, p. 5.

17. Ibid, p. 6.

18. Ibid.

19. Ibid, pp. 5-6.

20. Ibid, p. 6.

21. Interview with Mia Haunhorst, The Real Albert Goering, 3BM TV, 1998.

22. Mosley, L. (1974) The Reich Marshal: a biography of Hermann Goering, (London: Weidenfeld and Nicolson), p.9.

23. Ibid, p.7.

FOUR: BIRTH

1. Frischauer, W. (1950) Goering, (London: Odhams Press LTD), p. 21.

2. Manvell, R. & Fraenkel, H. (1962) Hermann Göring, (London: William Heinemann LTD), p. 5.

3. Mosley, L. (1974) The Reich Marshal: a biography of Hermann Goering, (London: Weidenfeld and Nicolson), p. 8.

4. Ibid.

5. Frischauer, W. (1950) Goering, (London: Odhams Press LTD), p. 21.

6. Maser, W. (2000) Hermann Göring: Hitlers janusköpfiger Paladin;

die politische Biographie, (Berlin: Quintessenz Verlags-GmbH), p. 19.

7. Mosley, L. (1974) *The Reich Marshal: a biography of Hermann Goering* ', (London: Weidenfeld and Nicolson), p. 9.

8. Ibid, p. 10.

9. Goldensohn, L. (2004) *The Nuremberg Interviews*. Ed. R. Gellately, 19th ed., (New York: Alfred A. Knopf), p. 104.

10. Mosley, L. (1974) *The Reich Marshal: a biography of Hermann Goering*, (London: Weidenfeld and Nicolson), p. 11.

11. Ibid, p. 12.

12. Irving, D. (1989) *Göring: A Biography*, (London: Macmillan London LTD) p. 33.

13. Miller, G (1998) 'The Death of Manfred von Richthofen: who fired the fatal shot?', "*Sabretache*": *the Journal and Proceedings of the Military History Society of Australia*, 39 (2).

14. Frischauer, W. (1951) *Ein Marschallstab Zerbrach: eine Göring-Biographie*, (Ulm: Münster Verlag), p. 28.

15. Albert Günther Göring's Military-Medical Records, Landesamt für Gesundheit and Soziales: Versorsungsamt-Krankenbuchlager, Berlin.

16. Frischauer, W. (1951) *Ein Marschallstab Zerbrach: eine Göring-Biographie*, (Ulm: Münster Verlag), pp. 36-37.

17. Ibid, p. 37.

18. Dr Margot Fuchs (Leitung Historisches Archiv, Technische Universität München) email to author, 23rd November 2006.

19. *Interrogation Report of Albert Göring*, compiled at the Ministry of Interior in Prague, 17th December, 1946; Ls V 242/47, Czech National Archives in Prague.

20. Interview with Jacques Benbassat, *The Real Albert Goering*, 3BM TV, 1998.

21. Goldensohn, L. (2004) *The Nuremberg Interviews*. Ed. R. Gellately, 19th ed., (New York: Alfred A. Knopf), p. 132.
22. Ibid, pp. 21-22.
23. *Interrogation Report of Albert Göring*, compiled at the Ministry of Interior in Prague, 17th December, 1946; Ls V 242/47, Czech National Archives in Prague.
24. Interview with Edda Göring, *The Real Albert Goering*, 3BM TV, 1998.

FIVE: A BOY AND A STUDY FULL OF BOOKS

1. Interview with Jacques Benbassat, *The Real Albert Goering*, 3BM TV, 1998.
2. Schleunes, K. A. (1972) *The Twisted Road to Auschwitz: Nazi policy toward German Jews, 1933-1939*, (London: André Deutsch LTD), p. 199.
3. 'Offenbar erlittenes Unrecht', *Der Standard*, 14th April 2006, p. 2.
4. Neubach, E. (1962) 'Mein Freund Göring', *Aktuell: deutsches Wochenmagazin*, 24th February, p. 22.
5. Ibid. Also supported by: Belach, H. (1986) *Henny Porten: Der erste deutsche Filmstar 1890-1960*, (Berlin: Haude und Spener), p. 120.
6. Belach, H. (1986) *Henny Porten: Der erste deutsche Filmstar 1890-1960*, (Berlin: Haude und Spener), pp. 137-138.
7. Göring, E. (1972) *My Life With Goering*, (London: David Bruce and Watson), p. 36.
8. Interview with Edda Göring, *The Real Albert Goering*, 3BM TV, 1998.
9. Interview with Jacques Benbassat, *The Real Albert Goering*, 3BM

TV, 1998.

10. Ibid.

11. Neubach, E. (1962) 'Mein Freund Göring', *Aktuell: deutsches Wochenmagazin*, 24th February, p. 20.

12. *Testimony of ALBERT GOERING, taken at Nuremberg, Germany, 25 September 1945, 1045-1240, by Ensign Jackson* (National Archives Microfilm Publication M1270, roll 5); Interrogation Records Prepared for War Crimes Proceedings at Nuernberg, 1945-1947; The International Military Tribunal (IMT) at Nuernberg, RG 238; NACP.

13. Ibid.

14. Heim, S. & Götz, A, (1987) 'Die Ökonomie der Endlösung.' IN: Götz, A. & *et al.*, *Sozialpolitik und Judenvernichtung: Gibt es eine Ökonomie der Endlösung?* (Berlin: Rotbuch), p.26.

15. Braham, R.L. (2000) *The Politics of Genocide: the Holocaust in Hungary*, (Detroit: Wayne State University Press). p. 247.

16. Testimony of Alex Neacşu. Cited in: Ioanid, R. (2000) *The Holocaust in Romania: The Destruction of Jews and Gypsies Under the Antonescu Regime, 1940-1944*. (Chicago: Irvin R Dee). p.181.

17. Albert Göring, *Menschen, denen ich bei eigenen Gefahr (dreimal Gestapo-Haftbefehle!) Leben oder Existenz rettete*, SAIC, Augsburg, May 1945. (XE002282); PNF 1939-1976, Goering, Albert; IRR; RG 319; NACP.

18. Interview with Jacques Benbassat, *The Real Albert Goering*, 3BM TV, 1998.

SIX: ÉMIGRÉ

1. Neubach, E. (1962) 'Mein Freund Göring', *Aktuell: deutsches Wochenmagazin*, 24th February, p. 20.

2. Ibid.
3. Ibid.
4. 'Austria is Finished', *Time*, 21st March, 1938.
5. Neubach, E. (1945) *Flugsand*, (Zürich: Pan Verlag), p. 35.
6. Neubach, E. (1962) 'Mein Freund Göring', *Aktuell: deutsches Wochenmagazin*, 24th February, p. 20.
7. Interview with George Pilzer, *The Real Albert Goering*, 3BM TV, 1998.
8. Ibid.
9. Neubach, E. (1962) 'Mein Freund Göring', *Aktuell: deutsches Wochenmagazin*, 24th February, p. 20.
10. Ibid.
11. Ibid, p. 21.
12. Linke, N. (2001) *Franz Lehár*, (Reinbeck, Hamburg: Rowohlt Taschenbuch Verlag), p. 118.
13. Neubach, E. (1962) 'Mein Freund Göring', *Aktuell: deutsches Wochenmagazin*, 24th February, pp. 21-22.
14. Ibid, p. 22.
15. Haffner, H. & I. (1998) *Immer nur Lächeln ... Das Franz Lehár Buch*, (Berlin: Parthas), p. 185.
16. Transcript of telephone call made by Sir N. Henderson in Berlin to the Foreign Office in London, 16th March 1938, FO 371/22316; Austro-German Relations; Foreign Office: Political Departments: General Correspondence from 1906-1966, POLITICAL: SOUTHERN: Austria; FO Records Created and Inherited by the Foreign Office: General Correspondence from Political and Other Departments; The National Archives of the UK in Kew, Surrey.
17. Schuschnigg, K. (1947) *Austrian Requiem*, translated by Franz von Hildebrand, (London: Victor Gollancz), p. 64.

18. Ibid, p. 65.
19. Neubach, E. (1962) 'Mein Freund Göring', *Aktuell: deutsches Wochenmagazin*, 24th February, p. 21.
20. Schuschnigg, K. (1947) *Austrian Requiem*, translated by Franz von Hildebrand, (London: Victor Gollancz), p. 73.
21. Heinrich Schuschnigg email to author, 24th February 2006.
22. Neubach, E. (1962) 'Mein Freund Göring', *Aktuell: deutsches Wochenmagazin*, 24th February, p. 21.
23. Ibid, p. 20.
24. Neubach, E. (1945) *Flugsand*, (Zürich: Pan Verlag), p. 74.
25. Neubach, E. (1962) 'Mein Freund Göring', *Aktuell: deutsches Wochenmagazin*, 24th February, p. 20.
26. Neubach, E. (1945) *Flugsand*, (Zürich: Pan Verlag), p. 74.
27. 'Part II: Special Report on Relations with Albert Goering', *Appendix E: Report on Dr Ladislao Kovacs*, Report on Conversations with Hungarian Personalities in Rome, 5th July 1944; HS 4/101, Assessment of Situation inside Hungary: List of Hungarian Personalities in Rome, 1944; Special Operations Executive: Eastern Europe: Registered Files, HUNGARY; HS Records of Special Operations Executive; The National Archives of the UK in Kew, Surrey.
28. Ibid.
29. Ibid.
30. Ibid.
31. 'Part I', Ibid.
32. 'Part II', Ibid.
33. Major Paul Kubala, *Final Interrogation Report: Albert Goering, Brother of the Reichsmarschall and Agent of the Skoda and Brno Works*, SAIC, 19th September 1945. (XE002282); PNF 1939-1976, Goering, Albert; IRR; RG 319; NACP.

34. Ibid.
35. Darley, J. M. & Baston, C. D. (1973) '"From Jerusalem to Jericho": A study of situational and dispositional variables in helping behaviour', *Journal of Personality and Social Psychology*, 27(1), pp. 100-108.

SEVEN: THE KING OF SWEDEN

1. Václav Rejholec email to author, 18ᵗʰ September 2006.
2. Svobodný, P. (2001) 'Josef Charvát (1897-1984) Mediziner: Die Kriegsjahre 1939-1945 im Lichte seiner Tagebücher.' IN: Glettler, M. & Míšková, A., *Prager Professoren 1938-1948: zwischen Wissenschaft und Politik*, (Essen:Klartext Verlag), p. 465.
3. *Testimony of ALBERT GOERING, taken at Nuremberg, Germany, 25 September 1945, 1045-1240, by Ensign Jackson*, M1270, roll 5; RG 238; NACP.
4. Krátký, V. (unpublished), *Göringů seznam*, Škoda Archives, Plzen.
5. Vilem Hromádko testimony to the Extraordinary People's Court in Prague XIV, 6ᵗʰ November 1947. Ls V 242/47, Czech National Archives in Prague.
6. Albert Göring, *Menschen, denen ich bei eigenen Gefahr (dreimal Gestapo-Haftbefehle!) Leben oder Existenz rettete*, SAIC, Augsburg, May 1945. (XE002282); PNF 1939-1976, Goering, Albert; IRR; RG 319; NACP.
7. Kubů, E., Novotný, F. & Šouša, F. (2004) 'Under Threat of Nazi Occupation: The Fate of Multinationals in the Czech Lands, 1938-1945.' IN: Kobrak, C. & Hansen, P. (Eds), *European*

Business, Dictatorship, And Political Risk, 1920-1945, (New York, NY: Berghahn Books), pp. 210-211.

8. Testimony of ALBERT GOERING, taken at Nuremberg, Germany, 25 September 1945, 1045-1240, by Ensign Jackson, M1270, roll 5;RG 238; NACP.

9. Vilem Hromádko testimony to the Extraordinary People's Court in Prague XIV, 6th November 1947. Ls V 242/47, Czech National Archives in Prague.

10. Charvát, J. (2005) Můj labyrint světa Vzpomínky, zápisky z deníků, (Prague: Galén), p. 198.

11. Ibid.

12. Interview with Elizabeth Goering, The Real Albert Goering, 3BM TV, 1998.

13. Krátký, V. (unpublished), Göringů seznam, Škoda Archives, Plzen.

14. SD report, Appendix 5: Albert Göring, ingenieur, Oberdirektor der Skoda-Werke, 23rd Oktober 1944. Ls V 242/47, Czech National Archives in Prague.

15. Krátký, V. (unpublished), Göringů seznam, Škoda Archives, Plzen.

16. Testimony of ALBERT GOERING, taken at Nuremberg, Germany, 25 September 1945, 1045-1240, by Ensign Jackson, M1270, roll 5; RG 238; NACP.

17. Interview with Jiřiná Rejholvová, The Real Albert Goering, 3BM TV, 1998

18. Svobodný, P. (2001) 'Josef Charvát (1897-1984) Mediziner: Die Kriegsjahre 1939-1945 im Lichte seiner Tagebücher.' IN: Glettler, M. & Míšková, A., Prager Professoren 1938-1948: zwischen Wissenschaft und Politik, (Essen:Klartext Verlag), p. 469.

19. Ladislaus Ervin-Deutsch, 'Night Shift in Work Camp III in

Kaufering, Dachauer Hefte 2.' *Slave Labour in the Concentration Camp*, Dachau Concentration Camp Memorial Site. Available at: http://www.kz-gedenkstaette-dachau.de/englisch/frame/geschichte.htm [Accessed 30th September 2006]

20. Svobodný, P. (2001) 'Josef Charvát (1897-1984) Mediziner: Die Kriegsjahre 1939-1945 im Lichte seiner Tagebücher.' IN: Glettler, M. & Míšková, A., *Prager Professoren 1938-1948: Zwischen Wissenschaft und PolitikII*, (Essen:Klartext Verlag), p. 470.

21. Interview with Jiřiná Rejholvová, *The Real Albert Goering*, 3BM TV, 1998

22. Interview with Christine Schöffel, *The Real Albert Goering*, 3BM TV, 1998.

23. Neubach, E. (1962) 'Mein Freund Göring', *Aktuell: deutsches Wochenmagazin*, 24th February, p. 21.

24. *Interrogation Report of Albert Göring*, compiled at the Ministry of Interior in Prague, 17th December, 1946; Ls V 242/47, Czech National Archives in Prague.

25. Charvát, J. (2005) *Můj labyrint světa Vzpomínky, zápisky z deníků*, (Prague: Galén), p. 18.

26. Per Svensson email to author, 15th November, 2006.

27. Sabine Stein (Stiftung Gedenkstätten Buchenwald und Mittelbau-Dora Archiv) email to author, 7th October 2006.

28. Charvát, J. (2005) *Můj labyrint světa Vzpomínky, zápisky z deníků*, (Prague: Galén), p. 201.

29. *Testimony of ALBERT GOERING, taken at Nuremberg, Germany, 25 September 1945, 1045-1240, by Ensign Jackson*, M1270, roll 5; RG 238; NACP.

30. Interview with Jarmila Modra, *The Real Albert Goering*, 3BM TV, 1998.

31. Interview with Jarmila Modra by author, 7th June 2006, Prague.

EIGHT: BARON VON MOSCH

1. Kubů, E., Novotný, F. & Šouša, F. (2004) 'Under Threat of Nazi Occupation: The Fate of Multinationals in the Czech Lands, 1938-1945.' IN: Kobrak, C. & Hansen, P. (Eds), *European Business, Dictatorship, And Political Risk, 1920-1945,* (New York: Berghahn Books), pp. 209-210.

2. *Testimony of ALBERT GOERING, taken at Nuremberg, Germany, 25 September 1945, 1045-1240, by Ensign Jackson,* M1270, roll 5; RG 238; NACP.

3. Ibid.

4. Ibid.

5. Josef Modrý testimony to the Extraordinary People's Court in Prague XIV, 6th November 1947. Ls V 242/47, Czech National Archives in Prague.

6. Albert Göring letter to Herrn Reichsprotektor Exzellenz von Neurath, 10th December 1940. Ls V 242/47, Czech National Archives in Prague.

7. František Zrno testimony to the Extraordinary People's Court in Prague XIV, 6th November 1947. Ls V 242/47, Czech National Archives in Prague.

8. Krátký, V. (unpublished), *Göringů seznam,* Škoda Archives, Plzen.

9. Ibid.

10. František Zrno testimony to the Extraordinary People's Court in Prague XIV, 6th November 1947. Ls V 242/47, Czech National Archives in Prague.

11. Krátký, V. (unpublished), *Göringů seznam*, Škoda Archives, Plzen.

12. Ibid.

13. Moravek Perou de Wagner, E. (2006) *My Roots Continents Apart: A Tale of Courage and Survival*, (Nebraska: iUniverse), p. 95.

14. Ibid, pp. 80-81.

15. Ibid, p. 81.

16. Ibid, pp. 90-91.

17. Ibid, pp. 100-101.

18. Ibid, p. 102.

19. Ibid, pp. 104-105.

20. Ibid, p. 122.

21. Ibid, p.123.

22. Ibid, p. 125.

23. *Testimony of ALBERT GOERING, taken at Nuremberg, Germany, 25 September 1945, 1045-1240, by Ensign Jackson*, M1270, roll 5; RG 238; NACP.

24. Ibid.

25. *Interrogation Report of Albert Göring*, compiled at the Ministry of Interior in Prague, 17th December, 1946; Ls V 242/47, Czech National Archives in Prague.

26. SD report, Apendix 5: *Albert Göring, ingenieur, Oberdirektor der Skoda-Werke*, 23rd Oktober 1944. Ls V 242/47, Czech National Archives in Prague.

27. *Interrogation Report of Albert Göring*, compiled at the Ministry of Interior in Prague, 17th December, 1946; Ls V 242/47, Czech National Archives in Prague.

28. Ibid.

29. Ibid.

30. Alexandra Otzoup testimony, Camp Mönchshof, 9th January 1947. Cited in: Neubach, E. (1962) 'Mein Freund Göring', *Aktuell: deutsches Wochenmagazin*, 24th February, p. 21.

NINE: BREDOW STRAßE

1. Charvát, J. (2005) *Můj labyrint světa Vzpomínky, zápisky z deníků*, (Prague: Galén), pp. 198-199.
2. Luža, R. & Vella, C. (2002) *The Hitler Kiss: A Memoir of the Czech Resistance*, (Baton Rouge, LA: Louisiana State University Press), p. 85.
3. Ibid.
4. Karel Staller letter to Extraordinary People's Court in Prague XIV, 6th December, 1947. Ls V 242/47, Czech National Archives in Prague.
5. Ibid.
6. Albert Göring, *Menschen, denen ich bei eigenen Gefahr (dreimal Gestapo-Haftbefehle!) Leben oder Existenz rettete*, SAIC, Augsburg, May 1945. (XE002282); PNF 1939-1976, Goering, Albert; IRR; RG 319; NACP.
7. Vilem Hromádko testimony to the Extraordinary People's Court in Prague XIV, 6th November 1947. Ls V 242/47, Czech National Archives in Prague.
8. Ibid.
9. SD report, Apendix 5: *Albert Göring, ingenieur, Oberdirektor der Skoda-Werke*, 23rd Oktober 1944. Ls V 242/47, Czech National Archives in Prague.
10. Ibid.
11. *Interrogation Report of Albert Göring*, compiled at the Ministry

of Interior in Prague, 17th December, 1946; Ls V 242/47, Czech National Archives in Prague.

12. Ibid

13. Krátký, V. (unpublished), *Göringů seznam*, Škoda Archives, Plzen.

14. Moravek Perou de Wagner, E. (2006) *My Roots Continents Apart: A Tale of Courage and Survival*, (Nebraska: iUniverse), p. 127.

15. Interview with Jacques Benbassat, *The Real Albert Goering*, 3BM TV, 1998.

16. Charvát, J. (2005) *Můj labyrint světa Vzpomínky, zápisky z deníků*, (Prague: Galén), p.199.

17. *Testimony of ALBERT GOERING, taken at Nuremberg, Germany, 25 September 1945, 1045-1240, by Ensign Jackson*, M1270, roll 5; RG 238; NACP.

18. 'Not a Person', *Time*, 3rd June, 1946.

19. Telex from SS Obergruppenführer Staatsminister Karl Hermann Frank in Prague to SS Obergruppenführer Dr Kaltenbrunner in Berlin, 24th August, 1944. Ls V 242/47, Czech National Archives in Prague.

20. Charvát, J. (2005) *Můj labyrint světa Vzpomínky, zápisky z deníků*, (Prague: Galén), p.199.

21. Elsa Perou. Cited in: Moravek Perou de Wagner, E. (2006) *My Roots Continents Apart: A Tale of Courage and Survival*, (Nebraska: iUniverse), pp. 143-144.

22. Charvát, J. (2005) *Můj labyrint světa Vzpomínky, zápisky z deníků*, (Prague: Galén), p.199.

23. Ibid.

24. *Interrogation Report of Albert Göring*, compiled at the Ministry of Interior in Prague, 17th December, 1946; Ls V 242/47, Czech

National Archives in Prague.

25. Gestapo (Prague) Report on Oberdirektor Albert Göring to SS Obergruppenführer Staatsminister Karl Hermann Frank compiled by the Staatspolizeileitsetelle Prag: Bredauer-Gasse 20, 14th October, 1944. Ls V 242/47, Czech National Archives in Prague.

26. *Interrogation Report of Albert Göring*, compiled at the Ministry of Interior in Prague, 17th December, 1946; Ls V 242/47, Czech National Archives in Prague.

27. Telex from Kriegsgerichtsrat Ehrhardt in Berlin to the Staatspolizeileitsetelle Prag, 30th December 1944. Cited in: Gestapo (Prague) Memorandum, 20th January 1945. Ls V 242/47, Czech National Archives in Prague.

28. Gestapo memorandum by SS Obergruppenführer Staatsminister Karl Hermann Frank, Prague, 2nd February 1945. Ls V 242/47, Czech National Archives in Prague.

29. *Interrogation Report of Albert Göring*, compiled at the Ministry of Interior in Prague, 17th December, 1946. Ls V 242/47, Czech National Archives in Prague.

TEN: 'REASON FOR ARREST: SUBJECT IS BROTHER OF REICHSFELDMARSCHAL GOERING'

1. Maser, W. (2000) *Hermann Göring: Hitlers janusköpfiger Paladin; die politische Biographie*, (Berlin: Quintessenz Verlags-GmbH), p. 427.

2. Fest, J. (2002) *Der Untergang: Hitler und das Ende des Dritten Reiches; Eine historische Skizze*, (Berlin: Alexander Fest Verlag), p. 102.

3. Ibid.

4. Maser, W. (2000) *Hermann Göring: Hitlers janusköpfiger Paladin; die politische Biographie*, (Berlin: Quintessenz Verlags-GmbH), p. 429.

5. Ibid, p. 434.

6. Ibid.

7. Interview with Dr Liselotte Schroth, *The Real Albert Goering*, 3BM TV, 1998.

8. Brigadier General Robert I. Stack (Assistant Division Commander) Eyewitness Account, *Capture of Goering*, The 36th Infantry Division Association Library. Available at: http://www.kwanah.com/36division/ps/ps0277.htm [Accessed July 25th 2007]

9. Maser, W. (2000) *Hermann Göring: Hitlers janusköpfiger Paladin; die politische Biographie*, (Berlin: Quintessenz Verlags-GmbH), p. 435.

10. B. F. Egenberger, *Memorandum for the Officer in Charge, Subject: GOERING, Albert, brother of Reichfeldmarschall Göring, Hermann*, Salzburg, Austria, 9th May 1945. (XE002282); PNF 1939-1976, Goering, Albert; IRR; RG 319; NACP.

11. Neubach, E. (1962) 'Mein Freund Göring', *Aktuell: deutsches Wochenmagazin*, 24th February, p. 27.

12. Major Paul Kubala, *Final Interrogation Report: Albert Goering, Brother of the Reichsmarschall and Agent of the Skoda and Brno Works*, SAIC, 19th September 1945. (XE002282); PNF 1939-1976, Goering, Albert; IRR; RG 319; NACP.

13. Ibid

14. Interview with Richard Sonnenfeldt, *The Real Albert Goering*, 3BM TV, 1998.

15. Sonnenfeldt, R. W. (2003) *Mehr als ein Leben*, (Bern: Scherz), p. 180.

16. Interview with Richard Sonnenfeldt, *The Real Albert Goering*,

3BM TV, 1998.

17. Richard Sonnenfeldt email to author, 3rd May 2007.

18. *Testimony of ALBERT GOERING, taken at Nuremberg, Germany, 25 September 1945, 1045-1240, by Ensign Jackson,* M1270, roll 5; RG 238; NACP.

19. Ibid.

20. *Testimony of ALBERT GOERING, taken at Nuremberg, Germany, 1100-1200, 3 September 1945, by Colonel John H Amen,* M1270, roll 5; RG 238; NACP.

21. *Interrogation of Goering,* SAIC, 3rd June 1945. (XE000996); PNF 1939-1976, Goering, Hermann; IRR; RG 319; NACP.

22. *Testimony of ALBERT GOERING, taken at Nuremberg, Germany, 25 September 1945, 1045-1240, by Ensign Jackson,* M1270, roll 5; RG 238; NACP.

23. Ibid.

24. Ibid.

25. Hermann Göring speech to the Reichstag in 1935, *Hermann Wilhelm Goering,* The Jewish Virtual Library. Available at: http://www.jewishvirtuallibrary.org/jsource/Holocaust/ Goering1.html [Accessed 20th August 2007]

26. Hermann Göring speech in Vienna, 26th March 1938, Ibid.

27. 'Part I', *Stenographic Report of the Meeting on "The Jewish Question" Under the Chairmanship of Field Marshall Goering in the Reichs Air Force,* Web Genocide Documentation Centre: Resources on Genocide, War Crimes and Mass Killing: The University of West England. Available at: http://www.ess.uwe. ac.uk/genocide/appropriation2.htm [Accessed 21st August 2007]

28. 'Part VII', *Stenographic Report of the Meeting on "The Jewish Question" Under the Chairmanship of Field Marshall Goering in*

the Reichs Air Force, Web Genocide Documentation Centre: Resources on Genocide, War Crimes and Mass Killing: The University of West England. Available at: http://www.ess.uwe. ac.uk/genocide/appropriation5.htm [Accessed 21st August 2007]

29. *Authorisation letter of Goering to Heydrich, July 31, 1941*, House of the Wannsee Conference: Memorial and Educational Site. Available at: http://www.ghwk.de/engl/authorization.htm [Accessed 18th July 2007]

30. *Testimony of ALBERT GOERING, taken at Nuremberg, Germany, 25 September 1945, 1045-1240, by Ensign Jackson,* M1270, roll 5; RG 238; NACP.

31. Ibid.

32. Ibid.

33. Moravek Perou de Wagner, E. (2006) *My Roots Continents Apart: A Tale of Courage and Survival,* (Nebraska: iUniverse), p. 127.

34. Albert Göring letter to 'the Commandant', Nürnberg, 10th September 1945. M1270, roll 5;RG 238; NACP.

35. Major M.N. Forrest of Section V in London telegram to United States, European Theatre (USFET) Main, *Major Albert GOERING,* 8th October 1945. (XE002282); PNF 1939-1976, Goering, Albert; IRR; RG 319; NACP.

36. Lieutenant Colonel Arthur A. Kimball letter to USFET Main, *Release of P.W.,* Nürnberg, 24th October 1945. (XE002282); PNF 1939-1976, Goering, Albert; IRR; RG 319; NACP.

37. *Application for Release,* Göring, Albert, Darmstadt, 5th July 1946. (XE002282); PNF 1939-1976, Goering, Albert; IRR; RG 319; NACP.

38. Interview with Getrude Parker, *The Real Albert Goering,* 3BM

TV, 1998.

39. Major Victor Parker, Preliminary Interrogation Report, Civilian Internment Camp No. 91, Darmstadt, 31st July 1946. (XE002282); PNF 1939-1976, Goering, Albert; IRR; RG 319; NACP.

40. Colonel C.B Mickelwalt, *Extradition of Alleged War Criminal*, Deputy Theater Judge Advocate, Wiesbaden, 15th March, 1946. (XE002282); PNF 1939-1976, Goering, Albert; IRR; RG 319; NACP.

41. Charvát, J. (2005) *Můj labyrint světa Vzpomínky, zápisky z deníků*, (Prague: Galén), p. 200.

42. Krátký, V. (unpublished), *Göringů seznam*, Škoda Archives, Plzen.

43. Alexandra Otzoup testimony, Camp Mönchshof, 9th January 1947. Cited in: Neubach, E. (1962) 'Mein Freund Göring', *Aktuell: deutsches Wochenmagazin*, 24th February, p. 21.

44. Ernst Neubach letter to Monsieur le Président de la République, Paris, 27th November1946. Ls V 242/47, Czech National Archives in Prague.

45. Alfred Baubin letter to the Extraordinary People's Court in Prague XIV, 5th November1946. Ls V 242/47, Czech National Archives in Prague.

46. Charvát, J. (2005) *Můj labyrint světa Vzpomínky, zápisky z deníků*, (Prague: Galén), p. 200.

47. Ibid, pp. 199-200

48. Ibid, p. 200

49. Ibid, p. 201.

50. Albert Göring letter to his wife Mila, Prague, 21st March 1947, 3BM TV Archive in London.

1. Interview with Elizabeth Goering, *The Real Albert Goering*, 3BM TV, 1998.
2. Interview with Jacques Benbassat by author, Greenville, South Carolina, 28th June 2005.
3. Interview with Elizabeth Goering, *The Real Albert Goering*, 3BM TV, 1998.
4. Interview with Jacques Benbassat by author, Greenville, South Carolina, 28th June 2005.
5. Telephone interview with Elizabeth Goering by author, 1st April 2009.
6. Ibid.
7. Brunhilde Löhner-Fischer, *The Real Albert Goering*, 3BM TV, 1998.
8. Ibid.
9. Jacques Benbassat email to author, 26 February 2005.
10. Telephone interview with Elizabeth Goering by author, 1st April 2009.
11. Brunhilde Löhner-Fischer, *The Real Albert Goering*, 3BM TV, 1998.
12. Ibid.
13. Interview with Christine Schöffel by author, Graz, Austria, 12th May 2007.
14. Ibid.
15. Neubach, E. (1962) 'Mein Freund Göring', *Aktuell: deutsches Wochenmagazin*, 24th February, p. 27.
16. Charvát, J. (2005) *Můj labyrint světa Vzpomínky, zápisky z deníků*, (Prague: Galén), p. 201.

1. Maser, W. (2000) *Hermann Göring: Hitlers janusköpfiger Paladin; die politische Biographie*, (Berlin: Quintessenz Verlags-GmbH), p. 466-467.